V.P. Dutt (1925-2011), former Pro-Vice-Chancellor of Delhi University, a former nominated member of Rajya Sabha, and a former member of the Parliamentary Consultative Committee on Foreign Affairs, headed the Department of East Asian Studies in the Indian School of International Studies, and subsequently the Department of Chinese and Japanese Studies at the Delhi University. He had been writing on India's foreign policy for the last half century. Among his major works include *India's Foreign Policy, India's Foreign Policy in a Changing World, India and the World, China's Foreign Policy, China After Mao* (Co-author) and *China's Cultural Revolution* (co-author).

Popular Social Science

INDIA'S FOREIGN POLICY

Since Independence

V P DUTT

nbt.india
एकः सूते सकलम्
NATIONAL BOOK TRUST, INDIA

First published in 2007
Reprints 2007, 2009, 2010, 2011 (twice), 2012,
2014 (twice), 2015, 2016, 2024 (twice), 2025 (*Saka* 1947)
by the Director, National Book Trust, India
5 Institutional Area, Vasant Kunj,
New Delhi-110070
Website: www.nbtindia.gov.in

Agartala • Bengaluru • Chennai
Cuttack • Guwahati • Hyderabad
Kochi • Kolkata • Mumbai • Patna

ISBN 978-81-237-4955-6

₹ 230.00

Printed at Magic International Pvt. Ltd., Greater Noida

To

Mavis and K P Jain,
Sarojini and Mohinder Dewan

Contents

Preface

This Book is primarily designed for the educated layman who would like to understand how our foreign policy has evolved, what the basic motivations and governing ideas were, the principles on which it was founded and the political milieu in which it developed, the various and sometimes very serious challenges that it confronted at different times and how the various Prime Ministers faced those situations, the directions that it took under the stress of those challenges, the changes as well as the continuities, both fundamental to the understanding of the evolution and development of India's foreign policy.

It is, however, the hope of this author that serious analysts of foreign policy would also find it of some interest and that research scholars could use it as a base for further study.

I am grateful to the Chairman of the National Book Trust, Professor Bipan Chandra, for inviting me to write this book. I should also like to acknowledge my debt of gratitude to my editor Binny Kurian, for his unstinted help. The mistakes are my own.

New Delhi
January 2007

V.P. DUTT

CHAPTER ONE

THE NEHRU ERA

Foreign policy of a country is determined by the times in which it is conducted. It is also influenced by its history and its geographical position. The recent past colours a country's collective subconsciousness. Where you are on the map makes a great deal of difference in interacting with the world just as your own view of your position in the world does. In other words geopolitics plays an important role in the evolution of foreign policy. Then there are particular requirements of a country at a given time which cannot be ignored. All these have to be factored in understanding and analysing a country's foreign policy.

India became independent in 1947 and had to evolve its own view of the world and chart its own course within the prevailing international situation. India's foreign policy bore the firm stamp of Jawaharlal Nehru, first Prime Minister of independent India. He nurtured it, gave it flesh and blood and shaped it in a myriad ways. But he did not invent it.

As Jawaharlal Nehru himself said, India's foreign policy was rooted in India's civilization and traditions, India's struggle for freedom, India's geographical position, and India's quest for peace, security, development and a place in the sun. To quote Nehru, "it is completely incorrect to call our policy 'Nehru' policy...I have not originated it. It is a policy inherent in the circumstances of India, inherent in the past thinking of India, inherent in the whole mental outlook of India, inherent in the conditioning of the Indian mind during the struggle for freedom and inherent in the circumstances of the world today".

Nehru was often accused of being an idealist and a moralist in foreign policy: he was neither. He showed great realism in steering the country through a minefield of the Cold War without sacrificing its interests or its autonomy in international affairs. People forget the circumstances prevailing—both domestic and foreign—in which Nehru had to shape India's foreign policy stances. When independence came in 1947 India had hardly any military or economic strength. India was hobbling both militarily and economically. The partition had been extended to the army and one part of it had gone to Pakistan. So far as the economy was concerned, as it used to be said at the time not a pin was produced in India.

The critical question before Nehru was: what should be the priorities of India? Should India invest its meagre resources in economic development or should they be utilized for military build-up on a priority basis ? The answer was obvious. Military strength not based on a strong economic foundation was ephemeral, as ephemeral as the chase for the will-o'-of-the wisp. The example of a number of countries was instructive. Those who had essentially relied on military buildup, with little economic backup, like Pakistan or Thailand at that time, were ruled by inherently unstable regimes, and remained inordinately dependent on other countries.

Nehru was quite realistic to recognize that economic strength was central to the stability and social coherence of the country. As he recognized, every paisa he spent on economic development was in the final analysis a surer guarantee of the security and viability of the nation. Military strength was important but it had to be acquired on a robust economic base. Equally important, you had first to build the factories that would build other factories. In other words you had to set up heavy industries which alone provided the sinews of economic strength. Hence, Jawaharlal Nehru concentrated on the construction of heavy industry like steel mills, engineering and infrastructure projects. India's present strength owes itself to the economic foundations laid in the time of Jawaharlal Nehru.

While Nehru was aware of India's various weaknesses, he was equally conscious of India's potential, its proud past, the civilisational urges, the vastness of the country and its implications. As he told the Constituent Assembly in March 1947, "if we had been some odd little nation in Asia or Europe it would not have mattered much, but because we counted and because we're going to count more and more in the future, everything we do becomes a matter of comment and many people do not like our counting so much. It is not a question of our viewpoint or of attaching ourselves to this or that bloc, it is merely a fact that we are potentially a great nation and a big power and possibly it is not liked by some people that anything should happen to strengthen us".

Primarily two approaches defined India's foreign policy—the awareness of current weaknesses and the belief in India as a potentially great power. One lead to remaining in the commonwealth and keeping intact India's economic links with the West and the other to nonalignment which we shall discuss presently. At the time there was considerable opinion against the Commonwealth, then known as the British Commonwealth, as a relic of colonial days. However, Nehru realized that the country needed some security from the hostile winds that were blowing in the world. Both the major power blocs, one led by USA and the other by the USSR (Union of Soviet Socialist Republics) were trying to inveigle (bribe or browbeat) other countries into their orbit. Membership of the Commonwealth was a signal to them to stay away. By joining the Commonwealth he was buying security for India "on the cheap", that is without any entangling alliances. It did not compromise the country's freedom in international affairs, yet it acted as some kind of a shield against predatory powers. The charge of lack of realism thus did not hold.

Despite many difficulties in the political relationship with Washington (discussed subsequently) Nehru retained not only a civil dialogue with USA but also very considerable economic interaction. Notwithstanding that he regarded nonalignment as "immoral", John Foster Dulles, then U.S. Secretary of State and high priest of the Cold War, came to India more than once for conferring with Nehru on important international issues. One of the just four Presidents of the U.S. to visit India came during Nehru's time.* Dwight Eisenhower visited India 9-13 December 1959 to a warm welcome. The economic relationship was even more extensive than the political relationship. Nehru's view was that until the country had fully evolved its economic policies and developed new economic ties, the old economic relations must be retained.

In Nehru's words, "we maintain our old ties with those countries because no nation can live in isolation. We wanted certain things that we cannot get from elsewhere. That some people obsessed by passion and prejudice disapproved of our relations with the Anglo-American bloc is not sufficient reason for us to break any bond which is of advantage to us". So "unless (and until) we develop new bonds, we shall have to continue as we are doing". This could hardly be described as naive idealism.

Certainly Nehru believed in principles and ideas—in the power of ideas—but he was against the ideologisation

* Written before George W. Bush's visit to India.

of foreign policy. He was not taken in by the din and noise about "freedom" by one bloc and the proselytizing zeal about socialism by the other. Behind these big words lurked national and often the narrow interests of those who were heading these blocs. The U.S. had no qualms about embracing dictators that offered hospitality to U.S. military and various other facilities and declamations against communism ("our s.o.b.s, are better than theirs", as a high U.S. official said famously); and the Soviet Union had no qualms in brutally suppressing popular movements in eastern Europe in the name of protecting socialism.

Nehru rejected fundamentalism in foreign policy, whether of the Western or of the Soviet variety. He was accused of preaching, but in fact he was against moralism in foreign policy. As early as March 1949, he told an audience of the Indian Council of World Affairs (where this writer was present as a young lad) that he disliked moralizing and preaching in international relations. He felt that it was the Western and the Soviet leaders who were most of the time preaching the virtues of their respective systems.

Indeed Nehru clearly told his people that India's interests were paramount in the interactions in foreign relations. He told the Constituent Assembly on 4 December 1947, "whatever policy we may lay down, the art of conducting foreign affairs of a country lies in finding out what is most advantageous to the country. We may talk about international goodwill and mean what we say. But in the ultimate analysis government functions for the good of the country and no government dare do anything which in the short or long run is manifestly to the disadvantage of the country".

Of course with all countries of the world pursuing their own interests, clashes of national interests were bound to take place. It was, therefore, necessary to harmonize the interests of various countries and achieve a consensus. It was Nehru who first used the words "enlightened self-interest", so as to harmonize the differing interests of various countries.

We might also note that Jawaharlal Nehru was against the use of vituperative language in international relations. He was for a civil dialogue both in domestic and international politics. The influence of Gandhi was there: fight against injustice but not against persons individually or nations as such. He called the left's protests against the Dulles visit as juvenile. India had to interact with leaders of other countries, whether we liked their policies or not.

This does not mean that Jawaharlal Nehru never made any mistakes. He was human and to err is human. He made mistakes and we shall have occasion to identify some of those mistakes. But the broad thrust that he gave to India's foreign policy has remained valid despite half a century having passed since. The durability of that thrust is evident from the adherence to it that every government has proclaimed in the last half-century.

The roots of India's foreign policy have often been traced to Asoka's conversion to peace and non-violence and the influence of Gandhi was palpable. The immediate background was, however, the struggle for independence. India's foreign policy was outlined in the resolutions of the Indian National Congress which were essentially drafted by Nehru. The principal element in these foreign policy declarations was India's commitment to the struggle against imperialism and colonialism as well as a commitment to the unity of the struggling nations of the world. India gave a ringing call for the freedom of all countries under colonial rule and solidarity with the worldwide anti-imperialist struggle.

The post-war world saw the collapse of imperialism and the emergence into independence of a large number of countries hitherto under colonial control. India was among the first countries to become independent. The struggle for independence was a long one lasting for nearly a century. In some cases the struggle continued for a long time even after the general collapse of imperialism.

Science and technology came to play a vastly more substantial role than before. Technology, particularly, raised the level of military warfare and civil development to new highs. The 10 mile-an-hour bomber was replaced by the far more terrifying B-52 by the end of World War II, whose lethality was demonstrated in the Vietnam war. Also came the atom bomb raining death and destruction in Hiroshima and Nagasaki. And then the hydrogen bomb and ballistic missiles and what was called the revolution in military affairs (RMA) accompanied by fantastic developments in communications and other scientific and technological achievements that have qualitatively changed the lives of people in the modern world.

There were other important changes taking place rapidly. A unified world market came into existence. Both military and economic power came to be concentrated in U.S. hands. Washington became the hub of economic activity. Its economic dominance coincided with its military dominance. While Europe disarmed and forgot about military power and China was engulfed in revolution and nation building, USA was investing in military modernization and leaped forward in this area leaving all others far behind. (Only the Soviet Union gave it some competition). All decisions about U.S. military power and many concerning economic power came to be concentrated in the hands of the President of the United States who become the most powerful person in the world.

It heralded a new world order: a unified world with its nerve-centre in Washington, a large part of the world under a domination centred in the United States of America, but with a secondary breach represented by the USSR. American military power was positioned strategically around the world. The possession of nuclear weapons changed the power equation, both in military and political terms. The U.S. became the headquarters of the new world system with the Soviet Union challenging it from the margins. A new assembly of world nations was formed as United Nations, but it too was an American inspired, American-financed and American-dominated agency for a long time.

The world economic system was hammered out at Bretton Woods and Dumburton Oakes. The new world order rested on two pillars: nuclear weapons and the new monetary system. It was greatly fortified by the rise of a highly centralized decision-making authority with unparalleled power in its hands, the U.S. presidency. No Emperor in history could match the power and authority of the U.S. President.

Yet as we have noted a breach had been made: Soviet Russia and its allied communist countries with an equally centralized headquarters became the nerve center of the emerging communist camp. The status quo has never been eternally maintained in history—where is the Roman Empire, the French Empire, the British Empire today? But the Americans have immense faith in their exceptionalism and triumphalism. In any case the contention between the two blocs was inevitable. Starting from a much narrower base the Soviets forged ahead in acquiring the attributes of power, particularly nuclear capability and broke the American monopoly.

USA became obsessed with building barriers to the spread of socialism and the destruction of Soviet communism, determined to roll back the "tidal mud" of communism. The cold war eroded the independence of many countries in the world with one camp claiming to speak in the name of freedom and democracy and the other extolled the virtues of social justice and egalitarianism. In this process whether or not a particular country had imposed a ruthless dictatorship became an irrelevant consideration, so long as it remembered to shout the right slogans about the free world. The other power stood for the ushering in of the millennium and vowed to strike down all foes of the proletariat. It regarded democracy as a bourgeois sin and suppressed any strivings for a liberal regime in any communist country with the help of Soviet troops.

It was within this international milieu that Indian foreign policy had to be evolved and shaped.

It was inconceivable that India would wrest freedom with one hand and gift it away with the other. There was no question of India joining the Soviet bloc as India was not a communist country and the Soviet bloc did not have any non-communist member country. That left the U.S.-led Western bloc. Prominent among the Western bloc were those very imperialist countries against whom India and many other Asian countries had struggled for a long time. The question of joining such a bloc could not arise. Becoming a part of the Western bloc militated against the traditions of the freedom struggle. Moreover USA seemed intent on stepping into the space vacated by the erstwhile imperialist powers. Nehru made at least a visible contribution to the Indonesia struggle by organizing an Asian conference to oppose Dutch efforts to reoccupy the islands— known as Indonesia—by sending an Indian pilot to rescue and bring to India the foreign minister of the proclaimed government by the freedom fighters. Possibly Nehru underestimated the pull of the cold war which drew many Asian countries into its vortex with the North Atlantic countries cajoling, bribing and browbeating them into becoming camp followers.

But he was right in believing that membership of a

bloc in those circumstances resulted in an unequal relationship and dilution of the freedom of choice in international relations. You were *ipso facto* on one side, no matter what the merit of a particular issue was. The extension of the cold war became a highly divisive event among and within Asian countries. It not only polarized the Asian countries, it polarized domestic politics also or generally led to the fuelling of dictatorial trends, if not the establishment of dictatorship, in many Asian countries. It sowed the seeds of tension, conflict and violence internally. Through the adoption of independence, a policy of support to the anti-imperialist struggles elsewhere and through a policy of promoting peace in the world, Nehru took foreign policy out of the turmoil of domestic politics and made it subserve the cause of unification and stability in the country.

Jawaharlal Nehru realized that nationalism remained the fundamental feature of the world. It dominated the thinking and actions of countries, all of whom were trying to look after their own interests. The attempt to subsume nationalism into loyalty to a military bloc with a strong head leader succeeded for a while but ultimately blew up in smoke. For a while, however, various countries were either bamboozled or dragooned into submitting to another country's interests. European conflicts took centre stage in the immediate post-war situation. As Nehru put it, Europe and the US "had got into the habit of thinking that their quarrels and controversies were the world's quarrels and controversies and, consequently, the world and specially Asian and African countries must submit to them". To him the major question of the day was not the mutual antagonisms of European countries but the readjustment of relations between Asia and Europe

To begin with India's foreign policy priorities did not concern developments in Europe but were focused nearer home. It was the neighbourhood that claimed first attention.

As early as 1949 Jawaharlal Nehru spelt out the natural directions of India's foreign policy. The nearby countries always had a special interest for India. Necessarily India's foreign policy first turned its attention towards countries bordering it by land and sea. Which were those countries? "If you start from the left, Pakistan; I would also include Afghanistan although it does not touch India, Tibet and China, Burma, Malaya (now Malaysia)", Nehru had defined as India's neighbours in 1949.

He was clear in his mind that India and Pakistan must have close relations and would have them so in the near future. They could not be merely indifferent neighbours or live in eternal hostility. "Ultimately, we can only have friendly relations, whatever period of hostility may intervene in between, because our interests are so closely interlinked", Nehru had said with great perspicacity. Today both in India and Pakistan people are searching for pathways to establishing peaceful relations.

As far as other countries were concerned, Nehru pointed out that relations with them were quite friendly. "Relations with Afghanistan were extremely friendly; so were relations with Nepal", Nehru said. If the neighbouring countries had the first place "in our minds", Nehru said that the second place went to the other countries of Asia with whom India was fairly intimately connected. Indeed India's geographical position made it important whether one thought in terms of China or the Middle East, or Southeast Asia. (The China issue we shall discuss in a separate section). The same logic extended to African countries. India reached out to the struggling countries there, expressed its solidarity with them, and took the lead in the international fora against racialism and colonialism in Africa. All this contributed to the coming together of an increasingly strong and influential Afro-Asian community.

Nonalignment

A major question before the world at that time was, as we have noted earlier, the adjustment of relations between Asia and Europe. The Cold War was an extension of European struggles and Nehru wondered why the European conflicts should distract the attention of Asian countries from the main problems through the fussy climate created by the Cold War. The main problem centred around development and not communism or anti-communism. "In each country of Asia—underdeveloped more or less—the main problem is the problem of food, of clothing, of education, of health. We are concerned with these problems. We are not directly concerned with the problems of power politics", Nehru told the Constituent Assembly on 8 March 1949.

We must keep in focus the international situation in which India's foreign policy was being evolved and given shape and substance. The wartime allies had fallen apart. Two antagonistic blocs had come to dominate the world. The communist bloc led by the Soviet Union and the North Atlantic camp with the United States at its helm. There was intense rivalry resulting in a highly vitiated atmosphere. Particularly the US was intent upon erecting barricades against the Soviet Union and absorbing more and more countries including Asian in an anti-Soviet grouping, euphemistically described as the "freedom" camp and dominated by Washington.

India's main concern at the time was to consolidate its freedom and to keep intact its options in foreign policy. To keep your option open and be able to take decisions according to your own interests and not because you have no other choice since someone else wants you to take a particular decision—that is the essence of an independent foreign policy. Independent foreign policy is a relative term. It does not mean you do not react or interact with other countries, nor even that you are not influenced by others or that you do not influence others. Interaction is a continuous process in international relations and compromises are inherent in dealing with the world community. But in the final analysis you should be able to take your own decision.

That was also the spirit of nonalignment. You interact with various countries of the world but you do not lose your identity by willy-nilly following another country, especially when it's a powerful country. Many countries also used such alignment for settling scores with their local rivals. Nonalignment was also the sister of non-violent satyagraha. The ferocity of the Cold War and the pressure of big powers was extending the area of contention and conflict and eroding the autonomy of the newly independent countries. India's resistance to Western-sponsored pacts and alliances became stiffer as they tried to divide Asian-African countries and suck them into their orbit. The prolonged struggle for independence heightened suspicions in the country about these attempts to inveigh smaller and weaker Asian countries by the imperialist powers.

The creation of military blocs in Asia and Africa was a manifestation of neocolonialism. It represented a determined attempt by the Western powers to re-establish and extend their spheres of influence and ensure their domination under the garb of anti-Communism and freedom. To quote Nehru, "the crisis of the time in Asia is colonialism versus anti-colonialism" and that "colonialism is digging in, in some areas, putting on new clothes". Delivering the presidential address of the Indian National Congress session on 24 January 1954, Nehru said, "the issue was colonialism and racialism". He abhorred racialism as much as colonialism.

In fact there were two struggles going on simultaneously in the world, the struggle against imperialism and colonialism, or more correctly neocolonialism, and the struggle for world peace. The two meshed in with each other, with the struggle for independence taking primacy in the initial years after the second world war and the demands of preservation of world peace occupying a higher priority in later years, as we shall see.

Kashmir and Indian Foreign Policy

The example of Kashmir was instructive in observing how the imperialist powers were functioning at the time. It was India which complained to the Security Council against Pakistan's aggression in Kashmir where the latter had first sent tribesmen to invade and maraud and when that was foiled it dispatched its regular troops. But the Kashmir issue was embroiled in international power politics. The Western powers pressed on with unfriendly resolutions on the Kashmir issue obliging India to look to the Soviet Union to use its veto power or the threat to use it to modify or moderate Western-sponsored resolutions. As Nehru himself observed in 1957, despite the fullness and clarity with which Krishna Menon had expounded the Kashmir question in the Security Council, the Western powers' sponsored resolutions was totally unacceptable to India. They were deterred only by the Soviet veto.

Most people have given insufficient attention to the impact of the Kashmir issue on India's foreign policy. The Anglo-American effort was to support Pakistan and enable it to snatch Kashmir away in order to reward it for making available its territory and bases for various activities aimed at the Soviet Union and China. It became a question of preserving India's territorial integrity. The Soviet leaders' shrewd analysis of the opportunity offered by the Kashmir issue for a new relationship with India yielded rich dividends and when Khrushchev and Bulganin visited India in 1954 and went to Kashmir and declared that Moscow considered Kashmir to be a part of India, Indo-Soviet relations entered a qualitatively new era. Kashmir defined our foreign policy in ways that our foreign policy practitioners and analysts have rarely dwelt upon. But this impact on our foreign policy also demonstrated that the charge of sheer idealism informing our foreign policy could hardly be sustained.

Nonalignment emerged in a certain historical context—to meet particular challenges in a particular international milieu. Nonalignment was not coterminous with foreign policy. It was an instrument of foreign policy—a concept that has remained valid for more than half a century and continues to remain valid until now. The core of nonalignment was the defence of autonomy of decision-making in foreign affairs, particularly in a situation in which the weaker Asian countries were being drawn into military blocs, like the SEATO (Southeast Asia Treaty Organisation) concluded at Manila and CENTO (Central Treaty Organisation) which was created in the Middle East often referred to as the Baghdad Pact, but with overlapping membership. Pakistan, for instance, was a member of both SEATO and CENTO. The military blocs were therefore not even genuinely regional. They not only overlapped but also included non-regional powers who established a toehold in the alliance and exercised pressure and control.

SEATO went beyond the confines of the countries in the region. To quote Nehru: "This area can be designated by those countries by merely declaring that any given place is in this area. This, I submit, is a dangerous extension of the idea of defence. The area which they mentioned was partly determinate and partly indeterminate. It would be the big and powerful countries that would decide matters and not the two or three weak and small countries who became members of the alliance".

Military Blocs

A brief look at the Asian alliances is instructive. First in order to pave the way for alignment with Pakistan, Washington pressurized Turkey to form an alliance with Pakistan. Turkey was reluctant for after all what did Pakistan have to do with Turkey's defence or vice versa. Under Washington's pressure Turkey signed a Pact of Mutual Cooperation with Pakistan in February 1954. This was followed by the establishment on 8 September 1954 of the Southeast Asia Collective Defence Treaty, subsequently known as SEATO, comprising USA, Australia, France, Great Britain, New Zealand, Pakistan, the Philippines and Thailand. The large majority of the members were non Southeast Asian states. Following a military agreement between Turkey and Iraq on 24 February 1955, came the CENTO,originally named Middle East Treaty Organization. Its members included USA, Britain, Iraq, Turkey and Pakistan. Again the majority was non-regional. These alliances were the product of Anglo-American pressure with promises of US military and economic largesse.

What was equally objectionable was the way "aggression" was defined in the Manila Treaty. "Aggression" was not only external aggression but also "a fact or situation created within this area" that could be construed as aggression. This curious wording entitled those countries to intervene in the internal developments of various countries. It affected the concept of integrity, sovereignty and independence. Pakistan had made no secret that it's sole purpose in joining SEATO was to derive leverage against India. It was hardly concerned about Soviet communism, much less Chinese communism. It regarded any quarrel or conflict with India as falling within the purview of "aggression".

It is another matter that most of those military alliances came to grief but that need not concern us here. Many of those military alliances were in fact extensions of the North Atlantic Treaty Organisation (NATO). Officially India's comments about European developments were kept in a low-key. But the creeping and continual enlargement of the ambit of NATO became a matter of considerable disquiet. The way NATO was expanded geographically and the way it developed conceptually could not be ignored, particularly as it was enlarged to cover the colonial possessions of the erstwhile imperialist powers. As Nehru put it in the Lok Sabha on 29 September 1954, how the maintenance and the continuation of the authority of those colonial powers over their dependent countries was a matter of defence of the North Atlantic community was not clear to him. The treaty members had started giving protective cover to the colonial domains of the powers concerned. Of immediate concern was the reference made by the Portuguese authorities to the North Atlantic Treaty covering Goa in its wide scope. As Nehru made it clear, India was not bound by treaties concluded by other countries affecting India's interests to which India was not a party.

India had to contend with persistent attempts by Western countries to decide about the problems of Asia in Washington or London or more often in tandem with each other. Nehru thought it would be a folly for Asian countries to allow themselves to be dragged into the European conflicts. But some in Asia were determined to commit that folly and become a part of Western-led military alliances. Nehru failed to realise his view of Asian resurgence which remained more a hope than a reality (it started becoming a reality nearly half a century later). Yet it should be recalled that more and more countries were coming around to the ideas and principles expounded by India under Nehru's leadership. The underlying principle of nonalignment was rationality. Differences among countries should be settled through dialogue and not through resort to force.

This was inevitably linked with the notion of coexistence which India advocated along with some other Asian countries.

Truth was many sided. The ancient Indian philosophy commended that there was not just black-and-white, but many shades of grey—that was the cosmic reality. In other words, tolerance, rationality and coexistence. No country or ideology could claim the monopoly of truth. As Nehru put it, "the only truth about the world was that truth was not confined to one country, one people, one ideology and one world". Nonalignment was an operational part of this pluralism. Nonalignment was not foreign policy but a tool of foreign policy in a given situation. Nehru's answer to the Cold War was the peace area, the maintenance of independence, the struggle for peace and the advocacy of peaceful coexistence. He called this peace area the "workshop of peace", as a bridge between contending countries, military alliances and their ideologies.

The world powers could only think in terms of black and white, no other shades. Nehru recalled that the "Russians pressed us for some time, but soon got reconciled to our independence. The Americans were more difficult because of Mr Dulles and his doctrine of military alliances.. When we refused to join them, they got Pakistan, a development which added to the tensions and troubles of this continent. Naturally, we reacted strongly against this process of intervention which brought the Cold War to our borders. For, if the Americans came in as a military force, the Russians were bound to follow suit".

The Temper of Peace

Thus there came to be two major objectives in foreign policy for India: the struggle against imperialism and racialism, and the quest for world peace. In fact, as the formal structure of imperialism began to collapse and more and more countries became independent and asserted their independence, the preservation of world peace became a more urgent necessity. Economic and social development would be seriously thwarted if peace of the world broke down. Along with Einstein and Bertrand Russell and some other world luminaries of the time, Nehru had come to the conclusion that the need for maintaining peace of the world had come to override the struggle against imperialism, or maybe he was deeply influenced by them. In any case bastions of imperialism were falling one after another and the emerging neocolonialism and the neoimperialism could be contested while keeping the focus on preserving world peace.

This was evident from Nehru's stand at the Belgrade conference of non-aligned countries in 1961. Much to the annoyance of some of the "radical" states who wished to concentrate only on anti-colonialism, and not to worry too much about the threat to world peace from the raging arms race, Nehru insisted that colonialism, vicious as it was, represented a dying force and that the question of war and peace was no less important. It was at his insistence that the conference dispatched two delegations, one to the Soviet Union of which Nehru himself was a member, and the other to USA to plead with their leaders to halt the testing of nuclear weapons.

Despite the deficit in military strength and the equally deficient economic power, Nehru brought India centrestage on the world scene. Not just that, the fact remains that the world powers used India's good offices to resolve the deadlocks over some cantankerous issues whose resolution helped to some extent the cause of peace. Despite the antipathy to Nehru and India in many quarters and notwithstanding other measures that USA reportedly took to obtain Chinese consent, like Eisenhower's reported threat to use the atom bomb, both the parties turned to India to unravel the knots in which USA and China had tied themselves up as a consequence of the Korean War in the early 50s. The war began when North Korea invaded the South in an effort to forcibly unify the Korean peninsula. The US entered the war and obtained UN sanction. General MacArthur, Supreme Commander of the US forces pushing back the North Korean troops also made a similar mistake of forcibly unifying Korea and racing to the Yalu river, the frontier between China and North Korea. The Chinese felt threatened by this action and sent their 'volunteer' forces to repel the US advance. The war resulted in a stalemate around the 38th parallel, and was equally stalemated on the issue of prisoners of war and allied issues. India was made the chairman of the Korean commission to sort out the problems relating to prisoners of war in the aftermath of the war in Korea.

Similarly with regard to the Indochina war, it may be recalled that the French had sought to re-establish their colonial control over Indochina after the second world war but were finally defeated by Ho Chi Minh's forces at Dien Bien Phu. An international conference was held in Geneva April-July 1954 to seek a political settlement of the wars in Indochina and Korea. The Americans managed to keep India out of the conference, but it is well-known that Krishna Menon played a substantial role from the sidelines. The Geneva accords established an International Control Commission of which India was made the chairperson with Canada and Poland as the other members to implement the accords and supervise free and fair elections in the two halves of Vietnam (South and North) for the emergence of a unified government. It is another matter that Washington had no intention to let the accords be implemented and it took another brutal war before Vietnam could become a unified, independent country.

The China Issue

The biggest challenge that India faced came not from Pakistan but from China. It was on the China issue that Nehru was flayed most sharply by domestic and foreign critics and called naive and idealistic and, of course, unrealistic. The irony is that many of his strongest critics have in recent years become the stoutest votaries of expansion of relations with China.

China went through a sanguinary revolution during 1945-47 marking the resurgence of China from what was described as "the sick man of Asia". A thoroughgoing land reform, described vividly by Mohit Sen in his autobiography, *A Traveller And The Road*, resulting in a great deal of bloodletting and the installation of a communist government riding the wave of a worker-peasent revolt. In the words of Mao Zedong, "China has stood up". The relationship of this new China with other influential countries of the world and its neighbours was a matter of great importance for peace in Asia.

Nehru was aware that what had happened was not a palace coup, but a fundamental transformation. "Our liking it or disliking it" was immaterial, as Nehru said. Putting it in very simple terms for his people, rice had been the major question in Chinese history. Empires had risen or fallen on their capacity to make rice available to the people on affordable prices. That was inextricably tied up with land relationships and landlord domination. It was also related to the establishment of a strong and effective government. Now a government had taken over which was effectively dealing with the question of distribution of rice and the land question. A strong central government had emerged after a century of war, disruption and warlordism.

The Chinese revolution also marked the upsurge of Chinese nationalism. Chinese nationalism, even more than Chinese communism had triumphed. The leaders of new

China were no doubt convinced communists and their goal was the establishment of a communist society. But in doing so they were sinifying Marxism. More than anything else nationalism had reasserted itself in China. That being so, the main question was what kind of policy and approach India should adopt in meeting this new phenomenon on its borders.

It should not be overlooked that the China policy had to be evolved in the context of the larger interests of the country. China's motives and intentions were raising serious questioning within the government, particularly after the march of Chinese troops into Tibet.

The Deputy Prime Minister and Home Minister, Sardar Vallabbhai Patel wrote to Prime Minister Jawaharlal Nehru on 7 November 1950 expressing serious concern over developments on the northeastern border. In Sardar's view China's abusive assertions about foreign influences on India and the use of armed forces in Tibet had opened a new, and dangerous perspective for India. The "disappearance of Tibet" as we knew it, Sardar pointed out, must invite the government's urgent attention. Communism did not exclude imperialism, as in Patel's opinion, Communists could be as bad imperialists as any. So for the first time, after centuries India's defence had to be concentrated on two fronts (the other being Pakistan). With the brittle situation in the North-East, "the Chinese and their source of inspiration, Soviet Russia would not miss any opportunity", Sardar wrote to Nehru, "of exploiting these two weak spots, partly in support of their ideology, but partly in support of their ambitions". Patel believed that this new development would enable the Indian communists to have easier access to ideas, commands and weapons from China and would constitute another threat. Patel's premonitions about the implicit troubles coming from the new situation in the North-East had a saddeningly prophetic ring about them. But the error in Sardar's thinking was his preoccupation with communism and insufficient consideration accorded to Chinese nationalism. The irredentism of Chinese nationalism was a more disturbing factor than Chinese communism. Indeed this very nationalism had impacted Indian communists also and the split in the Indian communist movement could be traced, in part at least, to the stirrings of nationalism among many Indian communists. Patel confused Chinese nationalism with Chinese communism.

Nehru did not err on that score, although he erred on some other scores as we shall see. Nehru was well aware of the new situation on the northern frontiers, nor was he blissfully ignorant of the challenges that could come from the new dispensation in China. In his speech to the Lok Sabha on 27 November 1959 Nehru said, "we know enough history to realize that a strong China is normally an expansionist China. This has been the case throughout its history. And we thought, or we felt the two factors, the great push towards industrialization of that country and the amazing pace of its population increase—taken together would create a most dangerous situation".

Elaborating on his understanding Nehru revealed while speaking in the Lok Sabha on 7 December 1961 that much earlier, soon after the Chinese revolution, "we came to the conclusion that our borders were going to be, well, threatened in some way. In what way, of course, we did not know. From then we had that picture". He conceded that "the government might have been overtaken by certain events and that all the steps that could have been taken were not taken because of the various difficulties, including the terrain and the financial difficulties, but thinking of a friendly China, we did not lose our perspective because the Government from the beginning was thinking of this perspective. A huge elephant of a country sitting on our borders..." Thus he denied the charge of complacency.

Nevertheless Nehru had pursued a course of caution for a variety of reasons. For one, as far as Tibet was concerned, India just did not have the military strength to send its troops and fight China. The Indian army had already been fractured with one part going to Pakistan after the partition of India. India had to send troops to Kashmir to fight first the tribesman who descended on Kashmir and then the regular Pakistani army whose attempt to seize Kashmir was thus foiled. The pot was not only boiling but was full. With one active front, only the most naive would wish to activate a second front against them. To fight simultaneously on two fronts even for a very strong army which the Indian army was not at the time—could hardly be appealing as a sound policy to Indian government leaders.

Equally notable was the fact that not only was no other country prepared to risk its own armed involvement, except for an odd one or two, certainly no big power was willing to recognize an independent Tibet, despite all the denunciation of "Red China" and the homilies to India about the perils of inaction.

However, even Nehru had erred in his deductions about Chinese history. First of all in old imperial days every empire tended to expand. Secondly, although Chinese empires had expanded on their peripheries traditional China still shunned contact with the outside world lest its peerless civilization be contaminated by contact with peoples at a lower level of civilization (referred to as barbarians which was a standardised way of putting it). What had happened now was Chinese nationalism pulsating with a revolutionary euphoria coupled with sinified Marxism that wanted to spread the message to the whole of Asia and at the same time to recover all the "lost territories".

Nehru felt that a clash with China could be a future possibility but he wanted to postpone, if not avoid, it. He advocated and pursued the path of peace with China. He wanted to give the country peace and time to develop its economic strength and achieve basic stability within the country and not be involved in exhaustive conflicts with other countries, more so in the context of an ongoing conflict with Pakistan. As he said, "there was a certain compulsion of events and no government, however much it may have differed from our ways of thinking, could have functioned very differently from what we did, always keeping in view the fact that the real thing before us was to strengthen India industrially and not superficially by getting an odd gun or an odd aircraft".

Nehru bent every effort to cultivate friendly relations with China, to remove misunderstandings, to establish the basis of cooperative relationship and to do everything possible to obtain a long period of peace with China. He accepted China as a great power. As early as 1950, he declared publicly that China was a great nation, able to shape its own destiny and which could not be ignored, "no matter what resolutions you might pass".

Nehru tried his level best to ensure that China was accepted into the international community with honour and dignity. Thereby, he was hoping, the Chinese revolution would be humanised and China become a normal member of the United Nations and its organs, particularly the Security Council where China was a founding and permanent member with veto power. The rump Kuomintang group led by Chiang Kai-shek in Formosa (now referred to as Taiwan) could not in all conscience claim to be the spokesman or representative of the vast country of China. Nehru's consistent and principled stand on the Chinese regime's membership of the UN and its various bodies seemed to have had a sobering effect on Beijing at the time, although subsequently China turned violently against him.

Nehru calmed the spat on Tibet with China and signed with Beijing a new accord which regulated trade on the borders between Tibet and India and by which India yielded all the facilities and the privileges enjoyed by British India in Tibet which the Chinese regarded as symbols of colonialism. The agreement on Tibet referred to the territory as "Tibet region of China"—a somewhat ambiguous term which definitely implied that it was not just a normal part of China, but this was also the phrase the Chinese themselves were using. The treaty became notable more because it enunciated the principles governing relations between India and China that came to be known as the Five Principles of Peaceful Coexistence:

1. mutual respect for each other's territorial integrity and sovereignty
2. mutual non-aggression
3. mutual noninterference in each other's internal affairs
4. equality and mutual benefit
5. peaceful coexistence

The enunciation of these principles made this agreement a landmark in diplomatic history, as similar declarations were made by many countries as directive principles for relations among countries, even though some of them did not exactly set a shining example on their observance.

The Americans were clearly dismissive of the five principles, and of course, of nonalignment. They considered it as immoral. But as the irony of history would have it, Nixon was obliged to enunciate these very five principles in the Shanghai Declaration that Washington signed with Beijing. Even as, domestic criticism against Nehru mounted, after a bitter revolt in Tibet was crushed and the Dalai Lama forced to flee to India in 1959. A senior Congress leader, Kripalani, said in Parliament that "nonalignment was born in sin". It was unfortunate that so many of his colleagues did not really understand the rationale and the compulsions behind his policies.

But the real tragedy was that Nehru's China policy was undone by the US administration's implacable hostility and its persistent moves to frustrate it. Nehru had hoped that recognition of revolutionary new China would tame some of the exuberance and that in this way China would gradually become a responsible member of the international order (that is what happened some three decades after his death). But this objective was unachievable without American cooperation. There was no way Nehru could have by himself enabled Beijing to realise its national objectives: acceptance as one of the great powers, membership of the Security Council with veto power and recognition as an equal consultant in resolving world issues. Only the Americans could have helped in realising these objectives. But successive American administrations excelled in inveterate hostility to China thus undercutting Nehru's China policy. Indeed US policy came to be to undermine Nehru and cut him to size.

The Border Issue

Going back to the agreement on Tibet, it must also be recalled that along with the new development in Tibet, what was exercising deliberations within the Government concerned the border issue. Chinese maps showed large areas of Indian territory (or at least regarded so by India) as within the Chinese borders. When the issue was raised with the Chinese authorities, the stock reply was that those were old KMT maps which they had not had the time to look into. When subsequently they made official claims to large chunks of Indian territory, the response was that all they had said was that those were old maps which they had not had time to look into but that did not mean that they were not correct; now that they had looked into the matter, they found that the maps portrayed the correct position! Beijing carried the "art of diplomacy" (or duplicity?) to a fine extent on the issue of its position on the Kashmir issue. During the period when India-China relations were good, on Indian questioning of its standpoint, since Beijing had not anywhere explicitly acknowledged the Indian position (unlike the Soviets), the repeated reply was: could you point out anything they had written that questioned India's position. Subsequently when Beijing came heavily on the side of Pakistan, including the Kashmir issue, the defence given to an Indian protest, as seen from India's White Papers on China, was: could you point out anything that we had written or spoken that endorsed your position on Kashmir!

Anyway, getting back to the issue, the Government deliberated on what stand to take, particularly around the time the Tibet agreement was signed. Looking at it from various angles, Nehru decided (as he revealed later) that, rather than confronting China at that time, India would make its position on the border alignment public and let the Chinese react or object to it. This was a serious mistake. As Beijing contended later it was not obliged to react to the statements made in India. It would have been a much better course if India had offered to fully accept China's sovereignty over Tibet in return for China's written agreement to a border alignment, with some suitable concessions from either side, approximating India's position on the border. At that time China needed India's friendship even more than India did of China's friendly hand. Possibly China would have refused such a deal, but then India would have known what to expect and the world would have been clearer about who was sincere and who was not.

Anyway, we have already noticed that India's China policy was caught up in the vortex of the Cold War and the intensity of the international rivalries. By 1957-58 Mao was getting impatient both with regard to domestic and international developments. He was swinging to a more radical domestic and foreign policy: the Hundred Flowers movement, the anti-Rightist campaign, the people's communes, "all reactionaries are paper tigers" thesis and so on. Simultaneously China sharpened its anti-American rhetoric. This leftward lurch in both domestic and foreign policy coincided with the Tibetan revolt, the use of armed forces to crush it and the flight of the Dalai Lama and his followers to India.

When the Dalai Lama escaped to India Nehru undoubtedly faced painful choices. There was no question of denying asylum to the Dalai Lama. That would have violated India's traditions as well as modern democratic practices. In addition some 60,000 Tibetan refugees also sought shelter in India. Public opinion in India was inflamed at the developments in Tibet. Jawaharlal Nehru insulated the Dalai Lama from domestic politics and international intrigue, made him at home in a hill station (Dharamsala) far from the madding crowd, and entrusted him with the work of rehabilitation of the Tibetan refugees. Nor did Nehru extend India's recognition to any Tibetan government in exile.

Border War

During this time the Chinese had extended the road to Aksai Chin in Ladakh and revived their border claims. Border skirmishes were taking place and Beijing sought to give it an ideological twist. Nehru had now become a reactionary pursuing an expansionist policy and serving the interests of world imperialism headed by the US—so ran the Chinese propaganda. The Soviets made one last effort to bring a reconciliation and persuade the Chinese leadership to send Zhou Enlai to India in response to a rather lukewarm invitation from New Delhi.

The two sides had already taken irreconcilable positions and with the Chinese making an ideological issue of the border dispute, there was little chance of a give-and-take on the border issue. The Indian opinion was already highly inflamed with the media in full cry about India's "honour" and "respect" the whole atmosphere hardly served any other purpose than hamstringing Nehru. Most of those shouting the loudest in print or otherwise gave no evidence of understanding the military realities on the ground.

The Chinese had, and in any case, decided to strike at an ill-prepared India in October 1962. We made another mistake in the assessment of Chinese motives and objectives. In panic we thought that the Chinese hordes would be rushing down the Assam hills and occupying large areas of Indian territory. This is what would explain the hasty letter Nehru wrote to the US President John Kennedy for immediate and large-scale assistance to meet the Chinese threat. The Chinese objectives were limited. They wanted to "teach India a lesson", undermine Nehru's image and India's nonalignment and to demonstrate to the world who was the stronger power. Having achieved that purpose they quickly withdrew to the positions generally held by them earlier.

Despite some mistakes, Nehru kept his head and did not allow a pure border dispute to degenerate into an ideological confrontation which was what Beijing wanted. Consequently, it became an unprecedentedly rare situation in which heads of both the rival blocs—USA and the Soviet Union—found themselves on the same side. Mr. Khrushchev made it amply clear that he did not buy Mao's argument that Nehru started the war to please the

Americans and had joined the imperialist camp. To make his position quite explicit he signed with India an agreement for the sale and production of MIG fighters. Mao never forgave the Russians for it.

The fact remains that Chinese policies did not succeed either. It was a testimony to the failure of their policies that they had ultimately to come around and adopt the very policy Nehru was advocating. The self-proclaimed "independent foreign policy" of China was a replica of Nehru's policy of non-alignment. Their approach towards India now approximated the approach advocated by Nehru. His policy of a friendly and civilized approach, seeking peaceful solution to various problems was in the vital interests of the people of India. Nehru's assessment of China was realistic and rational. Subsequently, even his sharpest critics joined the China bandwagon. Peace with honour with China was at the core of Nehru's policy. It still remains the only valid policy. Nobody has been able to suggest an alternative sounder policy and we are continuing to pursue the same policy towards China that Nehru had advocated and pursued.

CHAPTER TWO

FOREIGN POLICY UNDER INDIRA GANDHI

Jawaharlal Nehru was succeeded after his death by Lal Bahadur Shastri in 1965. Outwardly a mild-manner person, diminutive and without apparent charisma, he nevertheless showed great grit and leadership qualities. It was under his stewardship that the first real war between India and Pakistan took place in September 1965 and it was he who gave currency to the slogan, "Jai Jawan, Jai Kisan." The war partly helped restore the morale of the army that had been shattered by the border war with China in 1962, but was inconclusive. The United Nations helped arrange a ceasefire, and the Soviet Union for the first time took the initiative to bring about peace negotiations. Lal Bahadur Shastri met Field Marshal Ayub Khan, President of Pakistan, in Tashkent (now the capital of Uzbekistan) and under the persistent prodding of Alexei Kosygin, then Prime Minister of the Soviet Union, signed what came to be known as the Tashkent Agreement, by which the two countries agreed to follow the peaceful route to the solution of their problems, including Kashmir. However, the agreement was sharply denounced by Zulfiqar Ali Bhutto, who was then Pakistan's Foreign Minister and set him on the path to his own power.

Tragically, Mr Shastri passed away with a massive heart attack soon after signing the Tashkent Agreement. In January 1966 Indira Gandhi became the first woman Prime Minister of independent India. Mrs Gandhi took over the reins of power under a forbidding domestic and international milieu. First of all there were difficult domestic compulsions. Mrs Gandhi did not enjoy a clear majority in the Lok Sabha and was dependent on the left support (history seems to be repeating itself now). The balance of power had shifted from the Centre to the States. The new Government was further roiled by acute food shortages, the country troubled by floods and drought and was living from hand to mouth. Between December 1965 and May 1966 India had imported some 8 million tons of food grains under P.L. 480 from the United States itself which at that time was a pretty heavy burden, and some 23 countries had pledged food grains assistance to India. Forty six million people were affected by scarcity conditions spread over districts in Madhya Pradesh, Orissa, Rajasthan Maharashtra, Andhra Pradesh and Punjab. The pressure on the economy as well as on foreign exchange reserves could well be imagined. India had devalued its currency in the hope of easing the pressures and in expectation of large-scale assistance from USA which never really materialized. On top of it the security environment was none-too-benign. The wars with China and Pakistan had enervated the economy and relations were far from normal with either of the two neighbours.

Mrs. Gandhi began her innings in foreign relations first with a visit to Yugoslavia and the UAR (now Egypt) to re-emphasize their special relationship and the continued adherence to nonalignment, and then to the United States, perhaps believing that the era of abrasive relationship should be over and hoping to evolve a new relationship, what with the shared democratic values and the challenge posed by a militant Chinese foreign policy. These were the themes that she stressed during her visit, obviously nursing the hope of closer and more stable ties with the United States.

But she came back considerably chastened. Notwithstanding U.S. President Lyndon Johnson's public effusiveness ("give this girl whatever she wants"), privately, she told this writer in a special interview (19 March 1979) Johnson just sat tight over Indian requests for expedited food grains shipments. This arm twisting was meant to modify India's relationship with the Soviet Union. Johnson was also attempting to pressurize India to mute its criticism of USA's Vietnam war.

Mrs. Gandhi embarked upon an agricultural strategy that envisaged rapid growth of foodgrains production and vowed that never again should India be dependent on other countries to feed the people. Perhaps her greatest contribution lay in making India self-sufficient in foodgrains, thereby immeasurably fortifying India's independence in foreign affairs. She gave an indirect indication of this new approach in a speech at a civic reception in Colombo in September 1969. "Our new agricultural strategy hopes to add 25 million tons in five years, thus helping us to achieve self-sufficiency in foodgrains. This new approach to agriculture relied on intensive farming with the help of fertilizer, new varieties of seed, extension of credit and the bringing together of the farmers, the scientists and the extension workers", she told her audience. In fact India achieved virtual self-sufficiency much earlier than envisaged at that time.

The encounter with Lyndon Johnson reaffirmed the broad foreign policy principles enunciated and given shape by Jawaharlal Nehru. Mrs. Gandhi had to encounter and deflect a similar attempt by the Soviet Union to change the ground rules in South Asia. Soon after the Tashkent Agreement, in misbelief like that of the Americans, the Soviet leadership thought that they could take both India and Pakistan on board with them. Perhaps encouraged by the sweet-talking of the Pakistani ruling group, Moscow announced an arms aid programme for Islamabad. There was consternation and almost disbelief in India since the Soviets had come to be regarded as special friends. It was only after a hugely demonstrative reaction in India against the Soviet move that Moscow wound up whatever plans it had entertained in this regard. Mrs. Gandhi told this writer, on being asked why Moscow planned that action, that the Soviets thought they could get away with it. Moscow had to learn yet another time during the Bangladesh crisis that Mrs. Gandhi would set the terms for this friendship and would not accept anything that violated India's national interests. This much was acknowledged even by Richard Nixon and Henry Kissinger as we shall see.

Mrs. Gandhi's essential thinking was reflected in her ringing speech at a summit meeting of the Nonaligned in the African city of Lusaka in October 1970. It should also be recalled parenthetically that by that time Mrs. Gandhi had recovered considerable political ground and was emerging as the undisputed leader of her own party after a right-wing faction had split away. The economy was also reviving and the country was generally in better shape than before. The revolution of our times was unfinished, Mrs. Gandhi told the Lusaka Summit. Millions of people across the world had come into their own and they wanted that the decisions concerning war and peace and social, economic and political development "could be made only by us, in our own way and in our own countries. That was how nonalignment was born". The fact of the matter was that neither colonialism nor racialism had vanished. "The old comes back in new guise", Mrs. Gandhi said.

At an earlier foreign policy seminar in August 1970, Mrs. Gandhi had said significantly, "we see the world from where we are. Other countries see the world from where they are. There were common problems, common objectives, common difficulties and common threats that bound India and many Asian-African countries together. She wanted to be friends with all but on terms of equality.

Much of the leadership and the inspiration for the non-aligned movement was being provided by the troika of the leaders of Yugoslavia, Egypt and India. Nehru, Nasser and Tito held two formal meetings of what came to be known as the Tripartite Conference. The third was held in New Delhi in October 1966 when Mrs. Gandhi was Prime Minister. The speeches made by the leaders and the joint statement issued at the conclusion of the meet reflected the concerns of the non-aligned: the pressures being applied on the emergent countries, the threats of neoimperialism and the quest for world peace. The joint statement expressed particular concern at the "sufferings of the Vietnamese people", called for the cessation of the bombing of Vietnam (by the US forces) and the faithful implementation of the Geneva accords on Vietnam. This reference to Vietnam was rather a bold act on the part of Mrs. Gandhi because the country reeling under the impact of floods and drought was dependent chiefly on the US for food supplies and the Johnson administration had become particularly sensitive—and vulnerable—on the Vietnam's issue.

Bangladesh Crisis

While she was discovering her political elan and the country its economic revival, India came face to face with another crisis right at her doorsteps. Without going into too many details, which are outside the purview of this book, we may just recall that India's partition in 1947 had seen the emergence of two halves of Pakistan, West and East, separated by thousands of miles of Indian territory, but constituting one country on the basis of religion. The seeds of separation were sown in their very birth for, it had been observed the world over, that religion could bring but not keep countries together for a long time. In any case Pakistan came to be ruled by its western wing, and within the western wing by West Punjab. The East came to be treated as a poor relation, although it constituted the majority in Pakistan. Bengali was suppressed and Urdu promoted in its place. The East's resources were exploited but little attention given to the economic growth of East Bengal (or East Pakistan as it was then referred to). Gradually Bengali nationalism took hold and a Party, Awami League, and the leader, Sheikh Mujibur Rehman, arose to lead this nationalism.

The crunch came in December 1970 when after a protracted struggle elections were held throughout Pakistan in which Sheikh Mujib's Awami League swept the polls in East Bengal and secured a majority in the new National Assembly of Pakistan. Zulfikar Ali Bhutto's Pakistan Peoples Party secured a large number of seats in West Pakistan. Bhutto now advanced a new "democratic" principle that East and West Pakistan should be treated on a par and, therefore, he had equal right to form a government.

To cut the story short, the West Pakistan's elite had no intention of parting with power. Field Marshal Yahya Khan, then President of Pakistan, whose lapses in sobriety were legend, declared martial law, arrested Mujib and suppressed the Awami League. A brutal crackdown by the Pakistani army followed in East Bengal, the likes of which had not been seen in recent times.

While India had kept its own counsel, the rapidly escalating situation was willy-nilly dragging India into the Pakistani cauldron. Hundreds of thousands of East Bengalis were driven from their homes and were pouring into the safety of India. An ominous situation was developing. Within eight weeks three and a half million had crossed over to India in an endless track day and night. Some 60-70,000 were coming in every day from all social classes and communities—peasants, labourers, middle-class, Hindus, Muslims, Christians, men, women and children. The Pakistani army was obviously pursuing a policy of not just stamping out every vestige of dissidence but also to drive it out and away into India. This was putting intolerable social and financial pressure on India. Mrs. Gandhi told the Lok Sabha that there could be no military solution to the problem in East Bengal and that conditions should be created for the safe return of the refugees to their homes and lands.

India tried the path of arousing the world opinion and obliging the international community to pressurize the governing elite in Pakistan to halt the persecution and repression and restore democratic process so that nearly four million refugees could be sent back to their homes. The international media was doing a fair job of highlighting the atrocities being perpetrated on a hapless population, but the governments were guarded, particularly the U.S. government which remained unmoved. The Nixon-Kissinger team was fully aligned with the regime in West Pakistan.

The reader would recall that this was precisely the time that the Nixon-Kissinger duo with the active co-operation of the Government in Islamabad were determinedly making their opening towards China and the time when the Mao-Zhou duo were determined to end China's isolation, forge a new relationship with Washington and create a new front against the USSR. India was the common stumbling block. The Bangladesh developments could not have come at a more inconvenient time for the Nixon administration. Arranged through the good offices of General Yahya Khan, Henry Kissinger, then Secretary of State and chief security advisor of Nixon, ostensibly on a visit to Pakistan, had feigned illness and gone on a secret visit to China. The records of his meetings with Chairman Mao Zedong

(Chairman of the Chinese Communist Party) and Prime Minister Zhou Enlai clearly revealed their bias (and one can almost say venom) against India, and their preoccupation with "saving" Pakistan. Kissinger candidly admitted that he was constrained by domestic public opinion and encouraged Beijing to take military action against India, a bait which the Chinese leadership was not prepared to fall for. But not knowing all that was going on, India could not take a chance against this combination of USA and China.

It was under the circumstances that the Indo-Soviet Treaty of Peace Friendship and Cooperation was signed in August 1971. Again, Mrs. Gandhi had set the agenda. The Soviets agreed, perhaps reluctantly, that if there was aggression against any of the two parties, they would immediately consult each other on how to meet the aggression. Since there was no question of any aggression against the Soviet Union, the Treaty served as a warning to both Washington and Beijing not to think of military action against India in the unfolding Bangladesh crisis. The Treaty also praised India's policy of nonalignment.

Recent records show that it was a restraining factor in U.S. response to the crisis. Mrs. Gandhi said after the signing of the treaty that it would "discourage such adventurism on the part of countries which had shown a pathological hostility towards us". Responding to criticism in certain western circles that India was abandoning the path of nonalignment, Mrs. Gandhi made the withering remarks that those who were now criticizing India had always been hostile to India's policy of nonalignment. The Treaty won broad support in India, among its defenders being Jayaprakash Narayan and C. Rajagopalachari.

The crunch came on the third of December. Pakistani airforce struck in a pre-emptive move to decimate the Indian air force on the ground. The Pakistani plan went totally awry as India had already moved the planes into safer hangars. It is ironic but true that every war between India and Pakistan was started by the Pakistani military rulers under the naive belief that they could score a quick victory and humble India and, in some cases, grab Kashmir. The end result was generally the opposite of what they had planned for.

The December 3rd strike started yet another war between India and Pakistan. The Indian troops struck back on both the eastern and western fronts. More significantly, the Indian troops, actively aided and guided by the Mukti Bahini raced towards Dacca. India recognized the new state of Bangladesh on 6 December and the Pakistani troops in the erstwhile East Bengal surrendered to the Indian troops on 16 December 1971. Bangladesh had become a reality and soon afterwards Sheikh Mujibur Rehman was restored to power in his sonar Bangla. This was Mrs Gandhi's finest hour and won her the tribute of being India's "Joan of Arc" by her arch political rival, Atal Behari Vajpayee. Both China and USA made threatening noises and Mr. Nixon even sent the aircraft carrier "Enterprise" into the waters of the Bay of Bengal but they had been constrained by the Indo-Soviet Treaty.

Simla Summit

In Pakistan the political turmoil in the wake of the defeat in Dacca took its toll in political alignments. Yahya was forced to resign and Bhutto became Prime Minister, well on the road to achieving his life-time ambition of scaling the pinnacle of power in Pakistan. Despite being the progeny of a Hindu girl, Bhutto had militantly taken to Islam and hoped to be the leader of an Islamic bloc of nations in the world. However his immediate problem was to secure the release of some 90,000 prisoners of war being held in Bangladesh, the return of territories occupied by India in western Pakistan and to bring about some measure of normalization between India and Pakistan.

The summit between Indira Gandhi and Bhutto, assisted by their high-level aides, was held in the salubrious hills of Simla at the end of June 1972 to try to resolve some of the problems mentioned above. Those problems could be satisfactorily handled over time. But in addition the problem of Kashmir loomed large over the summit. India desired the total solution of the problem at one go. It hoped that the ground reality, with minor modifications, could be turned into a permanent border between India and Pakistan. Bhutto was both unwilling and unable to agree to any such settlement. Unwilling, because of his own mindset and political philosophy (see Bhutto's book *If I am Assassinated*), and unwilling because he could not have carried through such a settlement within Pakistan (even now Pakistani opinion was not ripe for it). Through Mrs. Gandhi's last-minute intervention and some generosity (see Benazir Bhutto's *Daughter of the East*) an accord was signed on 1 July 1972, known as the Simla Agreement that stipulated that the Kashmir issue should be resolved peacefully through bilateral negotiations.

Opinions differ on what actually transpired at Simla. Both the late P.N. Haksar and T.N. Kaul, high-level diplomats and foreign policy advisers, denied that there was any secret clause but Professor P.N. Dhar, also a former principal secretary of Indira Gandhi, maintained that it was secretly agreed by Bhutto to convert the LoC into a formal border as soon as feasible (that is when he was politically strong enough to do so). Since, however, there was no written slip of paper, Bhutto could and did deny the existence of any such secret agreement. In fact Bhutto disowned the spirit of the Simla agreement as soon as he could.

Relations with USA: The Aftermath

Soon enough Nixon-Kissinger duo had to reconcile themselves to the emergence of Bangladesh and they made efforts, reciprocated by India, to restore some normalcy in their relations with India. Both Nixon and Kissinger used rather offensive language against Mrs. Gandhi and India betraying their frustrations but as Kissinger said at the time they knew Indira Gandhi was "too cold-blooded" to barter away India's independence and national interests. There was one more troublesome development that riled the US and Western opinion—the nuclear explosion (or implosion as India claimed) at Pokhran on 18 May 1974. It took the West (and even the CIA) by surprise. However, outwardly at least, Kissinger took a calmer view of it and believed it did not radically change the balance in South Asia. He also indicated that now USA regarded India as a major regional power. Mrs. Gandhi made a major mistake at the time and her advisers must also take the lion's share of the blame. If India had declared itself to be a nuclear weapons state, it could have subsequently joined the Nuclear Non-Proliferation Treaty (NPT) as a nuclear state. USA also had not yet put domestic laws in place for imposing sanctions against states exploding a nuclear device. Instead, India chose to keep its nuclear explosion within the context of the peaceful uses of the Atom.

The real problem, however, between India and the U.S. was the perceptional difference between the two about what they regarded as their interests in the region. From India's point of view the chief problem was the determined and persistent attempts by Washington to create an artificial parity between India and Pakistan. This quest had combined with the repeated arms aid to Pakistan, some of which was at times meant to put pressure on India. Pakistan, in fact, became the hub of the problem between India and the United States. There could be no better evidence of it than the amusing sequence of events at this time. Kissinger came to India in October 1974 in search of a *modus vivendi*. In India he praised the vision of Jawaharlal Nehru and nonalignment and recognized India as a potentially big power. At a banquet hosted by Foreign Minister Y.B. Chavan, where questions and answers were allowed after the dinner, this writer pointed out to the U.S. Secretary of State that the central issue between the two countries was the U.S. policy of creating an artificial parity between India and Pakistan. Plumb came the reply from the top U.S. diplomat that they had abandoned this policy. There was no longer this approach. Yet as soon as Mr. Kissinger reached the shores of the United States, he announced a new arms package for Pakistan on the plea that India had changed the balance much to the disadvantage of Pakistan and, therefore, Washington had to step in to redress it !

Domestic Balance, Emergency and Foreign Policy

Even before the triumph of the Bangladesh war, Mrs. Gandhi had won a landslide victory for Parliament in the general elections of March 1971. But the political elan soon became a hostage to the economic difficulties that faced the country in the wake of the Bangladesh victory. People, particularly in India, often do not realize the economic costs of war. There had been acute economic difficulties after every conflict or war in which India was involved.

New economic difficulties stared the country in the aftermath of the 1971 war with Pakistan. Prices rose bringing distress to many in their trail. The distress was compounded by the inclemencies of weather, floods in some places, drought in others. The deteriorating economic situation coincided with the political crisis as it often does. The worsening economic conditions made way for a vociferous political campaign against Indira Gandhi. This campaign now led by the veteran leader. Jayaprakash Narayan was immensely fueled by a flippant judgment given by a judge of the Allahabad High Court setting aside Mrs. Gandhi's election as member of Parliament. Flippant, because he dismissed all the serious charges and picked on a few minor technical details, like the date of resignation of her personal assistant who had become her election agent and whether the police had helped making the arrangements like lighting for her election rally. The decision became the rallying point for the opposition to mount a sustained call for the Prime Minister's resignation. Calls were also issued to the police and the army to defy any "lawless" instructions issued to them. In general insurrectionary situation prevailed in the country and the climax came when the opposition announced that it would encircle the Prime Minister's residence and not let her function. Mrs. Gandhi declared emergency in the country and arrested a large number of opposition leaders and activists. The boiling political cauldron cooled down almost immediately but a heavy price had to be paid subsequently.

The impact on foreign policy was unfortunate. While the Soviet bloc countries supported the emergency, the West, the governments as well as the media, was highly critical. Mrs. Gandhi was unnecessarily riled for a while and sharply denounced the Western countries for their double standards in her public meetings and in Parliament. For the first time the pendulum moved too far away against the United States and other Western countries—at least politically. Mrs. Gandhi could have been perturbed at the possibility of U.S. effort to destabilize her Government and the country. Her fear was shared by many in India, although there were others who scoffed at it as a political gimmick. The revelations about CIA activities in other countries and the manner in which the Allende Government was forcibly overthrown in Chile through outside interference did nothing to mitigate these fears. They were reinforced by the developments in Bangladesh, the bloody *coup d'etat*, the murder of Sheikh Mujib and his family and the fuelling of anti-Indian sentiments, harking back to appeals in the name of religion and the installation of a government far less friendly to India—all these happenings on the borders of India deepened the suspicions about Western intentions and role in the subcontinent.

However, Mrs. Gandhi was not the one who would allow this kind of a situation. She knew very well the need for a more balanced relationship and she moved early to redress the tilt. The Indian ambassador T.N. Kaul met Kissinger's aides to begin a new dialogue and the Indo-U.S. Commission met in October 1974 as Indo-U.S. relations limped back to some kind of normalcy. However the real normalcy took place later.

The emergency had gone hopelessly awry. Mrs. Gandhi had herself realized it and ordered a general election. Mrs. Gandhi and the Congress party were badly defeated and the new government headed by Morarji Desai took over in New Delhi. Despite the antipathy towards Indira Gandhi and the talk of "genuine nonalignment", there was no basic change in foreign policy. Continuity has been one of the hallmarks of India's foreign policy. Desai went to Moscow and retained the special relationship with the Soviet Union. Perhaps the one change was the change in the U.S. attitude exemplified in Jimmy Carter's visit to India. The Desai government became a victim of internal feuding, was substituted by an interim administration headed by Charan Singh and paved the way towards another general election at the end of 1979 leading to the return of Indira Gandhi as Prime Minister with an absolute majority in Parliament in January 1980.

Afghanistan

Almost immediately she had to address the problem of Afghanistan which had witnessed what was called the Saur revolution led by communists, followed by considerable turmoil in a land dominated by tribes, the mullah and the Qazi, wracked by internal schisms within the revolutionary party, which in any case had a small base, and leading eventually to the entry of Soviet troops at the invitation of one of the ruling factions.

For India a doubly worrying situation had developed. On the one hand, foreign troops had entered an independent, non-aligned country, even if the troops were from a friendly country and had gone at the invitation of the government in Kabul, and on the other hand Pakistan had once again become the frontline state for the United States. Washington not only began a large-scale arms and economic assistance program, but also started on arms supply through Pakistan to elements that subsequently formed themselves into the Taliban and the Al Qaeda led by Osama bin Laden. These were all the creation of the United States through the good offices of General Zia-ul-Haq, the Pakistani army and its Inter-Services Agency (ISI), the high-profile intelligence agency of the army.

Faced with this kind of a situation, Mrs. Gandhi had to pursue a dual tight-rope policy. There was no question of India endorsing the entry of foreign troops. Mr. Andrei Gromyko, then Foreign Minister of the USSR was dispatched to New Delhi by the Soviet leadership to get Indian Prime Minister's endorsement but was to meet with disappointment. The former Prime Minister I.K. Gujral who was then India's ambassador to the Soviet Union, told this writer that on persistent prodding of Gromyko, Mrs. Gandhi told the Soviet Foreign Minister that in the current situation India could not approve of foreign troops in Afghanistan and advised him that the Soviet troops should leave as early as possible. Despite various set backs India continued to maintain contact with political elements in Afghanistan that came handy subsequently.

Mrs. Gandhi continued the efforts at rapprochement with the United States and managed to bring about a working relationship with Washington. She met U.S. President Ronald Reagan for the first time during a world summit at Cancun (Greece) in October 1981. Reportedly she struck a personal rapport with the U.S. President who became convinced that she was not a client follower of Moscow. She followed it with a visit to USA which she described as an "adventure in search of understanding and friendship" and which elicited a reciprocal sentiment by Reagan as a "dialogue of discovery". Indira Gandhi made it clear during her visit that India did not tilt to any one side, but "stood upright". It weighed the issues on their merit and in the perspective of India's interests. It may be added that she maintained all the economic links with the United States even during the troubled period.

Mrs. Gandhi and China

Realist and "cold-blooded" (Kissinger's words), as she was, Mrs. Gandhi understood the need for more flexibility in foreign policy, chiefly in mending fences with China that had been put on ice since the border conflict. She felt the need for a gradual but steady improvement of relations with such a big neighbour whom history and geography had destined India to coexist, and for that she was willing to take the initiative. The readers would recall that ambassadors had been called back from each other's country due to the border conflict. After private soundings, Mrs. Gandhi took the initiative to send an Indian ambassador to Beijing in 1977 and she chose a career diplomat known for his sobriety and maturity, K.R. Narayanan who subsequently rose to be the President of India.

When she came back to power in 1980, Mrs. Gandhi continued the policy of improvement of relations with China. She met Hua Guofeng, then Chinese Prime Minister, in Belgrade in 1980, and later Premier Zhau Ziyang at Cancun in 1981, both of them subsequently disgraced and now dead. Beijing too had been realizing the advantages of a better relationship. In June 1981 it dispatched to New Delhi one of its senior Vice Premiers, Huang Hua, who had an important place in the hierarchy of the Chinese Communist Party. The mission was designed to carry forward the process of improvement of relations. In a discussion with Mrs. Gandhi, she indicated her mind when she said to this writer, "we cannot take the approach that here we stand and here we shall stand for all time to come". Flexibility without sacrificing India's basic interests was the hallmark of Mrs. Gandhi's foreign policy.

It was Mrs. Gandhi who initiated the so-called "look East" policy, later pursued by succeeding Prime Ministers. She took special steps to improve relations with the Southeast Asian countries. She visited Malaysia, Indonesia (twice), Singapore, Thailand and the Philippines during her two tenures as Prime Minister. She established particularly close relations with Vietnam. The presence of Vietnamese troops in Cambodia (then known as Kampuchea) to put down the unspeakably tyrannical regime of Pol Pot and his henchmen, brought a temporary estrangement with some of the ASEAN countries (Association of Southeast Asian Nations), but she worked to bridge the hiatus and restore cordial relations. Emphasis was also given to the development of economic relations with the ASEAN countries. Later, the withdrawal of Vietnamese troops from Cambodia helped restore normalcy in the region. In fact both Vietnam and Cambodia were made members of ASEAN.

Relations with Nepal: Sensitivities of a Small Neighbour

There are not many instances in the world, apart from Nepal and India, where the relationship between two countries could be described as that between lips and teeth. History and geography have so bound them together that they are almost like a separable twins. India's natural boundary does not end where the Nepalese territory begins. It ends with the higher mountains which it shares with Nepal and which surround the Himalayan country from three sides. Nepal is a landlocked country whose only real outlets lie through India. This has entailed and resulted in many abrasive developments and situations. Many mighty rivers in India originate from Nepal and their harnessing requires co-operation from both the countries but has also led to contention at times. If they co-operate, estimatedly as much as 45,000 MW of electricity could be produced that could help the economies of both countries.

India and Nepal have many common mythologies, including the mythology relating to their mountains. As Nehru put it, the Himalayas were "intimately tied up with Indian history, traditions, faith, beliefs, literature and culture". They were "something much more than mountains to us, they are part of ourselves". And so for Nepal too.

India's security was inextricably tied up with Nepal. Particularly after the rise of a resurgent new China on the borders of India and Nepal, India's security was even more tightly bound up with Nepal. With utmost frankness Nehru told Parliament in December 1950: "Apart from our sympathetic interest in Nepal, we are also interested in the security of our own country. From time immemorial, the Himalayas have provided us with a magnificent frontier. Of course, these are no longer as impossible as they used to be, but are still fairly effective. We cannot allow that barrier to be penetrated because it is also the principal barrier to

India". With the same frankness he continued, "much as we appreciate the independence of Nepal, we cannot risk our own security by anything going wrong in Nepal which permits that barrier to be crossed or otherwise weakens our frontier".

For many long years India's relations with Nepal where governed by the Treaty of Peace and Friendship that India signed with Nepal on 31 July 1950. The Treaty provided that neither government shall tolerate any threat to the security of the other by an aggressor and enjoined upon them to consult each other and devise effective counter measures in case of any such threat. The Treaty also provided that Nepal would consult India before importing any war equipment from any country other than India but gave the right to Nepal after such consultations to import from or through the territory of India arms, ammunition, or warlike material and equipment necessary for the security of Nepal. Nevertheless Nehru was very keen that the independence and territorial integrity of Nepal should be maintained in full measure and the Treaty itself gave expression to it.

In lieu of this Treaty soft borders, in fact open borders, were established between India and Nepal. A very large number of people of Nepalese origin are working in India. Similarly some three to four million people of Indian origin, called Madhesis, are settled in the Terai region of Nepal whose issue of citizenship is not yet settled. It is well-known that the Indian army has been recruiting from British times a large number of Gorkhas from Nepal. An Indian official document puts the figure of Gorkha soldiers at about 40,000 and the amount of pensions paid to some 115,000 retired Gorkha soldiers at over rupees 450 crores a year.

The Treaty, however, itself became a bone of contention in later years. Nationalist feelings upsurged, or were aroused at this "unequal Treaty" and demands made for its annulment. In any case in recent years the Treaty has been observed only partially in letter and spirit. By the very nature of its geography and history India has often been drawn into the internal developments of Nepal from Nehru's time to the present days. Whenever popular movements have hit Nepal, many of the leaders, and even the King at one time sought refuge in India or solicited Indian help to resolve the situation.

When India became independent, Nepal was ruled nominally by the King but in effect by a Rana autocracy and popular pressures grew in Nepal for an end to the Ranas' rule and the establishment of a constitutional monarchy. Nehru took a middle course and tried to preserve Nepal's stability, restore the constitutional role of the King, while assuaging Nepalese popular aspirations. With India's help Nepal transited from Rana autocracy to constitutional monarchy. Jawaharlal Nehru himself went to Nepal in June 1951 to cement the friendly relations between free India and the new Nepal that was emerging from the recent constitutional changes (as *The Hindu* of 20 June 1951 put it). It was obvious that the developments in China and Tibet had made it all the more necessary for India and Nepal with their strong ties of history, geography and culture to come closer in their common interests.

Things, however, saw a downward slide in India-Nepal relations when King Tribhuvan passed away and was succeeded by King Mahendra. The new King turned out to be a different kind of person. He tried to accumulate power in his own hands and dispense with political parties and their leaders who had little option but to flee to India and carry on their movement from here. This further inflamed Mahendra who nursed a deep suspicion about India's attempts to dethrone him.

King Mahendra did his best to arouse anti-Indian nationalism and play the China card as well.

Demonstrations were held against India and Mahendra demanded that the international community ensure the rights of Nepal as a land-locked state. Nehru expressed sorrow at the erosion of democracy in Nepal but continued to pursue a moderate policy towards Nepal. King Mahendra was unpropitiated. As we have noted, China had with the assimilation of Tibet become an important new factor in Nepal as it had on the borders with India. Mahendra hoped to balance India with China and Beijing at that time was quite willing to play the game. Beijing began advancing substantial amounts of economic aid and some military materials to Nepal (although much later it ceased the attempt to match India's aid).

Anyway, this was the situation with regard to Nepal which Mrs. Gandhi had to grapple with when she became Prime Minister. Mrs. Gandhi continued with the soft policy towards its smaller Himalayan neighbour. She took an early opportunity of visiting Nepal in October 1966 and announcing the largest aid package until then. She was making a deliberate effort to calm down the tensions and restore the normalcy in relationship. The joint statement issued at the end of her visit spoke of the traditional friendship, common ties of history, geography and culture, their vital interest in the territorial integrity, prosperity and well-being of each other and reaffirmed their commitment to the principles of nonalignment and peaceful coexistence.

King Mahendra was, however, relentless in his pursuit of absolute power and the termination of any special relationship with India. He played upon the sensitivities of a small neighbour against the Big Brother the next door. He called upon India to withdraw its Military Mission group. That was done in August 1970. Mahendra continued to use the China card, declared Nepal would remain neutral in any conflict between India and China and even invited the Chinese to build a road in the Terai area which was too close to the border for Indian comfort. India was extremely anxious about the Chinese role in Nepal and worried about large-scale smuggling of goods from Nepal. There was no doubt about the cold anger in the corridors of power in India and equally undoubtedly there was arm-twisting of Nepal because of Mahendra's attitude and policies towards India.

Nevertheless India continued to persist with a moderate policy and assist Nepal in various developmental projects. King Mahendra's passing away in early 1972 and the succession by King Birendra brought relief to India-Nepal relations even though not all the contentious issues were put out of the way. Mrs. Gandhi went to Kathmandu a second time in February 1973 and was given a big ovation. She assured the Nepalese leaders of India's interest in the development and prosperity of Nepal and of its disinterest in fanning any rebel activity against the Nepalese government.

To bring the story forward, India remains the largest trade partner of Nepal, the biggest donor in Nepal's economic growth and the country most engaged in Nepal's developmental projects. India spent on an average rupees 60–70 crores annually in aid of Nepal. India has actively participated in construction of roads and highways and airport, in the harnessing of rivers and prevention of floods, in power generation, in small-scale projects and in the production of industrial goods like cement and sugar.

Subsequently another people's movement engulfed Nepal that again drew India into the vortex of the Nepalese politics, but these developments would be considered in a subsequent chapter.

Sri Lanka: The Intractable Issue

India had a number of unresolved issues with most of its neighbours and many of them blamed India. One central problem was that India's neighbours were not each other's neighbours. They were India's neighbours but not of each other. Therefore, all the sensitivities of smaller neighbours were reflected in their concerns about India, none against each other.

Yet another sensitive issue Mrs. Gandhi had to address was related to relations with Sri Lanka with some of the problems so built-in that they defied any easy solution. India has had intimate historical relations with Sri Lanka (the name itself evokes mythological memories in India). Despite such close contacts, relations were at times troubled and at times abrasive. The genesis of the problems lay in that Sri Lanka was home to one million Ceylon Tamils whose forebears migrated there way back in history, and another million known as Indian Tamils whose forefathers were taken to Sri Lanka by the British as indentured labour. The native Tamils were concentrated around Jaffna in the northern and eastern coast and the Indian Tamils generally lived in and around Colombo, Kandy and the port city of Trincomalee.

The tensions between the two major communities, the Sinhalese and Tamils kept boiling every now and then. The Jaffna Tamils gradually sought safety through the organization known as LTTE (Liberation Tigers of Tamil Elam) who desired to carve out a Tamil state, bifurcating Sri Lanka. The LTTE came to be a tightly controlled, highly authoritarian organization that brooked no dissent even among the Tamils in Sri Lanka. Another complicating factor in the early eighties was the sympathy factor for their ethnic brethren in Tamil Nadu. The developments in Sri Lanka tended to be dragged into the domestic politics of India. Many Sinhalese politicians alleged that the Tamil Nadu government under M.G. Ramachandran was covertly aiding the Tamil militants. Yet another disturbing development was the formation of a militant Sinhalese organization, JVP, and increasing army violence against Tamils in Sri Lanka.

Any detailed discussion of the developments in our neighbouring country is outside the purview of this volume. Here we are concerned with India's approach to those developments. Essentially there were two components of Mrs. Gandhi's policy. One, Sri Lanka's unity and integrity must be preserved. India was against any partitioning of Sri Lanka. Second, the Tamils in Sri Lanka must be assured safety and life with honour and dignity. Generally India favoured a federal or a devolutionary approach. Above all, India stood for a peaceful settlement of the Tamil issue in Sri Lanka.

This was an eminently sensible approach and has remained India's overall stance towards the island Republic. But it is one thing to adopt a sensible approach and quite another matter to tame the ground passions.

We may also add here that there was a small territorial dispute between India and Sri Lanka over the control of an islet in the sea between the two countries that went by the name of Kacchativu and that was of some interest to fishermen of the two countries. In order to win the goodwill of a smaller neighbour, Mrs. Gandhi graciously ceded the sea rocks to Sri Lanka thus diffusing any possible territorial tensions.

Conclusion

Mrs. Gandhi's handling of foreign policy was firm, realistic and dignified. She made a few mistakes, as we have noted, but no leader or country anywhere in the world can claim infallibility. Mrs. Gandhi kept the flag of independence afloat in foreign policy. She combined flexibility with firmness, determination with resilience. Whatever the flaws in domestic policy, she demonstrated very considerable aplomb in dealing with foreign relations and in managing critical challenges from abroad during her tenure.

CHAPTER THREE

RAJIV GANDHI AND FOREIGN POLICY

Rajiv Gandhi took over as the youngest Prime Minister of India in tragic circumstances following the assassination of Mrs. Indira Gandhi and the anti-Sikh riots in its wake. Despite his inexperience, he quickly got hold over the somewhat anarchic India and particularly its foreign policy, which is what we are chiefly concerned with here, showing considerable panache. A young man with a modern outlook, Rajiv Gandhi was a technophile with great faith in modern management ways (he was the one who introduced six-day working week).

Yet, Rajiv Gandhi's worldview did not turn out to be very different from his grandfather's. He displayed a similar touch of idealism coupled with great sense of realism in foreign policy. He was passionate about nuclear disarmament, but made his proposals at the United Nations contingent on a gradual basis under a verifiable system. He carried forward the traditions of his grandfather and mother in supporting and consolidating nonalignment but tried to give it a contemporary dimension. He was equally indefatigable in the struggle against racialism. And he had his share of errors of judgment and misapplied approach to certain issues in foreign relations.

Initially, perhaps, Rajiv Gandhi displayed the same optimism as his mother when she became Prime Minister about turning around India's relations with the United

States but equally quickly he came to realise the complexities of the relationship and the problem of the perceptional differences about their respective national interests. Rajiv Gandhi took an early opportunity to visit the United States in June 1985, struck a kind of personal rapport with Ronald Reagan, charmed many in the US with his youthful good looks and eloquent articulation. He drew the attention of the American elite about their shared values of democracy, freedom, justice and the rule of law. But he was also unsparing in pointing out the dangers of a rapidly nuclearising Pakistan (the American ruling elites knew about the nuclear proliferating activities of A.Q. Khan but chose to remain quiet about it in the interests of their other objectives). And he spoke strongly about peace and development. Rajiv Gandhi pushed the US door more open and created stabler ties.

But by the time he went again to the US coinciding with the 40th anniversary of the UN in October 1985, in the words of a US official, "the honeymoon is over". Apparently the Americans were hoping, against hope, that India would take a right about turn in its foreign and economic policies and dilute its relationship with the Soviet Union; and India was hoping, again against hope, that USA would reappraise its policies towards the subcontinent and moderate its ties with Pakistan—at least to the extent that they impinge on India. Both expectations were misplaced.

Nevertheless it would be wrong to draw any conclusion that the ties between India and the US had become abrasive or that any new tension had marred the relationship. There was very considerable interchange between USA and India in almost every field, political, economic, cultural and social. The economic ties remained particularly strong. India had always shunned extremist postures and adventurous policies.

Neighbours

Pakistan

Rajiv Gandhi's priorities necessarily centred around the neighbours and he played a proactive role in handling various issues with neighbouring countries. He gave very considerable attention to problems with Pakistan and with and within Sri Lanka. Equally necessarily success could not be ensured when dealing with such complex and complicated issues. On relations with both countries, Rajiv Gandhi expended considerable political capital and energy. He chartered out a road map for putting relations with Pakistan on a higher level of comfort and understanding, but soon realised that Islamabad was feverishly building up not only its armed forces, but more disconcertingly its nuclear capability. One might also note in passing that General Musharraf was not the originator of cricket diplomacy; it was General Zia-ul-Haq who began it. All the same Rajiv Gandhi and Zia signed a significant agreement as a confidence-building measure, by which the two countries agreed not to attack the nuclear installations of each other.

When Zia-ul-Haq was killed in a plane crash, the return of at least a measure of democracy saw Benazir Bhutto at the helm as Prime Minister of Pakistan, Rajiv Gandhi continued his attempts to secure better bonds with Pakistan. There was some euphoria in India about the return of democracy in Pakistan and even about Benazir as Prime Minister. Rajiv Gandhi went to Islamabad to attend the SAARC summit and held what were described as "constructive and cordial talks" with the Pakistani counterpart. There was optimism in the air about Indo-Pak relations entering a new era.

But optimism often runs ahead of reality. The reality was that Benazir was not master of her own house, so to say. Ms Bhutto could not move an inch in relations with India without a prior nod from the chiefs of staff of the Pakistan army and its ISI (Inter Services Agency)wing. As the popular saying in Pakistan went, whatever happened in Pakistan depended on Allah, USA, and the army. The army was the defacto ruler, no matter whether a democratically elected prime minister had taken over or not.

Another reality that soon came to the notice of the Rajiv Gandhi government was the feverish acceleration of Pakistan's nuclear capability. Whether Rajiv Gandhi learnt that Benazir Bhutto had gone to Pyongyang to negotiate a deal for the exchange of missiles and missile technology from North Korea in return for the know-how of manufacturing the atom bomb we do not know. But he certainly came to know of Pakistan's mounting acquisitions in the nuclear weapons field. So with all his passionate advocacy of nuclear and general disarmament he knew he had to safeguard India's security obliging him to give the green signal to the nuclear scientists to go ahead in the manufacturing of nuclear warheads. It was this decision that enabled India to forestall a possible nuclear blackmail. Relations with Pakistan and the real factors behind the apparent issues need to be considered in some depth and this we shall do in the subsequent chapter.

India and Sri Lanka

The happenings in another neighbouring country that claimed a great deal of Rajiv Gandhi's attention was Sri Lanka. The Sri Lankan development added to the troubled relations with some of the neighbouring countries. Rajiv Gandhi had to grapple with a deteriorating ethnic situation in Sri Lanka that had a direct impact on Tamil Nadu. The escalating violence against the Tamils in Sri Lanka was generating passions in the Tamil state in India where, in addition, a number of politicians were not above exploiting the sentiments of the people. The plight of the people in and around Jaffna under siege from the Sri Lankan army facing conditions of starvation and looming chaos led to spiraling passions in Tamil Nadu with rising calls for some action to help the Tamil "brethren" in distress in Sri Lanka.

The Rajiv Gandhi government too felt the heat from the touch and go situation in Madras (now Chennai) and that led to the decision to airlift supplies of essential commodities for the people in Jaffna. Naturally this was viewed as an infringement of Colombo's sovereignty over its airspace, evidence of the arrogance of a bigger and more powerful neighbour, and created more bad blood between Colombo and New Delhi.

Nevertheless, the action seemed to have induced some rethinking in Colombo. Instead of Sri Lankan army pursuing the mirage of a military solution, then President Junius Jayewardene negotiated with Rajiv Gandhi the India-Sri Lanka Accord in August 1987. The Accord held on to three basic premises of India's Colombo policy. The first reiterated the maintenance of the unity of Sri Lanka and opposition to any bifurcation of the state, while emphasizing the requirement of the surrender of arms by the LTTE cadres. The second envisaged substantial and effective devolution of power so that the Tamil majority areas could live in peace with honour and exercise self-rule. The third obliged Colombo not to provide bases and allied facilities to any foreign power. This was in the context of the reported move by Colombo to provide the Trincomalee port as a base to the United States and various facilities to the Voice of America to operate from Sri Lanka, both moves viewed with very considerable suspicion in New Delhi.

The Accord envisaged the dispatch of Indian Peace Keeping Force (IPKF) to Sri Lanka to supervise the ceasefire, the surrender of arms and the peace arrangements in the Tamil areas in the North and the East. History has yet to give its final verdict on the wisdom of this move but, on the face of it, the move was fraught with hidden and not-so-hidden dangers. It was bound to inflame the opinion of many sections of the Sinhalese people as an obvious abridgement of Sri Lanka's sovereignty and arouse nationalist sentiments directed against India. Rajiv Gandhi had taken the precaution (though it turned out to be a chimera) of bringing secretly the LTTE leader Prabhakaran to New Delhi and, after intensive negotiations with some arm twisting, securing his consent to the agreement. Prabhakaran agreed to surrender the LTTE arms in return for provincial autonomy in the Tamil-dominated areas. Prabhakaran made only a token surrender of the arms under the possession of the LTTE and had no intention of abiding by the agreement. It is well established that Prabhakaran had little commitment to the establishment of democratic values. He was totally intolerant of any dissident opinion and resorted to the use of suicide bombers and assassinations. He had become an icon among the Sri Lankan Tamils because he had provided them with relief from the depredations of the Sinhalese militants and the Colombo army.

Nor had the Sinhalese nationalists any intention either to abide by the Accord. A Sinhalese extremist organisation, JVM, had already arisen with its programme of violent retribution against Tamils. The JVM carried on a relentless movement against the Accord. Both sides were fanning base passions but what was much more unfortunate was that some of Jayewardene's closest colleagues were unalterably opposed to the Accord. Chief of them was Premadasa, the designated successor of Jayewardene.

The IPKF willy-nilly became chiefly engaged in confrontation with the LTTE and, at considerable loss in officers and men, recovered a large area for Colombo's rule which was earlier under the thumb of the LTTE. However, the Sinhalese nationalists were unreconciled to the presence of Indian troops on Sri Lankan soil. As soon as Premadasa became President, he called for the withdrawal of the Indian troops. Premadasa had cut a deal with the LTTE, but this only resulted in LTTE capturing back the areas that had been restored by the IPKF to Colombo's rule as a consequence of the withdrawal of the IPKF. By then Rajiv Gandhi had been assassinated by a LTTE suicide group at the command of Prabhakaran. It should be noted that this murder most foul by Prabhakaran's henchmen dissipated the widespread sympathy enjoyed earlier by Prabhakaran in Tamil Nadu. He and his armed group no longer remained an active factor in Tamil Nadu's politics.

India-China: A Breakthrough

One of the real success stories of Rajiv Gandhi's foreign policy was relations with China. He moved with careful preparation but he moved decisively. Even more than Mrs. Gandhi who had to be more cautious in handling the China issue, Rajiv Gandhi recognised the need to speed up the process of mending ties begun by his mother in 1977. He believed that the time was ripe for a bolder move. He had sent the late P.N. Haksar on a peace errand to Beijing. Haksar met the then Prime Minister Zhao Ziyang and he came back with encouraging signals from the Chinese side for speeding up the process of normalization. Although Zhao became a victim of the Tiananmen uprising in 1988, the process continued because the dominant Chinese leadership was equally convinced to put the past behind and begin the track towards better ties.

Rajiv Gandhi went to China in December 1989 and was greeted by a warm and long handshake by the then paramount leader Deng Xiaoping. The prolonged handshake lasting many seconds became a symbol of the new beginning. The tension had been taken out and the thaw had begun in full earnest. India had in fact accepted the Chinese viewpoint that the central border issue should not be made the lone issue and that strengthening and broadening exchanges in other areas should not be made contingent on the resolution of the border issue and that these would in fact over the long run help resolve the territorial dispute in a relaxed atmosphere. This was the logic that Deng had advanced years earlier when he held a session with an Indian Council of Social Science Research delegation headed by G. Parthasarathy who was also then adviser to Mrs Gandhi. Deng told a delegation, of which this writer was a member, that the two countries should put aside the border dispute for the time being and concentrate on developing relations in a variety of areas so that a proper environment could be created for a settlement of the border issue.

At that time we did not think it was possible for us to accept that approach, but by the time Rajiv Gandhi took power, the country was far more relaxed about China and Rajiv Gandhi realised that it was a sensible approach. From then on India and China were on a course of rapid expansion of relations. This was only briefly halted when India exploded atomic devices in May 1996. The course set by Rajiv Gandhi was resumed after a short interregnum of adverse reactions in China and wordy retaliation by India.

Big Powers: Nonalignment and Disarmament

We have already noted Rajiv' Gandhi's efforts to improve relations with the United States. Although the quality of that relationship did not rise to the level that Rajiv Gandhi had hoped for, for reasons that have also been mentioned earlier, but they did improve considerably and the tension that existed earlier during certain periods had been dissolved during Rajiv Gandhi's tenure. One of the important steps that Rajiv Gandhi took in promoting relations with the United States was the signing of an agreement in March 1988 for the transfer of high technology and the subsequent acquisition of a super computer. Economic ties also remained strong. Both sides chose a dual approach towards each other. They used the option of continuing expansion of exchanges and promotion of trade but also retained their respective countervailing relationships. Washington indicated it was paying increasing attention to what it had began describing as a growing Indian market that was of interest to the US, and more public recognition of India's growing military strength. Yet, military relations with Pakistan remained strong and there was to be no dilution. Despite the criticism of Pakistan's determined acquisition of nuclear capability, it virtually winked at Islamabad being so near towards becoming a nuclear weapon country (and not too much later Nawaz Sharief who had stepped into the hot seat vacated by Benazir Bhutto announced publicly that Pakistan had a bomb on the shelf). The United States was averse to letting go the leverage exercised through Pakistan, not just against the Soviet Union, but also, in fact, against India.

Rajiv Gandhi was equally protective of India's ties with the Soviet Union. This relationship was beneficial to both the countries. The people realised the value of these ties and thus Indo-Soviet friendship came to be embedded in public consciousness. It enabled India to fend off many hostile challenges that came from abroad—from China, from Pakistan, from the West in the form of support to Pakistan over the Kashmir issue as well as the supply of military hardware that was principally directed against India. Each time the Soviet support to India played a crucial role in meeting the challenges. India's friendships with the Soviet Union was of considerable benefit to Moscow too as it enabled it to contend with the isolation the West sought to impose on it, enlarge its ties with non-aligned countries, expand the mobilisation of public opinion against war and explain many of its actions to the world.

Symbolic of this relationship was the fact that Rajiv Gandhi went on his first visit abroad as Prime Minister to Moscow 21-26 May 1985 and had wholly satisfactory and fruitful talks with the Soviet leaders. They expressed understanding of India's anxiety about the Pakistani race towards the bomb and their views coincided with those of the Indian Prime Minister on issues of war and peace and disarmament. Moscow announced new economic aid to the tune of 1160 crores of rupees as well as the construction of new projects such as the Kahalgaon thermal station with a capacity of 840 MW.

Rajiv Gandhi came back fully satisfied with the results of his visit. He expressed his view that Moscow had stood by India at every critical juncture and that the Soviet support had been of considerable help in meeting various crisis situations. National interests dictated the continuation of these close ties with Moscow.

The return visit by the Soviet President Mikhail Gorbachev to India in November 1986 was a landmark in more ways than one. Not just the deepening of relations with India but the new philosophy for the Soviet Union to accept and endorse, broke new ground in international relations. The Delhi Declaration, as the joint statement by Gorbachev and Rajiv Gandhi came to be called, endorsed Mahatma Gandhi's philosophy of nonviolence as the desirable code of conduct among nations, but also, more significantly, within society itself. Rajiv Gandhi said in the Parliament after the signing of the declaration that with it the USSR had "joined India in a common vision of a nuclear-weapons free and non-violent world" and that the declaration had given expression to "the ideas of Gandhi and Lenin". He noted that the document would be issued as an official document of the United Nations that highlighted its importance. The vision spelt out by the Delhi declaration closely approximataed Jawaharlal Nehru's vision which in turn was heavily influenced by Gandhi.

New agreements were signed between India and the USSR on economic and technical cooperation. Rajiv Gandhi told a joint press conference that the future thrust of their cooperation in science and technology would be on joint research and joint production in many areas. These technologies centred around nuclear power, space technologies, and high temperature physics.

Another area of concern was developments in Afghanistan. The constant feuding among the contestants at the top of the Saur revolution had been overcome with the accession of Dr Najibullah at the helm. Dr Najibullah was maintaining very close contact with India. He began suggesting to Moscow to withdraw its troops and sought India's good offices in this regard. As we have already recounted, India had differences with the Soviet Union on the presence of Soviet troops in Afghanistan, but by the time Gorbachev came to India Soviet troops had already vacated Afghanistan. But a different kind of scenario was opening up. India for geopolitical reasons was deeply interested in the developments in Kabul so as to ensure that the reactionary fundamentalist groups did not seize Kabul. Rajiv Gandhi stepped up support for Dr Najibullah and invited him to visit India. He was somewhat dismayed that Moscow was losing interest in Afghanistan and possibly argued with Gorbachev for continued, tangible support to Najib and his party, the PDPA.

World Peace and Nonalignment

Rajiv Gandhi's deep commitment to universal nuclear disarmament has been recounted. He used various fora to spread the message. He also continued with the informal world group set up during Indira Gandhi's time for deliberating upon issues of war and peace. This group spawning four continents, composed of heads of governments of six countries—Sweden, Mexico, Greece, Tanzania, Argentina and India—held a second meeting in New Delhi presided over by Rajiv Gandhi soon after he became Prime Minister. The new and youthful Prime Minister of India appealed to the five nuclear powers (USA, Russia, France, Britain and China) to halt all further production and testing of nuclear devices as the "first credible and reassuring step" towards nuclear disarmament and begin reducing their stockpiles. The joint statement issued by leaders of the six countries called for a stop to all nuclear testing and appealed to big powers to refrain from militarisation of outer space that should be reserved for peaceful research.

Another summit of the six nations was held in Stockholm in January 1989. It issued a joint appeal to the nuclear powers to reduce their stockpiles by half during the next six months. This time its appeal included the reduction of conventional forces also. While the leaders in the four continents welcomed the INF treaty between Moscow and Washington, they remained unconvinced that this constituted a credible resolve towards nuclear disarmament.

Rajiv Gandhi continued the tradition of strong commitment to nonalignment and the struggle against imperialism and racialism. Racialism, chiefly in Africa, had become a primary issue as the main form of the campaign against imperialism. Rajiv Gandhi took up the cause against the racial challenge with passion and some tangible action on the part of India. Speaking at a ministerial meeting of the non-aligned coordination bureau in New Delhi in April 1985 Rajiv Gandhi spoke strongly against settler colonialism in South Africa and gave a ringing call for defeating racialism and colonial control over Namibia and South

Africa. And he announced India's full diplomatic recognition of South-West African People's Organisation (SWAPO) as the genuine representative government of Namibia. He also expressed solidarity with the struggle of the Palestinian people for a homeland and the freedom to live in peace and with dignity.

Rajiv Gandhi directed his efforts towards achieving more cohesion in the non-aligned movement (NAM) and to turn its attention towards meeting new challenges in a changing world, particularly towards the increasingly important economic issues. There is no doubt that the success of NAM was turning it into a flabby movement lacking a sharp focus. NAM did not constitute the creation of a military bloc. Its members were sovereign countries who came together voluntarily to fend off the tentacles of the Cold War, maintain their independence and increase their leverage in world affairs. The great influx into the movement was a testament to its expanding attractiveness and influence. It became a mini UN. Inevitably this influx contributed to its flabbiness. It began to pass all-encompassing resolutions suited to the needs of various countries and regions, thereby lacking punch and power. It was relevant in protecting the broad interests of the non-aligned countries and possibly in helping stave off a world war, but it found it more difficult to meet the rising economic tasks especially in an age driven by the knowledge revolution. Rajiv Gandhi spent considerable human and time capital to maintain the coherence of the non-aligned movement and to turn its attention to the creation of a new economic order, besides meeting the onslaughts of racialism and colonialism. This was the message he took to the non-aligned summit in Harare and the subsequent meet at Belgrade.

Conclusion

Rajeev Gandhi came young, raw and inexperienced. Whatever his occasional flip-flops internally, in foreign policy he displayed a sure footedness that was remarkable. He dealt with world leaders on a basis of equality. He took initiatives in the international fora without recourse to adventurism and he upheld the traditions of Indian foreign policy in the spirit of "enlightened self-interest". Foreign policy cannot be all pluses and no minuses. This was so in the Nehru era or during Indira Gandhi's tenure, as also in Rajiv Gandhi's time, as the virtually intractable ethnic problem of Sri Lanka demonstrated. But the pluses outweighed the minuses and Rajiv Gandhi's handling of foreign policy issues would be given high marks.

CHAPTER FOUR

FROM NARASIMHA RAO TO I.K. GUJRAL TO ATAL BEHARI VAJPAYEE

End of An Era

Rajiv Gandhi lost power in the beginning of 1990. That marked the end of an era both in domestic and international politics. Within the country the V.P. Singh government took over with I.K. Gujral as the Foreign Minister. Gujral was both sober and shrewd in his understanding of foreign policy. But the government lasted for too brief a period to leave any lasting impression in foreign policy. Gujral, however, had a second and more productive stint as Foreign Minister and then as Prime Minister of India. Nevertheless some seminal world developments took place during this period.

Not satisfied with his armed attack against Iran, in which hundreds of thousands of people lost their lives, Saddam Hussein decided in August 1990 to invade Kuwait, a sovereign country and member of the United Nations. This had incalculable consequences some of which we are still contending with. If the warring countries had been in some other region, the US perhaps would not have mounted such a massive and high-tech attack to repel the invasion of Kuwait, but this was a strategic region. It was because of one word, as the then US Senate majority leader put it, "OIL." The Secretary of State James Baker confirmed it, "the economic lifeline of the industrial world runs from the Gulf and we cannot permit a dictator such as this to sit astride that economic lifeline".

Even after the Iraqi defeat in Kuwait and the pell-mell withdrawal of its armed forces, the pressures on Iraq continued. Iraq was bombed day in and day out and there was a virtual blockade relieved only by some humanitarian relief work by the United Nations. The people of Iraq have had no peace since then. The poor starved children suffered from prolonged undernourishment and emaciation. The sanctions against Iraq between 1991 and 1998 resulted in the slow death of half a million Iraqi children, according to a study by a United Nations Children Fund.

Anyway getting back to the first Gulf War, India's dilemma was the result of many factors. Iraq was one of the few more secular states in that region. It had stayed away from the Organisation of Islamic States, had not been a party to the anti-Indian resolutions passed there and had taken the most understanding attitude towards the Indian position in Kashmir. There was also a disturbing economic dimension. Already, the Iran-Iraq war had inflicted considerable damage on Indians as the number of Indian firms operating their dwindled from 100 to less than 30,and 50,000 workers, engineers and technicians employed there to less than 9000. In 1985 Iraq owed $ 1 billion to both public and private Indian companies of which only $ 500 million had been realised. Iraq was also a significant source of oil imports. India had reached an agreement with Iraq in March 1990 to import 2.5 million tons of oil for 1990-91, with 30 per cent of the proceeds to be adjusted against the Iraqi dues towards India.

India's anguish and the delayed reaction to the first Gulf War may be seen in this perspective. However, India could not endorse Iraq's invasion of Kuwait and supported the UN resolution for the withdrawal of Iraqi troops from Kuwait and abided by the sanctions imposed by the UN. Foreign Minister Gujral had gone to Baghdad at the start of the Iraqi attack, but was confronted with Saddam's recounting of how many tanks and armoured cars he possessed and how many soldiers he had. Equally helpless was the Soviet Union which had a much bigger stake in Iraq and which in any case was hobbled domestically. India had to confine itself to arrangements for a well-organised evacuation of Indians from the region.

The first Gulf War unfolded an accumulating and dramatic alteration in the balance of power in the world. It began with the easy triumph of American armed superiority over Saddam's much vaunted army and ended with the breakup of the Soviet Union for very different reasons with which we need not be concerned here. It certainly marked the end of the post World War II political order. It left in its place a world system dominated by a sole superpower—United States of America—and in consequence unleashed new trends which we are still grappling with.

The American triumph in the desert war was so rapid and so complete that in the words of the US commander of the desert war Gen Norman Schwarzkopf, it was like "a beagle chasing a rabbit". It had been all "pleasant surprises" with the hunter pursuing the prey without risk to himself. An even more portentous development was the breakup and dissolution of the Soviet Union. The collapse of the communist regimes in Eastern Europe earlier and now the demise of the Soviet Union drew the curtain on the existing world order. A new post war world order had not yet emerged but whatever remained left the US unrivalled. The chief successor state, Russia, was so beggared and bedraggled that with all its nuclear weapons that could still destroy the world it was struggling for survival and stability. The last five years have witnessed new notable changes in the international political and economic scenario but these will be discussed subsequently.

The assassination of Rajiv Gandhi in the midst of a general election in 1992 saw the return of the Indian

National Congress to power with a wafer-thin majority and with Narasimha Rao as Prime Minister. Rao had to contend not just with an international situation which had left India almost naked but also with a crumbling economy at home. The crisis had been compounded by political instability and economic profligacy. India faced a gargantuan balance of payment crisis that left its foreign-exchange reserves for only two weeks' requirements. Narasimha Rao had brought in as his Finance Minister Manmohan Singh to begin a second wave—far more substantial this time—of economic reforms to halt the economic slide and boost production. The good doctor, as he was called, a veteran of Delhi University, had been economic adviser to the government of India for a number of years and subsequently Governor of the Reserve Bank of India. The economy limped back to the growth track followed, however, by another spell of political fluctuations.

During his tenure Narasimha Rao, bowing to the demands of the international situation, began a process of adjustment involving primarily relations with the United States and China. The dialogue with the United States was intensified and a series of continual talks between senior functionaries of the two sides marked the Narasimha Rao regime's attempt to explore a new relationship with the US but remained shackled by the goals of Washington during Bush senior and Clinton administrations to cap and roll back Indian and Pakistani nuclear and missile programmes and maintain parity between the two countries. (The change towards India began only in the dying years of the Clinton administration gathering momentum in the second term of George W. Bush as President).

The dialogue that Narasimha Rao's aides had begun with the aides of Bush senior was initially vitiated by the aides of the new Clinton administration. Particularly the statements of the new assistant secretary of state Robin Raphael were viewed in India as unnecessarily insensitive and even alarming. Raphael, who had been earlier a counselor in the US embassy in India and was "helicoptered" into the new position because of "school ties" with Clinton, seemed to question the very instrument of accession of India's independence and was dismissive of Indian allegations about Pakistani-sponsored militancy in Kashmir. "I think it is very important to point out that whatever outside support might have been or might be for the insurgency in Kashmir, in our view there are very strong indigenous elements to that insurgency. And one can even argue that at this point it is really self-sustaining"—that was the lady's exposition of the US view in October 1993. A little later she compared the insurgency in Kashmir with the civil war in Afghanistan.

The pincer movement of US pressure at the time focused on human rights in Kashmir on the one hand and the nuclear and missile programmes of India and Pakistan on the other. The pincer movement also ensured that India and Pakistan would be treated on a par with each other. Clinton himself said in January 1994, while accepting the credentials of the Pakistani ambassador, Maleeha Lodhi, "we share Pakistan's concerns about human rights abuses in Kashmir". Earlier speaking at the UN General Assembly on 1 September 1993 Clinton had referred to "bloody ethnic, religious and civil wars" that were raging "from Angola to the Caucasus to Kashmir".

A slight tilt towards Pakistan could also be noticed as the administration lobbied with the Congress to abolish the Pressler amendment that stood in the way of providing military materials to Pakistan and when that failed to ask for a one-time waiver in order to sell 38 F-16 aircrafts to Pakistan. It may be recalled that American policy was governed by an amendment to existing laws moved by Senator Larry Pressler that provided for automatic suspension of aid for any country that carried out or was believed to be engaged in carrying on a nuclear weapons programme. The aid to Pakistan had been suspended in the last years of Bush senior's administration as the President could no longer certify to the Congress that Islamabad was not engaged in the pursuit or production of nuclear weapons. It may also be recalled that for nearly half a decade the US had winked at Pakistan's nuclear programme because of the felt need for an alliance with Pakistan in view of the developments in Afghanistan. The Soviet withdrawal from Afghanistan had changed the perspective.

The other side of the US pincer pressure on India related to the nuclear non-proliferation concerns. In order to wriggle out of the pressures that the senior Bush administration was putting on Islamabad, the Pakistani establishment advanced a proposal of a five-power conference comprised of USA, Russia, China, India and Pakistan to ensure non-proliferation in South Asia. This was a clever gambit to have USA and China sitting on India's head and dictating its nuclear policy. It was quite unacceptable to India but the senior Bush's administration made determined efforts to get India accept the proposal. Through some clever diplomacy India managed to secure Washington's acceptance of broadening the scope of the discussants to go beyond South Asia.

All that was now being undone by the newly installed Clinton administration whose chief objective appeared to be, in the words of Lynn Davis, US undersecretary of state for international security, "looking at India and Pakistan equally and together as we seek to craft a non-proliferation strategy to limit their deployment of missiles, to gain the support for a cut off of.. material for nuclear weapon purposes, their adherence to the comprehensive test ban treaty". The general impression in India was that Narasimha Rao was buckling under this intense pressure to some extent. He had earlier given the green signal to the atomic scientists for conducting a nuclear weapons test, but the Americans came to know about it and it had to be called off at the last minute under their pressure. From available evidence, combined with the other statements being made at the time, it could be concluded that the new administration had made a new strategic assessment of its requirements in Southwest and Central Asia and the role Pakistan could play in the new situation.

Premised on the Islamic arc of instability, volatility and infiltration of terrorism, Washington appeared keen to revive its alliance ties with Pakistan. Pakistan in fact had always allied itself with the US. Islamabad could be helpful in dealing with the uncertainties and the dark side of developments in this region, besides keeping India constrained. According to the briefing given to *New York Times*, Pakistan would be a better ally in the region if the proposed sale of arms materialised. Yet, with all this new understanding, the complexity of the international situation demanded that India should not be pushed off the board. India was too large a country to be marginalised. The economic link was meaningful for both countries. India was an emerging market: it was already on the path of economic revival. The Indo-US trade volumed at $7.4 billion in 1994 could rise exponentially, US Commerce Secretary Ronald Brown believed. USA was also pressing India to further open its markets for international trade. India was equally aware of the economic and political compulsions for a sustained relationship with the US while resisting its pressures where its own vital interests were concerned. It was obvious that both sides had evolved a dual approach towards each other. More of it later.

A New Beginning with Russia

As we have already remarked, the cold war world order lay in tatters as the Soviet Union dissolved into 13 states with Russia as the chief successor state. In many ways India had to rebuild and reorder its relations with Russia on the basis of continuing common interests but in the absence of a special relationship that had marked Indo-Soviet ties. Soviet Russia had provided a countervailing power support in international politics that had now melted away. Many serious problems required a solution to reclaim a new relationship with the successor state of Russia encompassing political and economic ties. The gravity of the new problems for India stemmed from Soviet Russia having been the second-largest economic partner and by far the largest supplier of military hardware.

Russia, besides hobbling politically and economically, was no longer a centralised state with Moscow controlling all political and economic activities. The latter had particularly been decentralised to an uncomfortable degree. India could no longer just do business with Moscow. It had now to negotiate new contacts and contracts at the ground level. Trade and economic relations were hit the hardest. Soviet Russia had been the second largest trading partner of India. The more worrying problem was the supply of spare parts needed by the military. There was no single point of contact and most contracts had to be renewed—at what level and with whom was not too obvious. This was critical and a matter of grave worry for the defence of the country, as the army relied for nearly sixty percent of its requirements on the Soviet Union; the air force and the navy were also similarly handicapped.

The exchange rate between the rupee and the rouble had to be renegotiated. The volume of India's rupee debt to the successor states had to be determined (it was finally fixed at rupees 31,093 crores); so also how it was to be paid back. Significant also was India's reliance on Moscow for meeting its energy needs with 25 percent of its oil imports supplied by the Soviet Union. The Power Ministry was also on tenterhooks as there had been heavy Soviet credits for many power projects. All these painful problems were part of the agonising process of re-establishment of ties on a new basis. Other red herrings were thrown into this process of rebuilding ties. The new establishment in Moscow was divided on the approach to be adopted towards the subcontinent. Some of them were anxious to bury all vestiges of a special relationship with India. They advocated reaching out to Pakistan and some of them even made their way there to assure Islamabad that the tilt towards India was over and that henceforth Pakistan's concerns would also be kept in mind. This was immediately denied by others in position in the foreign policy establishment.

Many in the West put in their weight behind Moscow ending its tilt towards India. This was all too evident on the issue of the supply of cryogenic engines for India's space program for peaceful explorations which Moscow had undertaken to supply but reneged under intense US pressure on the plea that these engines could have military-related uses. The Russians finally gave in even though a senior official of the Russian space agency exclaimed, "no space expert in the world would say such a thing. No one has ever used super-cooled liquid oxygen-hydrogen engines for military purposes".

Nevertheless the stamp of the start of a renewed relationship was forcefully put by the then president Boris Yeltsin during a visit to India soon afterwards. In his address to Parliament members and in his press conference Yeltsin reiterated Russian support to India's position on Kashmir and underlined the value of India-Russia ties in the new international situation. India must maintain its integrity and stay united and undivided, he told a press conference on 28 January 1993. The earlier Indo-Russian Treaty of Peace, Friendship and Cooperation was substituted by a new 14-clause Treaty of Friendship and Cooperation, valid for

20 years, which stipulated that the two countries would refrain from taking any action that might affect the security interests of the other, pledging support to each other's territorial integrity and non-interference in internal affairs.

Gradually various problems were sorted out and a close relationship developed again, particularly under Vladimir Putin, that we shall have occasion to revisit a little later.

Central Asia and the Oil Game

Central Asia was once the cradle of civilisation. It was the caravan route for trade for centuries. Basra and Bukhara are well-known names in history. But Central Asia also became the battleground for competing imperial invasions that laid waste much of the region. Came the Soviet revolution and gradually the Central Asian states were absorbed in the new Soviet leviathan with both its advantages and serious disabilities. There was remarkable progress in the areas of education and health but all the economic activity was tied up with Moscow. Most of the present rulers in the various Central Asian states were functionaries of the Soviet Communist Party with its strict discipline exercised by the centralised party apparatus.

These republics, chiefly Kazakhstan, Uzbekistan, Turkmenistan, Kyrgyzstan and Tajikistan were ill-prepared when suddenly independence was thrust on them in December 1991-January 1992. They were economically fragile and politically volatile. The demographic mosaic was challenging. There was a large Russian minority population in most of them, so also Uzbeks in sizeable numbers in some of them. The ethnic divisions were complicated by Islamic militancy, the economic weakness fuelling religious extremism and sectarian politics. There were also a huge differences in population and resources between them: Kazakhstan had a population of 17 million and sizable oil deposits and other minerals, Uzbekistan blessed with nearly 26 million people and natural resources, Turkmenistan astride an area comprising 488,000 square kilometres, sparsely populated, but claimed the world's fourth largest gas reserves. The other two were both poorly populated and poorly endowed with natural resources except that Kyrgyzstan had gold reserves.

India had grasped early the need for establishing immediately diplomatic and economic relations with Central Asian republics but was unwilling or rather unable to make the kind of economic commitment that they desperately needed. India had historic contacts with Central Asia, particularly through the silk route and held particular attraction for the new Central Asian states as a non-threatening major state near the borders. That India gave importance to the region was demonstrated by the fact that Narasimha Rao went twice to this region during his five-year tenure. India tried to develop multiple political and economic contacts with the Central Asian countries. By 1996 India's trade volume stood at Rs 58 million with Uzbekistan, 56 million with Kazakhstan and only 1½ million with Kyrgyzstan. Even in the financial year 2003-2004, barring Russia, CIS (Commonwealth of Independent States set up after the dissolution of the USSR) and Baltic states, India's exports with the rest of CIS countries, essentially the Central Asian nations, stood at about $ 312 million and imports at over $ 300 million. Specifically with Kazakhstan Indian exports for this period were valued at nearly $ 70 million and imports at just over $9 million. This constituted a pittance in their or India's overall foreign trade. The leaders of these states initially looked up to India as their safest bet for development but were disappointed. Apart from the fact that India did not have a direct trade route to these countries, they required massive investments in roads, railways, pipelines, storages, etc, on a scale that India did not have the means to make, nor was there a political will to make sacrifices for such purposes. They began looking elsewhere. Russia once again became the paramount power in the region followed by USA and China. USA established bases in Uzbekistan and Kyrgyzstan. It has recently been ejected from Uzbekistan but retains its base in Kyrgyzstan.

It is only recently, partly in the wake of the developments in Afghanistan, but much more because of the worldwide hunt for energy resources that India began to expand its presence here. The Central Asian region is now recognised as a strategically important region. In view of the volatility in the Persian Gulf region and the regional conflicts in West Asia (what the West calls the Middle East), Central Asia's substantial oil and gas resources have enhanced the attractiveness of this region (just as it has pinpointed the importance of some African countries like Sudan, Nigeria, Angola and some others for similar reasons). Prime Minister Manmohan Singh said that energy security was second only in our scheme of things to food security. Both India and China have become active actors in the search for oil; their energy resources are new magnetic poles for the countries of the world. China much more than India has invested heavily in building roads, infrastructure and pipelines in some of these countries. Already the 625-mile long Kazakhstan-China pipeline has opened new possibilities for the supply of oil and gas to China. Along with Russia, China has helped establish Shanghai Security Organisation (SCO) that includes all the countries of the region in addition to Russia and China. India, Pakistan and Iran have observer status at the SCO.

India too is now actively engaged in developing relations with the region and is staking its claim for oil exploration in countries like Kazakhstan and Uzbekistan and offering whatever expertise and financial resources it can muster. Like many other countries, India has become fully alive to its relationship with Central Asian countries in the new era of the search for energy security. Consequently Indian diplomacy became active in the region in the last five years, looking for oil and economic agreements and becoming a part of what has been rather facetiously called the great game.

Symptomatic of this was Prime Minister Manmohan Singh's visit to Uzbekistan, a leading central Asian country with a population of 26 million, with 594 million barrels of proven oil reserves and among the world's top 10 natural gas producers, in April (2006). Manmohan Singh said in Tashkent: "We see Uzbekistan as an important element in any effort to optimally utilize the energy resources of Central Asia. India will also cooperate with Uzbekistan in exploration and development of its vast geological and mineral resources". As part of their agreement India was to set up an Entrepreneurship Development Centre in Tashkent and to provide satellite based tele-education and tele-medicine connectivity between India and Uzbekistan. Manmohan Singh also inaugurated the Jawaharlal Nehru India-Uzbekistan Centre for Information Technology at Tashkent. Karimov offered the allocation of geological territory to Indian companies to explore gas, oil and other mineral resources with revenues from any finds to be shared equally between the two countries. In the joint communiqué Singh and Karimov noted the propinquity of their views on various international issues and vowed to fight together in all its manifestations and forms the menace of terrorism which they described as the most serious threat to international peace and security.

India is also helping Tajikistan develop an air base which many Western writers have described as an Indian base. There is inevitably some competition between India and China which has been far more active in the region with the advantage of proximity, but they are also trying to cooperate with each other and avoid a mindless race for the black gold. Relations between India and Central Asia remained very cordial and non-conflictual.

Pakistan: Continuing Acrimony

Relations with Pakistan remained tense for many years to come. In fact for most of the period under consideration Pakistan had been raising its stakes and involvement in the Kashmir insurgency and gradually in militancy in the rest of the country. It had also accelerated its race towards the possession of nuclear weapons, considerably assisted in acquiring a nuclear capability by China and missile capability by North Korea and China. Then Foreign Minister Yakub Khan visited Delhi in 1990 using undiplomatic and threatening language about "dark clouds hanging over Jammu and Kashmir" to be told in "unmistakable language" by I.K. Gujral, Foreign Minister in the short-lived VP Singh government that India would not allow the secession of Jammu and Kashmir.

The Indo-Pakistan waters were further muddied by the mindless destruction of the Babri masjid on 7 December 1992 by swayam sewaks and shiva sena zealots. It raised the communal temperature and gave comfort to all the forces of intolerance and irrationality. While most people in India were distressed and shamed by the events and regarded it as a failure of the Narasimha Rao government, vandalism was officially encouraged by Pakistan and more than 30 temples were destroyed in Pakistan. The emotions of religious bigotry and fanaticism were aroused much to the delight of their Indian counterparts. Then came the Bombay blasts in March 1993 further tumbling the already deteriorating India-Pakistan relations with the prime suspects, Dawood Ibrahim and his kinsmen and associates fleeing to Dubai and on to Pakistan. Since then Pakistan has feigned ignorance about the whereabouts of Dawood.

While Indo-Pak talks to normalise the relations continued fitfully and fruitlessly, the language of threats rose by quite a few decibels. Assef Ahmed Ali, who had become Foreign Minister, spoke at Tashkent on 8 January 1994 about the danger of a fourth war in South Asia that might become a nuclear war. Benazir Bhutto, Prime Minister of Pakistan at the time herself went to Pyongyang to negotiate (and sign ?) a deal with North Korea for the acquisition of missile technology while terminating the negotiations process with India on the ground that it would send a wrong message to the people of Kashmir. She claimed subsequently (when she was not in power) that Pakistan had acquired nuclear capability in 1987.

Bhutto was summarily dismissed by Pakistani president Leghari, apparently in concert with the army, and Nawaz Sharif became Prime Minister in the elections that ensued. Nawaz Sharif threw a "bombshell" while speaking at a public meeting in Pakistan-occupied Kashmir when he claimed that Pakistan actually had a nuclear bomb on the shelf and that in case of war it would be used.

There is ample evidence to show that China had materially contributed to Pakistan's nuclear capability. The *New York Times* revealed (22 June 1995) that between February and May, China had delivered to Pakistan important components that could be used in M-11 missiles. Despite Pakistan's denials, US sources insisted on the authenticity of the report. The *Washington Post* (2 July 1995) quoted US intelligence resources asserting that Beijing had given Pakistan complete medium-range ballistic missiles and that storage crates at Sargodha contained more than 30 Chinese-made M-11 missiles. In response to US pressure and protests, while denying any wrongdoing, Beijing promised that it would tighten exports controls on companies dealing with military-related items. Pakistan also took the stand that it was responding to the security threat posed by the development of the Prithvi missile (and subsequently the Agni missile) by India. Later, US Senator John Glen, first American astronaut and subsequently member of the Senate Armed Services Committee and the Senate Select Committee On Intelligence asserted (4 December 1997) that Beijing had provided Pakistan with a proven Chinese design for a nuclear bomb that had been tested many times in China.

Foreign Policy Under Gujral: The Gujral Doctrine

I.K. Gujral became Foreign Minister in June 1996 and then Prime Minister in March 1997. As we have noted earlier, Gujral was intellectually above many of his predecessors (or successors) and was more knowledgeable too, besides being articulate and sober. While a votary of the Nehruvian vision, he had developed his own approach about foreign policy in the changed circumstances. His ideas on foreign policy came to be known as the Gujral doctrine. At the core of his ideas was the belief that as the dominant state in South Asia, India need not weigh the concept of reciprocity in numerical or arithmetical terms. As the largest country in the region India could afford to be more generous while protecting its fundamental interests. It was not a case of all give and no take but India could give a little more than it took. If the neighbour was willing to move an inch forward, India should be willing to move a yard forward. Certainly India was too big and mature to trade insult for insult, invective for invective and India must more actively pursue opportunities for establishing a new quality of relations with neighbours. These ideas could influence public opinion in the neighbouring countries even more than those of the governments there. In any case India's sober and constructive responses would have a beneficial impact on relations with neighbours.

Bangladesh, Sri Lanka and Pakistan

Before we consider relations with Pakistan in the light of Gujral's new approach, it is appropriate to take note of developments in relations with some other neighbours like Bangladesh and Sri Lanka. A serious effort was made to move forward with Bangladesh with whom relations had been in the freeze since the assassination of Sheikh Mujibur Rehman. These relations deteriorated in the wake of the demolition of the Babri masjid, when communal elements in Bangladesh used the opportunity to vandalise a large number of Hindu temples and attacked the houses of the minority community while Khaleda's government merely looked on. The freeze was further congealed by the ever present resentment against a bigger neighbour fanned by appeals to religion in the struggle for power within Bangladesh. Gujral drafted the good offices of the prominent CPI (M) leader, Jyoti Basu, then Chief Minister of West Bengal, to negotiate a settlement of the issue of the utilisation of Ganga waters—a particularly thorny issue between the two countries. (The sharing of waters is not only an inflammable issue among countries but also within a country among its different parts and regions—as we have seen in India and elsewhere). It helped that at the helm at the time was Begum Hasina Wajed (daughter of the late Sheikh) who unlike her predecessor (and later successor also) Begum Khaleda Zia (wife of the late President, Zia ur Rehman), was not driven by antipathy to India (either genuine or the product of the felt need to garner political support by utilising the anti-India card).

Jyoti Basu hammered out with the Bangladesh Foreign Minister Abdus Samad a 30-year treaty on the sharing of the Ganga waters. This had been a major dispute between the two countries and the agreement took some tension out of the troubled relationship and was celebrated in Bangladesh. Hasina speaking in India at the signing of the treaty underlined the need to overcome poverty and stagnation—the common task of the two countries. The treaty was expectedly opposed by Begum Zia and various Islamist elements. There should be no mistaking that there were elements in both countries whom the friendship between the two countries did not suit and who would in the name of religion fan passion and prejudice against the other.

Gujral's success in finding a solution to one of the most divisible issues in Indo-Bangladesh relations was partially undone by subsequent developments in which the extremist Islamist forces in Bangladesh were utilised by Begum Zia to return to power compounded by some wrongheaded decisions in New Delhi. It is generally believed that during the last election in Bangladesh which saw the re-emergence of Khaleda Zia as Prime Minister, Indian Prime Minister Vajpayee tried to secretly extend assistance to both the contending parties. If this was true, it was the worst possible policy to be pursued. It gave no help in any real sense in generally repairing relations with Begum Zia and her supporters, some of whom belonged to extremist Muslim organisations, but it helped a great deal in gravely damaging Hasina and the secular forces in Dacca.

Relations with Sri Lanka were also favourably impacted by the Gujral doctrine. Then Sri Lankan Prime Minister Premadasa's implacable hostility had resulted in the premature withdrawal of the Indian Peacekeeping Force (IPKF) from the island Republic. Premadasa had struck a deal with the LTTE who were naturally keen to see the backs of the Indian forces, but paid a heavy price for soon after suspected LTTE agents assassinated Premadasa. The ruling UNP was losing steam rapidly and in the ensuing elections Chandrika Kumaratunga (daughter of the erstwhile Prime Minister Srimavo Bandaranaike) heading the coalition of parties, People's Alliance, in which her own Sri Lanka

Freedom Party was the major complement, took over power in Colombo on a peace platform. Gujral had developed particularly close relations with the Sri Lankan leaders easing any lingering tension. The late Laxman Kadirgamar, who was then Foreign Minister in the new government, described the relations between India and Sri Lanka as being "in excellent condition".

We may note in passing and bringing the story forward that ever since Rajiv Gandhi's assassination at the hands of LTTE agents, India had virtually taken itself out of Sri Lankan politics and developments. Norwegian government emissaries have been facilitating, somewhat fitfully, peace negotiations between Sri Lankan governments and the LTTE leadership, keeping India briefed and perhaps occasionally taking counsel, but New Delhi has studiously kept away since the banning of the LTTE in India and its involvement in the killing of Rajiv Gandhi, despite recent overtures by the LTTE. The fact of the situation in Sri Lanka is that on the one hand the LTTE has neither given up its goal of a separate Tamil state and its intolerance of any dissident opinion or its policy of violence and assassination, nor, on the other hand, has Colombo evinced its readiness to agree to a genuine federal structure in Sri Lanka and opinion within the Sinhalese majority community remains sharply divided.

Pakistan

We have already touched upon the nuclearisation of Pakistan. After making bold claims the Pakistani leadership, perhaps realising the damage, hedged about the possession of a nuclear bomb. Both Bhutto and Nawaz Sharif retracted from some of their earlier statements and took the position that Pakistan had the capability but had not actually exercised it. We shall come back to this theme a little later. Gujral's approach had a balming effect on relations with

Pakistan. In the first instance, he decided that India would not engage in verbal warfare with Pakistan and India and would not react to Islamabad's fulminations at various international fora. Just as one could not clap with one hand, one-sided tirade soon loses steam.

Gujral was keen on moving on in relations with Pakistan. He and Nawaz Sharif, who became Prime Minister after the dismissal of Benazir Bhutto and the ensuing elections, met on the sidelines of the ninth SAARC summit to revive the dialogue process under the auspices of the respective foreign secretaries that went on fitfully because of basic differences. For Pakistan there was a one-point programme: Kashmir. India wanted to move ahead on various fronts, political, economic, social and cultural to create an atmosphere for the resolutions of the most cantankerous issue. On top of it was the issue of terrorist activities in India aided and abetted from across the border. Mr Gujral told parliament that Pakistan was not only providing sanctuary to terrorists but was also supplying them arms and ammunition and assistance in infiltrating into India. Nevertheless, he said, he was keen on continuing the India-Pakistan dialogue. But these problems have continued to hobble ties between the two countries.

China

One of the areas where discernible progress took place was relations with China which maintained their upward curve. The process which Rajiv Gandhi pushed was gaining momentum. A high point was the visit of the Chinese President and General Secretary of the Communist Party, Jiang Zemin in November 1996. It became even more significant because, coinciding with his visit, an agreement was signed between India and China to maintain peace and tranquility at the border and provided a mechanism for maintaining it. Since then India-China border has been quiet and tranquil. It was also significant that visiting Pakistan after his India visit, Jiang publicly advised the Pakistani leadership that if certain issues could not be resolved for the time being, they could be shelved temporarily so that they would not affect the normal state-to-state relations. The reference to Kashmir was unmistakable. However, in view of Pakistani sensitivities, Beijing did not publicly repeat this admonition nor did it lead to any lessening of their aid to Pakistan in various areas.

Clinton: A More Sophisticated Approach?

The Clinton administration's primary concerns, at least so far as this region was concerned, centred around securing non-proliferation. A Comprehensive Test Ban Treaty (CTBT) had been drafted that would oblige all signatory states to stop any more nuclear tests. The treaty would have permanently divided the world into those who had and those who did not have. Those who had (atomic weapons) would keep what they had and those who did not have could not aspire to possess them. This was in addition to the Nuclear Non-Proliferation Treaty (NPT). The two together would establish a wholly discriminatory regime as the new world order. The Clinton administration's chief effort was to get India fall in line and sign the CTBT, if not the NPT as this would effectively forestall any attempt by India to possess a tested bomb. Pressure was mounted on India to acquiesce in the US strategy. We have also noted Clinton administration's initial tilt towards Pakistan. It is possible that gradually some rethinking was taking place at the highest levels that called for a more nuanced approach towards India (this rethinking was partially reversed by India's nuclear tests but finally materialised in a shift only towards the last two years of the Clinton regime at the turn of the century). The goals remained the same but a softer approach was adopted. Clinton, who was also meeting

Nawaz Sharif, requested Gujral to advance his trip to New York to meet him on the sidelines of the UN General Assembly which Gujral was also addressing. Gujral took his finance minister, P. Chidambaram and the two had a 40-minute meeting with Clinton and his aides on 22 September 1997. The Indians did most of the talking while the Americans listened apparently with greater understanding than before. The Indian Prime Minister explained the country's security concerns as the context in which India could not adhere to the CTBT, and Chidambaram outlined the economic perspective and opportunities as well as India's requirements. The atmospherics between India and USA became more cordial.

It must be mentioned that economics exercises a profound influence on foreign policy. It is not just politics that drives economics, it can often be the other way around. In any case the economic situation and economic requirements leave an enduring impact on the country's foreign policy. In this perspective it is pertinent to keep in mind that for years now USA had been India's largest export market and that India has generally enjoyed a favourable balance of trade with the US. Even when political relations with USA were not the most friendly economic contacts were kept intact both in Nehru's and Indira Gandhi's time.

The Vajpayee Government And Foreign Policy

The Gujral government fell as the Congress withdrew its support leading to fresh elections which ushered in a government of the National Democratic Alliance, a conglomeration of 32 right-wing centrist and regional parties, led by the BJP's leader Atal Behari Vajpayee as the Prime Minister. It is generally believed that Narasimha Rao told Vajpayee on his assumption of power to do what he himself could not do—go for a nuclear weapon test. The Vajpayee government remained in power for nearly six years. It is appropriate to look at its foreign policy in greater detail.

Nuclear Tests and After

One of the first acts of the Vajpayee government was to conduct nuclear tests. On 11 May 1998 at 3:45 p.m. India conducted three underground tests in succession at Pokhran, one of them a thermonuclear test indicating a hydrogen bomb capability. Two days later India conducted at the same side two more underground tests with a low yield to obtain "additional data for improved computer simulation of designs", and to obtain "the capability to carry out sub-critical experiments, if considered necessary". With these tests, codenamed Shakti 1-V, India had become a nuclear-weapons state with a capability to miniaturise nuclear weapons and mount warheads on Prithvi and Agni missiles. This completed the process that Indira Gandhi began in October 1974. In fact even Jawaharlal Nehru, despite all his abhorrence for nuclear weapons, had left the option open for future generations with the kind of nuclear research that he had permitted to be undertaken. It's equally obvious that the Vajpayee government could not have undertaken these tests if the groundwork had not been already in place. Pokhran 1 was thus succeeded by Pokhran II and Pokhran III. Pokhran I had been declared to be designed for peaceful uses of atomic energy, although demonstrating India's nuclear capability. A joint statement of the Department of Atomic Energy (DAE) and the Defence Research and Development Organisation (PRDO) claimed that India had acquired state-of-the-art nuclear weapon capability after testing a 45-Kiloton yield hydrogen bomb on 11 May at Pokhran and that the country had been conferred the capability to vacate nuclear threats.

It would only be fair to note that some foreign and domestic commentators cast doubt on the credibility of the thermonuclear bomb blast, a few of them even claiming that it had failed. However, that was not the understanding of the scientists directly involved, chiefly Dr Abdul Kalam, chief scientific adviser (now President of India) and Dr R. Chidambaram. Moreover, Dr Kalam claimed that the tests had made possible future tests to be sub-critical. In plain language it may no longer be necessary to conduct above ground or underground tests for further advancement: that purpose could be served through laboratory tests.

The Prime Minister declared that India had no need for more tests and undertook a voluntary moratorium on further testing. This promise came handy in future negotiations with the West. The Prime Minister also declared on behalf of the country that India would not be the first to use the atomic weapons; the recourse to them would only be in the self-defense. There was broad support in the country for the tests. Most political parties, barring the Left, expressed endorsement. The leader of the chief opposition party, Indian National Congress, Mrs Sonia Gandhi put on record the "pride we feel in the achievement of our nuclear scientists and engineers for putting India's nuclear capability in the front rank". She also recalled "with equal pride that successive Congress governments have ensured that India's nuclear capability remained up to date so that our security is not compromised". She also remarked that the Congress remained committed to a nuclear weapons-free and a non-violent world which remained the "sheet anchor" of India's policy.

The Fallout

The immediate calculations, rather the miscalculations of the government betrayed a certain immaturity and considerable lack of finesse in dealing with the new situation. The government did not seem to have either anticipated or factored in the atomic blasts that took place immediately afterwards in Pakistan. At the least one did not get the impression that New Delhi knew what would be coming, although there should have been no mistaking the consequences. There was ample evidence, as we have already noted, about the nuclearisation of Pakistan. The American pressure had restrained the Pakistani establishment from overt testing but once the Indians did it, Islamabad had its opportunity. There is no evidence that the government had taken this into account in formulating its strategy.

Even more unfortunately, the government tried to placate the Americans by citing the Chinese and Pakistani threat. Prime Minister Vajpayee wrote a letter to US President Clinton citing the threat from these two countries as the justification for the Indian tests. Besides enraging the Chinese, it served no other purpose. The Clinton administration immediately leaked the letter to *New York Times*, making an already difficult situation even more difficult. This was also the time when the Defence Minister, George Fernandes, had been pointing at China as number one threat to Indian security.

Unnecessarily also highly jingoistic statements were made by some senior ruling party leaders, besides the chauvinism displayed at the lower levels. One senior Minister in the Government even challenged the whole world and claimed India was ready for it. This was not the time for such bravado. This was the time when India should have put its best foot forward, showed its most benign face to the world and heavily underlined its responsible quality. This was the time for diplomacy to have taken over, when the rationale for our decision should have been squarely ensconced in the iniquities of the international system. It was the iniquities that had led Indira Gandhi to give the go-ahead signal for Pokhran 1, the same consideration with Narasimha Rao's decision to conduct nuclear tests, even though the decision was aborted. The decision might have been hastened by reports of Pakistan's nuclearisation programme, as both Rajiv Gandhi and Narasimha Rao perceived, but essentially the driving factor now as with Indira Gandhi was the grossly unjust world order in which there would be only five permanent first-class travellers and all the others would ever be obliged to travel by the third class.

The US argument that the possession of nuclear weapons did not confer any special position or special rights was disingenuous and was disproved immediately by the fact that it was the P-five (the five nuclear powers) who met to deliberate upon the response to the nuclear tests and the resolutions denouncing India (and Pakistan) were meant to be relevant for the whole world. The chief target was India and even though immediate success would not have been achieved India's diplomacy could and should have been focusing on the demand for nuclear disarmament. The NPT by which nuclear powers were swearing had also enjoined upon them to enter upon negotiations for gradual nuclear disarmament so that the world could finally become a nuclear weapons-free world. The nuclear powers had willfully ignored their own obligations while insisting on everyone else's. This should have been the thrust of our proactive diplomacy around the world demanding that nuclear powers begin serious and sustained negotiations for verifiable, under international supervision, nuclear disarmament and loudly proclaiming our own willingness to be a part of the process of nuclear disarmament.

In any case, some pain would have been there, no matter what. The American laws were applied immediately and India came under sanctions. Not just US sanctions, in fact under international sanctions. The US pressured the World Bank and International Monetary Fund to withhold new assistance and the ban was extended to a number of other financial institutions. The nuclear powers had also organised themselves into the so-called Nuclear Suppliers Regulatory Group that decided on whether any or which country would be given or denied (and how much) nuclear-related materials even if for peaceful purposes (like heavy water or uranium for a nuclear reactor). Russia and France too were obliged to follow its guidelines. Every effort was made by Washington to deny high technology to India. The scientific exchanges were severely restrained and handicapped. India's scientific community withstood the international pressures and acquitted itself well but the pain and the costs could not just be discounted. Russia was of considerable help, and even France did its bit but their constraints were obvious.

It was only with the passage of time that the US began to realise that a country like India could not just be ostracised and some via media be found to turn around the relationship. The Kargil conflict perhaps was a catalyst in this regard. Kargil was also important for analysing India-Pakistan relations but what preceded Kargil was no less significant as episodes in the zig-zag course of India-Pakistan relations.

The Bus Diplomacy

Prime Minister Vajpayee took some bold steps to break the logjam with Pakistan and pushed through a process of reconciliation. A bus service between Delhi and Lahore was inaugurated in February 1999 and Vajpayee himself took the inaugural bus service (in parts) and met Nawaz Sharif, then Prime Minister of Pakistan, February 20-21 at Lahore during his two-day visit. The visit generated tremendous enthusiasm in the two countries, perhaps more so in Pakistan than India. Nawaz Sharif and Atal Behari Vajpayee signed what came to be known as the Lahore declaration.

This was followed by the signing of a Memorandum

of Understanding between the foreign secretaries of the two countries reaffirming their unilateral moratorium on further nuclear testing and spelling out other confidence building measures. While new hope was aroused in the two countries for a reconciliation, the army brass in Pakistan was taking a very dim view of the goings-on between India and Pakistan. All the evidence suggests that General Musharraf and some of his closest comrades-in-arms had begun planning secretly a new military campaign in Kashmir even before the signing of the Lahore agreement.

Kargil and After

While Vajpayee was facing domestic Parliamentary instability, the Kargil conflict erupted in May-June 1999 as the Pakistani army hiding behind a facade of militants moved across the line of control and captured vital peaks in the Ladakh area. It may also be recalled that the national highway connecting Srinagar with Leh (the capital of Ladakh) cuts through Kargil. Besides occupying strategic heights the Pakistani army could cut off Ladakh from the rest of Kashmir and could then overlook the Indian army there. The Pakistani army's gamble was obvious. Moreover the rupture between Kashmir and Ladakh would force India to withdraw from the Siachen glacier. The Pakistani army's aim to force India to negotiate a settlement to the advantage of Pakistan could hardly be doubted.

The Kargil conflict was scripted by Gen Musharraf who had been appointed chief of army staff by Sharif in 1998. Musharraf said later that everybody was "on board", including Nawaz Sharif, but whether Sharif was really briefed properly on all the details was doubtful. That he had been hiding the preparations from his Prime Minister was amply evident from the telephonic conversation that Musharraf had with his deputy, General Aziz, from Beijing where he had gone for a visit in May 1999. Musharraf asked

Aziz whether he had ensured that "he" (meaning Nawaz Sharif) did not know what they had planned. Aziz replied that everything had been taken care of. India was able to pick up this conversation as a friendly East European country had given it the technology to eavesdrop on such overseas Pakistani conversations even from their "secure" communication lines. (This information has been conveyed to this writer by an extremely highly-placed source). So, while it was true that New Delhi was taken unawares when Kargil happened, it was able to reinterpret this conversation subsequently and rebut Pakistan's disclaimers about its army's involvement. In fact Musharraf himself conceded later that he had planned the Kargil adventure a month before Vajpayee's visit to Lahore.

Yet the fact remains that New Delhi, no less the army command, was caught unawares when Pakistan moved across and captured some vital hilltops that would enable it to choke the Indian army in Kashmir. Intelligence failures could not be denied, nor the complacency of the army command which ignored whatever warning signals that had been given to it by some of the command structure at the hilltops. But this failure and complacency was in stark contrast to the extra ordinary grit and determination displayed by the armed forces in recapturing the lost territory. There were heavy casualties on both sides. The Pakistani estimate of the Indian casualties was 800 killed and 2200 wounded, whereas the Indian estimate of the Pakistani casualties was 4000 killed and 1400 wounded. Notwithstanding the tall claims by General Musharraf in his recently released memoir *In the Line of Fire*, the fact remained that the Pakistani army was decisively defeated with the Indian army capturing back most of the hilltops. With defeat staring the Pakistani army in the face, Nawaz Sharif was left holding the baby as he headed towards Washington to meet President Clinton to secure American intercession.

As is well-known, Clinton told Sharif that he had to pull back his troops, while informing him that his army chief was moving nuclear tactical weapons forward (denied by Musharraf in his memoir) in case India after recapturing the mountain tops carried the campaign into the Pakistani territory. In fact India had no intention of doing so. The army, including the air force, was under strict instructions not to cross the Line of Actual Control (LOC). Britain and the European Community were applying similar pressure on Islamabad as the US that Pakistan must withdraw behind the LOC thus giving considerable international sanctity to the LOC.

Musharraf's Kargil gamble had failed. But the peace process lay in tatters. The Lahore declaration was dead as dodo. Yet it had opposite effects in India and Pakistan. In India it bolstered the position of Vajpayee. The NDA came back to power with a handsome majority in the elections that followed. In Pakistan, without going into the dramatic developments surrounding Musharraf's *coup d'etat*, Nawaz Sharif, the elected Prime Minister, was deposed and General Musharraf took over as the Chief Executive on 13 December 1999 and subsequently in a dubious referendum became President. The American intercession prevented the execution of Nawaz Sharif, resulting in his exile to Saudi Arabia. As Clinton told I.K. Gujral, "I could save his neck, but not his empire"!

Agra Summit

As Musharraf consolidated his control and gave indications of his desire to revive talks with India, Vajpayee took another initiative and invited the General now President as well as commander of the armed forces for talks at Agra in July 2001. The summit was held without any ground work having been done and without an adequate basis having been laid. The talks failed to achieve a breakthrough. There was no joint statement either. It was believed that Pakistan insisted on the inclusion of Kashmir as the "core" issue, rejected by India, while India asked for the inclusion of "cross-border terrorism" in the proposed joint statement, that was rejected by Pakistan. The Pakistani media briefed informally by the Pakistani officials claimed that both Vajpayee and Jaswant Singh had agreed to a joint draft that just mentioned Kashmir and with the word "core" taken out and terrorism put in without the addition of "cross-border", but that Advani had adamantly turned it down. The truth would not be known for many years but the fact of the matter was that the position of the two countries on both the issues was as yet unbridgeable.

From the public relations point of view the Agra summit was a fiasco for India. The Government choked off all information or sources of information to its own media, and therefore its own people, while Musharraf and his aides made full use of the opportunity to publicise their point of view. Particularly, General Musharraf had a field day in the breakfast meeting he had with senior Indian editors and media people before the Vajpayee government shared its own perspective with the Indian people. With regard to the violence in Kashmir Musharraf claimed, "We are not encouraging violence. It is an indigenous freedom struggle". Only once was Musharraf riled during his virtuoso performance when Prannoy Roy of the NDTV asked him that he was pushing for free elections in Kashmir but was not willing to grant the same to his own people in Pakistan.

Kandahar Episode

On the eve of Christmas 1999 an Indian Airlines flight IC 814 from Kathmandu to New Delhi was hijacked. Mysteriously, the aircraft that had remained parked in Amritsar for a full 40 minutes was allowed to take off and finally landed in Kandahar in Afghanistan. The hijackers threatened to blow the plane along with the passengers if their demands for the release of 36 captured militants by India and a ransom was not met and in fact killed one of the passengers to make their intent clear. After negotiations through the Taliban negotiators, to the standing discomfort of India, the Government decided to hand over three militants to secure the release of the passengers. What was more galling was that the then External Affairs Minister, Jaswant Singh decided himself to take the three militants, including Maulana Massood Azhar, head of a notorious terrorist organization, to Kandahar in a special plane. The hijackers as well as the militants released were Pakistan-based. Relations with Pakistan were hardly helped by this episode.

India-USA: A New Beginning?

The India-Pakistan relations took another turn with the 9/11 attack on the United States and the 13 December onslaught on the Indian Parliament. But as certain decisive changes were taking place on the world platform, we need to look at the India-US relations first. As we have seen, Indo-US relations had begun to mutate during the last years of the Clinton presidency. The Clinton administration began to adopt a tougher stance towards Pakistan-based terrorism against India, advising Pakistan to take action against the militants operating from its territory. The changing perception was also evident from Clinton's visit to India in March 2000—the fourth US President ever to visit India (after Dwight Eisenhower, Richard Nixon and Jimmy Carter*). Even before the visit there was already considerable political support for India in the United States. In a resolution carried by 396-4 votes in November 1999,

* Written before George W. Bush's visit to India.

the US House of Representatives lauded India as "a shining example of democracy for all of Asia to follow" and urged Clinton to visit India and "broaden our special relationship with India into a strategic partnership". Clinton spent three days in India and even though he stuck to the themes of nonproliferation and the CTBT, he did not let these deter him from pursuing a new agenda of a new relationship with India. Clinton brought American businessmen along with him to underline the importance of Indo-US economic relations. Businessmen from both the countries signed agreements totalling $ 3 billion. The deals represented over $ 2 billion in commercial ventures and $ one billion in US export-import financing. They involved various business houses of the two countries and included provision of electronic communication system, wireless broad band access, energy and financial sectors. His visit to India was in sharp contrast to his 6½ hours stop in Pakistan amidst the tightest possible security and where he used the opportunity to address the Pakistani people on the merits of civil and democratic rule.

Apart from the growing political support within the US elite, two additional factors were no less significant. One was the increasing realisation in the US that India was an emerging market and an emerging power. To take only one example of this emerging awareness, Clinton told the Nebraska University students in December 2000: "In Silicon Valley there are 700 high-tech companies headed by Indians—700 in one place. This was totally off the radar screen of American policy during the cold war". Clinton added, "do you know how many people live in India? 980 million. In 30 years, India will be more populous than China".

The second additional factor was the role of the Indian community in the United States. Smaller in numbers, but growing rapidly, many of them well-educated and professionally influential, they were getting better organised and more vocal in US politics. As the Oakland mayor put it: "They have the brains, they have the wealth and they are strategically positioned and interested in shaping American politics".

Even before Clinton's visit, with the approval of Vajpayee and Clinton, Jaswant Singh (then Foreign Minister) and Strobe Talbot, then Deputy Secretary of State, had begun a track 2 dialogue, away from the glare of publicity to try to reach a *modus vivendi* for some of the outstanding problems arising from India's nuclear tests and the US administration's sanctions against India and the demand for adherence to the NPT and the CTBT. The talks proceeded somewhat leisurely, but if one goes by Strobe Talbot's account, Jaswant Singh made amazing offers to the American for which there appeared to be no mandate. He was virtually committing the Government to sign the CTBT, particularly if the sanctions were removed and Clinton visited India. Equally incredulous was the offer one fine morning to Strobe Talbot that India would be willing to accept the line of control in Kashmir as the international boundary between India and Pakistan. On whose authority was such an offer made was not clear.

Anyway the Clinton administration was on its way out. In came the Bush administration with a wholly new set of ruling elite. But, interestingly, the Bush Administration did not change the course of searching for new relationship with India. It, on the other hand, intensified this effort, even more effectively in the second term of George W. Bush as President. Before we consider that interaction, we must note briefly the characteristics of the new administration and its changed approach towards the world as well as the seminal developments during 2001-2006 as the backdrop.

A word of caution, however, would be appropriate about American approaches. These are necessarily moulded by America's perceived national interests and are often seen to change quickly. Because of America's global interests there is more volatility in its friendships. How many times was Pakistan made an ally and how many times did the pendulum shift, even if slightly, towards India! The limits of Indo-US friendship often became patent even while commentators and analysts were writing euphorically about them.

Domestic Factors and US Foreign Policy: Rise of the Vulcans and the Neoconservatives

The Bush administration changed the political landscape of the United States. More particularly a new interpretation on the use of power, the unique position of USA and the its new role and goals in the world. All this was tied up with the fixation on one region: the Middle East, and a remix of the security, arms and oil dimensions. Many analysts have pointed out that George W. Bush's family had long associations with the oil business, the security agencies and the armament industry. In addition, George W. Bush, who had an early history of alcoholism, had reinvented himself as a born-again Christian and had carefully nursed his religious constituency. "Aristocrat as fundamentalist" was how the noted American writer Kevin Phillip put it. Bush had subsequently confided to his friends that he felt chosen by God to lead the nation in a "crusade" after the 9/11 attack. All these strands combined to make the sum and substance of Bush's foreign policy. It also coincided with the accession into power of some new groups who had been preparing themselves for such an eventuality.

We shall describe these groups presently but we take note of another seminal development that provided the basis for the policies of the new groups around George W. Bush. Unlike Europe, whose main preoccupation was centred around economic development and regional economic integration, the US made revolution in military affairs a major objective. Between 1995 and 2000 the US spent $ 1691 billion on the military, while the combined military spending of Britain, France, Germany, Russia, China and Japan totaled $ 1225 billion*. After the year 2000 US military expenditure went through the roof. As the noted historian, Paul Kennedy pointed out, that ever year the US "outspends the next nine largest defence-spending countries put together". The US thus emerged not only as the only superpower but also in fact as a military behemoth whose reach and range were unequalled in human history.

Bush's own knowledge and experience of foreign policy was very limited, but he prided himself in having gathered together a team of conservative specialists who were very well versed in foreign affairs as well as in bureaucratic labyrinths, having served in earlier Republican administrations. The core of his first-term team was constituted by Dick Cheney as Vice President, Donald Rumsfeld as Defence Secretary, Colin Powell as Secretary of State, Condoleeza Rice as Chief Security Advisor, Paul Wolfowitz as Deputy Secretary of Defence and Richard Armitage as Deputy Secretary of State. Even though there were serious differences among some of them, they had far more in common with each other than with Bush's opponents in the Democratic Party.

The Vulcans

First in jest and then more earnestly this group began to refer to itself as the Vulcans. Vulcan was the legendary god of fire and iron mongering. The modern-day Vulcans believed their outlook was characterized by steely determination like that of the Vulcan. They all had a defence background, "their wellsprings" being the Pentagon. These

---

* Figures deduced from SIPRI estimates.

top level foreign policy formulators and executors under George W. Bush were grounded in matters relating to military power, Cheney (vice-President) and Rumsfeld were two former Secretaries of Defence, Rumsfeld the current one also; Colin Powell was a former chairman of the Joint Chiefs of Staff, Wolfowitz was a former undersecretary of defence, and Armitage a former assistant secretary of defence. Condoleeza Rice too served the Joint Chiefs of Staff at the beginning of her career.

The Vulcans were ideologically and uncompromisingly anti-Communist. They did not believe that it was necessary to share power with other states. They were mortified by the Vietnam syndrome and worked for its demolition. They were convinced that the US was and would remain the greatest power on earth and should use this power to spread American values and way of life. Condoleeza Rice was the least ideological of them but she too was a staunch conservative, even though she was more of a pragmatist than some of the others. Whatever differences there were between Cheney, Rumsfeld and Wolfowitz, on the one hand, and Powell and Armitage on the other, were due to their different experiences. Neither of the former three had participated in any action on the ground for one reason or the other, nor had George Bush himself (some of them took the route of the National Guards to escape being drafted in Vietnam) whereas both Powell and Armitage had served in Vietnam. Powell, therefore, took a more cautious view of use of force for political objectives and had concluded that resort to military force should be take only when there was assured public support and then overwhelming force should be used (and not hold back on the number of troops to be employed as it was done by Rumsfeld in Iraq) to ensure quick victory.

The Vulcans were in fact a set of people who had organised themselves to help frame ideas and policies during Bush's election in November 2000. The original team had eight people, most of them veterans of the previous administrations. In addition to Rice and Paul Wolfowitz, it included Richard Armitage, Richard Pearle, Dov Zakheim "specialist on defence budget under Ronald Reagan", Stephen Hadley, Robert Blackwell (subsequently ambassador to India) and Robert Zoellick. All of them later occupied senior positions in the Bush government.

Alongside also rose to prominence and power another group, not mutually exclusive with the Vulcans, known as the neoconservatives (or neocons in short). Many of the names were common to them. Two self-proclaimed conservatives (not neocons)* have written at length about the personnel and the philosophy of the neocons, and it is perhaps appropriate to follow how the conservatives in the US analyse the neoconservatives. This is hugely important in order to understand US foreign policy, its functioning in the world and the impact on India. So far as the leading lights of the neoconservatives movement is concerned, apart from Wolfowitz, among the others could be counted: individuals in the administration, like Karl Rove, the powerful political adviser of Bush, Chief of Staff to the Vice-President, I. Lewis Libby; Special Advisor to the President, Elliott Abrams; Deputy Secretary of Defense, Paul D. Wolfowitz; State Department officials John R. Bolton and David Wurmser. On governmental advisory bodies one finds Richard Perle and Eliott A. Cohen on the Defence Policy Board; in the academy Yale professor Donald Kagan, Princeton professors Bernard Lewis and Aaron Friedberg, Pepperdine Professor James Wilson and others; in the media *Weekly Standard* editor William Kristol, *Washington Post* columnist Charles Krauthammer, and most foreign policy

* Stephan Halper and Jonathan Clarke: *America Alone: The Neoconservatives and the Global Order.*

editorialists on the *Wall Street Journal* editorial pages and the Fox News Channel; in business former CIA Director James Woolsey, among others; and in research institutions Max Boot at the Council on Foreign Relations, Norman Podhoretz and Meyrav Wurmser at the Hudson Institute, any member of the Project for the New American Century, and most foreign or defense studies scholars at the American Enterprise Institute.

Vice President Dick Cheney and Defence Secretary Donald Rumsfeld have been described as "American nationalists" but they have been the patrons-in-chief of the neoconservatives, have shared their views and have placed them in strategic positions with the full consent of President George W. Bush.

What do the neocons stand for and how it has impacted foreign policy? In the words of the above-mentioned conservatives, the neocons believed passionately in the primacy of military power. They asserted that "the fundamental determinant of the relationship between states rested on military power and the willingness to use it". The USA was the superpower, a military behemoth and necessarily the US must not hesitate to use this military power to reshape the world according to American values. The exceptionalism of the US was the running theme (that was, though, common to most Americans). They "disdained conventional diplomatic agencies such as the State Department" and were "hostile towards non-military multilateral institutions and instinctively antagonistic towards international treaties and agreements" which they believed constrained and controlled American power. The watchword was "global unilateralism", some analysts called it "militant unilateralism".

They believed in American imperium and were in fact, if not in theory, advocating the exercise of "benign" American imperialism to spread the message of American values in the world. The threats to the US could come from any direction and hence it was necessary to adopt the approach of preemption. They paid "little heed to the role of non-military factors, such as economic initiatives, poverty alleviation, soft power, environmental loss, or international commerce." The exercise of American military power became the principal option for them. They were also the first to give the call for preventing the emergence of any military peer to challenge the military might of the United States. Most of their views became part of the official lexicon in the US.

The chief focus of the neoconservatives was West Asia, or the Middle East in Western lingua. And within the Middle East they were fixated on Iraq. Most of them were demanding regime change in Iraq, even if it entailed US invasion, much before the 11 September assault on the World Trade Center in New York and the Pentagon in Washington, DC. As one of them said, imagine what would be the consequences if we could secure Iraq. Oil, dominance, security, in the process the spread of American values and what not. The Al Qaeda attack provided precisely the opportunity the neocons were looking for. They succeeded in putting the spotlight on those states, like Iraq, Iran and Syria, that had been "within their sites for at least a decade before 9/11". By directing attention on the "terror masters", as they described those states, they were able to influence the decision-making process towards their long-held positions involving attacking Iraq.

The neocons believed in the domino effect in an inverse way. Iraq was the linchpin in their thinking. If Iraq fell to the American way and to American dominance, the whole of Middle East would fall. American values would be secured in the entire region, so would be American bases and American dominance. The rest of the world would follow. Thus Iraq constituted the central piece in their "benign imperial" design for the world. Iraq must be invaded and Saddam must be overthrown—this had become their refrain even before the 9/11 attack.

As many analysts have noted, another distinguishing characteristic of the neocons was their commitment to Israel. Some of them were open supporters of the very right-wing party, Likud of Israel and had even written its platform when a hawkish Netanyahu was its leader.

The 9/11 gave the neocons their chance. A transformed Bush, (who had earlier shown little interest in the neocons' worldview and had disdained nationbuilding in other countries as the US goal during his election campaign), embraced the neocon's ideas in the wake of 9/11. The first indication of it came in Bush's state of the union message to the Congress in January 2002 where he gave the now famous phrase "axis of evil" referring to Iraq, Iran and North Korea. Although Bush decided to first retaliate in Afghanistan, the neocons perceptions were sanctified in the national security doctrine for 2002 presented by President Bush to the US Congress on 20 September 2002. The 33-page document frankly stated the determination of the United States to do everything possible to maintain its status as the world's sole superpower. The essential role of the US military strength was to "build and maintain our defences beyond challenge". The doctrine stipulated: "our forces would be strong enough to dissuade potential adversaries from pursuing the military buildup in the hope of surpassing, or equalling, the power of the United States". It added, "we will not hesitate to act alone, if necessary, to exercise our right of self-defence by acting preemptively". Thus military superiority, the threat to take unilateral decision and willingness to intervene around the world from wherever a threat could arise in the view of the US administration were at the heart of the new doctrine.

We can now consider the impact of the 9/11 happening

on India's foreign policy, on Indo-US relations and on the even more zigzag relationship with Pakistan.

9 / 11 and After

The terrorist attack on the United States on 11 September 2001 shocked India almost as much as it did the US. There was an outflow of sympathy for the United States which was expressed forcefully by Vajpayee in his address to the nation. The United States had now come face to face with the menace of terrorism of which India had been the victim for many long years, nurtured, fed and equipped from across the border. It became fairly obvious that the real sponsor of the attack was Afghanistan-based Al Qaeda under the leadership of Osama bin Laden, a Saudi exile coming from a rich family with visions of ruling the world according to his own tenets and interpretation of Islam. After a brief fugitive life in Sudan he had settled in the more hospitable surrounding of Afghanistan and ruled by his soulmate (and, it is generally believed, son-in-law) Mullah Omar and his equally fanatical party the Taliban. Osama had vowed retribution against four enemies of Islam—USA, Russia, Israel and India. The terrorists against whom India was struggling came from Pakistan but many of them were trained in Afghanistan.

Within two days of the attack, Foreign Minister Jaswant Singh went on record that India had established contacts on all political, executive and operational levels with the United States and that India had expressed its readiness not just to give logistic help but also provide the staging ground for the US military operations. This was even before the US had decided on military operations against the Taliban. For all his erudition and his "feudal" politeness, the Foreign Minister seemed to have a penchant for confusing his country, his friends and even his enemies, if not himself (remember his convolutions on the mole issue that he had alleged in the Narasimha Rao government). He seemed to have forgotten geography while rushing to offer India's services to the United States. No doubt USA would be very appreciative of the offer but, for its operations against Afghanistan, it was not India but Pakistan that it needed. And it was to Pakistan that it turned, presenting Musharraf with 7 demands ranging from access to Pakistan's border (with Afghanistan), its naval and air bases and complete intelligence sharing on the Al Qaeda and the Taliban. Are you with us or are you against us?—was the message from Washington.

Musharraf's acceptance of the demands was followed by a tense 7-hour conference of the army commanders (on 14 September) where it was brought home to them that they had only one option and that was to align themselves with the United States. Musharraf's acquiescence won a new legitimacy for him. Bush ordered a new aid package to reward Pakistan for allying itself once again with Washington—the aid package described as the "largest mobilisation of low-interest loans and debt relief" since the aid extended to Egypt during the Persian Gulf war. This time the alliance was not going to be short-term, temporary or evanescent, as Condoleeza Rice repeatedly assured Pakistan. Subsequently Pakistan was made not only a non-NATO ally, but the US National Commission on Terrorism enjoined upon the administration to develop a long-term strategic partnership with Pakistan.

Patently the United States had now other priorities and Indo-US relations had the subcontext of the US-Pakistan alliance. Richard Haass, then director of the US foreign planning division and coordinator for Afghanistan, told his Indian interlocutors in New Delhi, Kashmir was not an issue for which Americans were going to jeopardise their "good relations" with Pakistan. Washington had to display considerable nimble footedness in managing relations with both India and Pakistan. Visiting Pakistan, Secretary of State Colin Powell said in Islamabad (16 October 2001) that in the US view a peaceful resolution of the Kashmir dispute was central to ending hostility between India and Pakistan and urged them to open a dialogue. But the line, the tenor and the tone changed on arrival in New Delhi where he emphasised that ties with Pakistan would not be at the expense of relations with India. This dual line became the leitmotif of American policy in this subcontinent.

However, it was tested sorely in the subsequent developments that had very considerable impact on India-Pakistan relations also. But we may first note the invasion of Afghanistan. The Afghan war started in October 2001 with the US Army groups helping the Northern Alliance which provided the main fighting force to roll down towards Kabul. Gradually the US also enlisted NATO troops to assist in the task of pacifying Afghanistan. The US was also building an international coalition against terrorism to which the large majority of the countries of the world declared their support. In Afghanistan the Northern Alliance quickly overran the Taliban positions. The Northern Alliance was constituted predominantly by non-Pushto speaking tribes. The Taliban rule collapsed within a short time and the remnants of Mullah Omar's and Osama's loyalists took shelter in the border areas between Afghanistan and Pakistan. An interim government under Pushtun leader Hamid Karzai took charge in Kabul. India had maintained close contact with the leaders of the Northern Alliance and had provided sizable assistance to them. India remains one of the most substantial donors for the reconstruction of Afghanistan. The collapse of the Taliban was the bitterest pill for Pakistan to swallow as it had regarded Taliban-ruled Afghanistan as providing the depth it needed in any conflict with India. Both Osama's Al Qaeda and Omar's Taliban had, in fact, been the creations of USA (at one time) and Pakistan.

Attack on the Indian Parliament

Cross-border terrorism had been stepped up in the last quarter of 2001. First came the attack on the Kashmir assembly and then on the House Of Indian Democracy, Parliament, on 13 December. There was a running battle between the security guards and the militants inside the precincts of Parliament House. The Vice President, Krishan Kant, had a narrow escape. Although the attack was foiled, relations with Pakistan came to a boil. India amassed its army on the borders in Kashmir in what was described as Operation Parakram, but did not take any immediate action, giving Pakistan time enough to also bring its troops to the border. The face off lasted for many months until India called back the troops. The question remains unanswered whether the Government was at all serious or whether it was a ploy for inviting American intercession, was it a ploy from both sides to hope for intervention by Washington to pull up the other? Former chief of the army, General Roy Chaudhary described Operation Parakram a "disaster". India had mobilised some 700,000 soldiers in this operation, he said. There was some sabre rattling or rather nuclear rattling from Pakistan but its hope appeared to be the same: US intercession.

America's dilemma was obvious. Leading an international coalition against terrorism it could not turn the other way in the face of the terrorist attacks in India whose perpetrators had their headquarters in Pakistan. On the other hand, USA needed Pakistan government's assistance in fighting the Al Qaeda and the Taliban who were regrouping in Pakistan-held territories and had sympathisers and supporters throughout Pakistan. The Americans had to lean on Pakistan to tame its militants (who continued to enjoy ISI's patronage) but not too hard since they needed Islamabad's cooperation. Then they leaned on India not to be provoked and not to retaliate.

The new strategy was perhaps most aptly summed up by David Sanger, a senior correspondent of *New York Times* (7 January 2002). In the weeks following the deadly attack on the Parliament, President Bush and his foreign policy team had scrambled to avoid war in South Asia with a simple formula: "daily phone call to both sides." Sanger might have added, fortnightly visits to both countries by high dignitaries, such as Secretary of State, Secretary of Defense, Deputy Secretary of State, and many lesser functionaries. They reframed the conflict as a battle over terrorism, not territory, of which Pakistan too was a victim, with the terrorists trying to threaten Pakistan as much as they threatened India. Sanger acknowledged that this was "a convenient fiction" for it glossed over the fact that the terrorist groups that Bush wanted to be crushed had often acted "as a surrogate for Pakistan's intelligence service."

Musharraf came under considerable pressure as Bush told him that he must deliver on his pledges that he was fighting terrorism. Consequently, Musharraf went on the air on 12 January 2002 denouncing terrorism. He took care to focus his speech on domestic terrorism but he had to make a public disavowal of assistance to terrorism abroad, meaning India (including Kashmir). The fiction of terrorist acts under the garb of a freedom struggle could no longer be sustained. India-Pakistan stalemate, however, continued. The year ended with two significant elections, one held in Jammu and Kashmir in September and the other in Pakistan in October. In Kashmir, under the strict supervision of the Election Commission headed by James Lyngdoh and the intensely watchful monitoring of the international media and the diplomatic community, and despite the visible rise of level of violence perpetrated by the militants to thwart the election process, elections were held for the Kashmir Assembly that were generally regarded as free and fair.

Around the same time elections were held in Pakistan

for the National and provincial assemblies which, to say the least, convinced few outside observers, and not many inside either, about their fairness and impartiality. As the noted Pakistani journalist Najam Sethi wrote in his *Daily Times*: "Thank you General Pervez Musharraf for delivering us from the likes of Nawaz Sharif and handing us over to Qazi Hussain Ahmed and Maulana Fazalur Rehman". The rightwing religious parties combination Muttahida Majlis-e-Amal became the "third force" in Pakistan's politics, the ruling party in the Frontier Province and near power in Sindh. There was an unwritten understanding between the Islamists and the General who retained his uniform even as President because of that understanding. As the International Crisis Group quoting Samina Ahmed, South Asia Project Director, wrote in its report 18 April 2005: "the choice that Pakistan faces is not between the military and the mullahs, as is widely believed in the West. It is between genuine democracy and the military-mullah alliance that is responsible for producing and sustaining religious extremism".

A. Q. Khan's Nuclear Shopping Mall

It is pertinent to consider here the shenanigans of Pakistan's nuclear scientist Dr A.Q. Khan. Metallurgist Abdul Qadeer Khan, dearly loved in Pakistan as the father of Pakistan's nuclear bomb, had established a world-wide network for the sale and supply of nuclear components. He could also be described as the father of nuclear proliferation in the world. Having himself being helped by Beijing in acquiring nuclear capability, he set about the task of establishing a chain of supply of nuclear parts and designs to various countries, and in the process enriching himself (and who others one still does not know). The trail of his nuclear business ran through at least three continents and seven countries from Pakistan to Japan to Malaysia, through UAE and South Africa to Germany: "a remarkable network that was able in the end to provide a turnkey gas centrifuge facility and the wherewithal to make more centrifuges", according to the then IAEA inspector David Albright. Among the recipient countries were Libya and Iran. It was Libya which blew the public whistle on the goings-on. A lengthy investigation by American and European intelligence agencies and international nuclear inspectors forced Musharraf and his government officials to question Khan and his associates and openly confront evidence that the country was the source of crucial technology to enrich uranium for Iran, North Korea, Libya and possibly other countries.

In fact the Americans knew for a long time what was happening. They had advised Holland against prosecuting A.Q. Khan because, the CIA told the Dutch, it wanted to keep a tab on him. The nuclear proliferation activities became public in December 2002—January-February 2003. Neither the Americans nor Musharraf have come clean on what all they know. Musharraf took the escape route of disclaiming all knowledge of it, blaming it all on Khan and his aides, washing away any dirty linen of his own and of the government or the military and claiming that the tap had been fully closed. Khan was obliged to become almost the lone fall guy and was quarantined. No foreigner has been allowed to meet him and Musharraf ruled out any international questioning or probing of Khan and his activities. Whether Abdul Qadeer Khan could set up an international atomic bazaar on his own without any knowledge of the government or of the army defies logic and is incredible, to say the least.

Unfinished Business: Shift to Iraq

It was the most unfortunate happening that just when the Al Qaeda and the Taliban were on the run and when it was possible to hunt down and largely eliminate the perpetrators of terrorism based in certain areas in Afghanistan and Pakistan, the Bush Administration decided to concentrate its attention on Iraq and prepare for its invasion on fictitious grounds. A great opportunity was missed. If the United States had continued vigorously the tracking down of the Al Qaeda rabble and the depleting forces of the Taliban, it was well within the range of probability that the Allies could have caught their leaders and radically altered the ground situation in Afghanistan. If at the same time, instead of fixating on Iraq, Washington had used its resources and opportunities and leverage to find a fair solution to the Palestinian issue, instead of letting it fester, the threat from Islamic militants could have been hugely reduced and the terrorist menace so lowered as to have become a negligible force. The Al Qaeda and all the various terrorist organisations would not have been able to feed on the Muslim rage that came to the boil after the Iraq attack, the suppression of Palestinians and finally the Israeli invasion of Lebanon.

Washington, however, let go the opportunity in the neocons' obsession with Iraq and the Middle East, and Osama and his hordes got a new lease of life. Washington's obsession with Iraq and the subsequent developments have unleashed forces and elements that the world finds it almost impossible to control. It appeared as if the neocons were intent upon proving the correctness of the theory of the clash of civilisations propounded earlier by an American academic whose prognosis was rightly rebutted by both intellectuals and politicians in many parts of the world, including USA.

As we have already recounted earlier, the neocons' fixation with Iraq began much before 9 / 11. They got their opportunity with the 11 September happening. This was the "great conjuring trick"—a political discourse that "hard wired the public mind to link a global assault on Al Qaeda with the territorial assault on Iraq". Seemingly out of nowhere, Iraq was represented as an immediate danger to the US. Just one day after the 9/11 attack, Wolfowitz, with support from Cheney and Rumsfeld, pleaded for attacking Iraq, instead of Afghanistan. Chairman of the Counterterrorism Group and a member of the National Security Council at the time, Richard Clarke has recorded that in the deliberations just a day after, both Wolfowitz and Rumsfeld insisted, without any real supporting evidence, that they should invade Iraq, as Saddam was behind the attacks and was the real source of terrorism. Even Bush asked Clarke that his group should "go back over everything" and "see if Saddam did it".

Even when Bush decided to go after the Al Qaeda and the Taliban, Iraq was never taken off the radar of the Bush administration. Within 72 days of the invasion of Afghanistan the Bush administration began planning for the war in Iraq. Even though Colin Powell prevailed upon Bush to go to the UN Security Council to get a second resolution passed by the world body authorising the invasion of Iraq, the US president's heart was not in it. According to a secret British memo written by Blair's chief foreign policy adviser, leaked by *New York Times* (27 March 2003), Bush made it clear to Tony Blair at a private two-hour meeting in his Oval office on 31 January 2003 that he was determined to invade Iraq without the second resolution, or even if international inspectors failed to find unconventional weapons.

In response to a tough message from the UN Saddam had caved in and a team of international inspectors headed by Hans Blix with the reputation of being a no-nonsense person, had gone to Iraq, did not find any weapons of mass destruction (WMD) but had yet to give their final report. Bush would not wait any more and even without any authorisation by the UN ordered the invasion of Iraq citing imminent threat of a nuclear attack from Saddam Hussain. Tony Blair even talked of this horrendous possibility within 78 hours. The invasion began on 20 March 2003.

Oil Politics

In this entire Iraq "enterprise" we have so far only mentioned in passing a very critical dimension relating to the importance of the Middle East: Oil. It is appropriate now to take note of the importance of this factor.

With the oil prices touching the roof and this non-renewable energy source getting depleted alongside the rising demand for it, the need to secure and corner the strategic areas producing the black gold can hardly be overstated.

The war in Afghanistan had already extended the American presence into Central Asia and extended its grip on the West Asian countries. And the war in Iraq was to consolidate this grip. The US now controlled the ocean and land arteries in the flow of oil. West Asia claims nearly two-thirds of the world's proven oil resources with Saudi Arabia presently holding 269 billion barrels and Iraq some 112 billion. Central Asia has proven reserves of 30 billion barrels but could potentially hold 140 billion barrels of oil. The figure for the consumption of oil and sources from which it comes by major oil countries make a telling picture. North America consumes 24 million barrels daily, Europe 14 million, and the Asia Pacific region 20 million. For the United States 60 per cent of its oil consumption is imported, for the European Union 75 per cent and for Japan 80 per cent. It is significant to note that a high percentage of the total import of oil by these countries or their formations comes from the Gulf region, 22 percent of the total import of oil of the United States, 36 per cent of the European Union, 80 percent of Japan, 44 percent of China and 73 percent of other Asian-African countries.

As the senior Bush's Secretary of State James Baker said to Former Prime Minister I.K. Gujral: "Oil is our civilization". Or as one U.S. administrator said of the plan to invade Iraq, "If the Gulf produced kumquats, would we be doing this".

Bush, Cheney and even Rumsfeld have had previous association with the oil industry and were only too well aware of the critical factor of oil. Rumsfeld was reported to have remarked at a meeting of the National Security Council in 2001 "Imagine what the region would look like without Saddam and with a regime that's aligned with U.S. interests. It would change everything in the region and beyond it".

Oil is, therefore, one vital factor in the strategy of the United States. Indeed oil has never been far from the minds of the leaders of all the big powers in contemporary history. Oil security has become even more critical a factor with the demand for oil growing by leaps and bounds. China and India were the late entrants, particularly China whose appetite for oil has sent the demand through the roof. USA is the topmost voracious guzzler of the "black gold". The USA now had bases or a huge presence in almost all the major oil producing areas in the world barring a few notable exceptions.

For all the denials that oil had anything to do with the Iraq adventure, Mr Bush finally cited this as an important reason to stay the course in Iraq. "You can imagine a world in which these extremists and radicals got control of energy resources" of Iraq, Bush said at a rally in Colorado. That would be the day of Armageddon, it seemed. So the ghost came out of the closet. Oil as a factor in Bush's strategy had become open and openly stated factor.

Myths of Iraq

The delusions on which the Iraq war was based were indeed

flabbergasting. The intelligence reports were cherry-picked or "sexed up" (to use the words of a BBC reporter). Even Bush's point man appointed to report on the state of WMD in Iraq, David Kay, finally reported Saddam did not have them. To Bush the issue was incidental. As a British chief of intelligence wrote in a memo after meeting his counterparts in USA, the CIA chief and other officials of the agency did not believe the WMD intelligence mattered because war was coming one way or another.

More delusions: the Iraqi people were waiting for liberation; American troops would be jubilantly welcomed as heroes; there was no need to have a large army to pacify Iraq and even less need for any detailed plans for post-war construction. Things would automatically fall in their place once Saddam was removed, Bush and his senior aides, with the exception of Colin Powell, believed. The new Iraq, in the words of the British ambassador to the US at the time, would inject stable democracy into a region of autocrats and tyrants and offer a haven for US military bases. And so, we might add, the whole of Middle East would fall into the embrace of the "city on the hill".

Bush's Reelection and New Goals for US Foreign Policy

Before we consider Indo-US relations in the context of Iraq war and beyond, for the sake of continuity, we mention the reelection of George Bush as President and the new goals that he set up for US foreign policy. Unlike his last election in 2001, Bush was elected for a second term with a credible majority in November 2004. He not only retained his conservative following in middle and southern America, but also expanded his religious constituency—a combination of evangelical Christian Church and orthodox Jewish organizations—who worked with religious fervour for Bush's success at the hustings. Fortified by his clear victory, Bush set forth new and more ambitious goals for

US foreign policy. In his inaugural speech for his second term on 20 January 2005, Bush gave notice that from then on US policy was "to seek and support the growth of democratic movements and institutions in every nation and culture, with the ultimate goal of ending tyranny in the world".

Bush also made a couple of important changes in his Cabinet. Out went Colin Powell and in came Condoleeza Rice as Secretary of State. Despite the boost that the exit of Colin Powell, who had a running feud with Rumsfeld and to some extent with Cheney over policies and approaches, gave to the neoconservatives, it should not be ignored that Rice, although one of the original Vulcans, was less of an ideologue and more of a conservative pragmatist. She had the ear of the President, which Powell did not have, and quickly established her hold over foreign policy.

Elections had been held in Iraq and an elected coalition government had assumed office but Iraq continued to slide into confusion and chaos. Saddam's brutal rule was not substituted by the establishment of peace and order, rule of law and growth of democratic institutions. The Kurd and Shia areas were awash with oil, the Sunni areas were barren and arid. Increasingly the country was lapsing into sectarian violence, trifurcation into Kurd-dominated, Shia-dominated and Sunni-dominated areas, and general lawlessness. There were "shadows behind shadows" (to use the words of Robert Fisk in London's *Independent*) on the streets of Baghdad and many other cities. Not just the private militias, but the state's security forces were equally partners in the looting and killing. On the average 100 Iraqis were being killed everyday. There was an exodus of Iraqi professionals and intellectuals from the country. The Iraqi society was dissolving under the stress of cumulative violence, according to the assessment of the UN Assistance Mission for Iraq.

The Iraq imbroglio is destined to be with us but meanwhile we turn our attention to the more central issue from our point of view—Indo-US relations.

India, Iraq War and Indo-US Relations Despite Iraq War

The Iraq war fractured the international coalition against terrorism. A large majority of countries in the world were unconvinced of the US justification for war and worried about its consequences. It posed a piquant situation for India. Whereas India had wholeheartedly supported the war against the Taliban and Al Qaeda, and against terrorism anywhere in the world, there was a definite turning away of public opinion against the American war in Iraq. It also created hurdles in the way of the Vajpayee government's concerted efforts to construct a new relationship with Washington. There was fairly strong US pressure on India to send troops to Iraq especially after the Saddam regime fell rather easily and it appeared that Iraq was ready for a new chapter—or so the Americans believed, but the level of violence there was rising by the day. It is well-known that in order to obtain American concessions on the issues of sanctions and provision of high technology and even acceptance of India's nuclear tests, Vajpayee, Advani and Jaswant Singh were keen on acceding to US request for dispatch of Indian troops to Iraq. They were supported by a section of the security and foreign policy elite. But public opinion was strongly opposed to it and the opposition put up a stiff resistance that obliged Vajpayee to drop the idea. Eventually Parliament passed a unanimous resolution deploring/condemning (depending on how you want to translate the Hindi word *ninda* used in the resolution) the Iraq war. The Indian decision gave a reprieve to Pakistan which too was under US pressure to send its troops.

However, the US took India's decision in its stride and a determined effort was made to take India-US relations to a higher level. It must be stated that whatever his approach and attitude to many other countries, George Bush adopted a friendly stance towards India. Necessarily there were distortions and meandering because of US perceived interests in Pakistan, but US foreign policy continued to be transformed in relation to India. The Bush Administration began a sustained dialogue with India on what was called a "trinity of issues": civilian nuclear technology, space shield and facilitation of dual-use high tech trade. Bush lifted the post-Pokhran sanctions against India (and Pakistan) in October 2001 in the wake of the 9/11 attack, but trade in high technology was still restricted. The dialogue began under the rubric of Defence Planning Group set up by the two countries that first met in Washington between 20-23 May 2002. India and USA signed a framework agreement, "statement of principles", in Washington on 6 February 2003 to boost high-technology trade between the two countries. The dialogue was expanded to include nuclear safety issues. All these talks, however, came up against the wall of US laws passed by Congress and restrictions imposed by the nuclear suppliers group (NSG). These various discussions led to a joint statement issued on 13 January 2004 by Prime Minister Vajpayee in New Delhi and President Bush from, significantly, Monterey while he was visiting Mexico, pledging expanded cooperation in civilian nuclear programme and high-technology trade. Described as the "Next Step in Strategic Partnership" (NSSP), the expanded cooperation also included US assistance in promoting safety in India's nuclear facilities and talks on a missile defence. Partners in the war on terrorism and in controlling weapons of mass destruction, Bush said, "the vision of US-India strategic partnership that Prime Minister Vajpayee and I share is becoming a reality".

Bush's Reelection and India

Indian reactions to the presidential elections in the US and George Bush's reelection make interesting reading. Much of the foreign policy elite and most of the mandarins of the Foreign Affairs Ministry, as they are often referred to (no slight intended), decidedly favoured George Bush. As a former Foreign Secretary and former ambassador to the United States, brilliant as he was, explained at an address in New Delhi, John Kerry might be better able to carry with him Europe and some other erstwhile US allies, George Bush was good for India as he was clearly friendly towards it. This perception was shared by many (though not all) in the higher echelons of the foreign policy decision makers or those on the fringes of it.

Another reason why Kerry did not excite much enthusiasm in India was his vocal opposition to outsourcing which he thought was taking jobs away from the United States, but preventing outsourcing would also affect jobs in India. Bush had made no adverse references to outsourcing. Perhaps for the first time the Indian community in USA was also more divided than ever before. It had traditionally been pro-democratic, but now an influential pro-Republican group had emerged that actively lobbied and made financial contributions to the Republican "war chest".

Yet it was equally true that on the popular level, including the spread-out elite and the professionals, Bush did not command much admiration, mostly because of the general perception that the Bush administration was pursuing a policy of might is right, taking inordinate recourse to the use of American military power, adopting unilateral decisions, and arm twisting other countries into acquiescence.

Thaw with Pakistan

A SAARC summit in Islamabad at the beginning of January

2004 provided the opportunity for India and Pakistan to resume the peace dialogue. Vajpayee met Musharraf on the sidelines of the SAARC summit resulting in a thaw in the frozen relationship since the attack on Parliament. The then Prime Minister of Pakistan, Zafarullah Khan Jamali conceded that the peace process had been facilitated by some other powers. The reference to USA was too obvious. As this writer remarked earlier, both countries, Pakistan directly and India indirectly, had acquiesced in the US becoming the third party in the India-Pakistan relationship. Vajpayee and Musharraf issued a joint statement embodying the agreement to commence and carry forward the process of the composite dialogue in February. Musharraf assured Vajpayee that "he will not permit any territory under Pakistan to be used to support terrorism in any manner". He emphasised that a sustained and productive dialogue addressing all issues, including Kashmir, would lead to positive results.

The General still went on linking the phenomenon of cross-border terrorism to the solution of the Kashmir issue. In his address to the joint session of Pakistan's parliament, while denouncing the jehadis whose intent upon exporting jehad had done "enormous damage to Pakistan", he still held that the only way to tackle the allegations of cross-border terrorism was a peaceful and just solution of the Kashmir problem. The contradictions in such statements were obvious and there was a widespread view, held even by many foreign scholars and journalists, that the ISI had not given up on selective use of jehadi organisations who provided training and assistance in arms and finances elsewhere too as the various incidents in Britain demonstrated. An international non-governmental organisation, International Crisis Group reported that over the two years since Musharraf's 12 January speech, there had been little movement on the promises made by him to crackdown on terrorism and end the jehadi culture. The failure to curb rising extremism, the report said, stemmed directly from the military government's unwillingness to act against its political allies among the Islamist groups. Having coopted the religious parties to gain constitutional cover for his military rule, General Musharraf was highly reliant on the religious right for his regime's survival. Pakistan had developed an India-specific foreign policy and an India-specific nuclear programme. We may not dwell here on the foreign-acquired nature of Pakistan's nuclear weapons and missiles to which reference has been made earlier. Pakistan had spent, as we have seen, very considerable effort and energy on the acquisition of missile capability. A more advanced 2000-kilometres range missile, Shaheen 11 or Hatf 1V, was test fired on 9 March 2004 that could strike at targets deep inside India. The troubling aspect was Islamabad's increasing proclivity in the last decade to brandish the threat of nuclear strike whenever relations with India were tense.

To take an overall view of the defence capabilities of the two countries, according to an estimate of *Jane's Defence Weekly* in August 2005, Pakistan's defence budget for 2005-06 was $ 3.75 billion and it was believed to possess 50-100 nuclear warheads. Pakistan had 619,000 active troops, 513,000 reserves, 290,000 paramilitary forces, 2460 tanks, 2000 artillery pieces and 1250 APCs. Pakistan's air force had 415 combat aircrafts and the navy had eight submarines and seven surface combatants. Missile types and ranges in the Pakistani arsenal included Shaheen 1 (600 km), Shaheen 2 (up to 2000 km) Ghauri 1 (1500 km), Ghauri 2 (2300 km), Hatf 1A (100 km) Hatf 2 (180 km) Hatf 3 (290 km) and cruise missile Babur (500 km). Two new missiles capable of being nuclear tipped have recently been added to Islamabad's nuclear armoury.

India's $ 19 billion defence budget for 2005-06,

although far exceed that of Pakistan, was still smaller in GDP terms than that of Pakistan. India was estimated to have 100-250 nuclear warheads. India had 1,325,000 active troops, 535,000 reserves and over one million paramilitary forces. It had 3898 tanks, and about 4500 artillery pieces and 388 APCs. The Indian air force had 680 combat aircrafts and the Navy 16 submarines and 25 surface combatants, including one aircraft carrier, eight destroyers and 16 frigates. It should however be kept in perspective that India has many times over the land and sea border to protect than Pakistan. Missiles in the Indian arsenal included Agni 1 (range 2500 km), Agni 2 (3000 km; upgraded to 3500 km), Prithvi SS-150 (150 km), Prithvi SS-250 (250 km), and supersonic cruise missile Brahmos (290 km).

Nevertheless, there were few options before India and Pakistan other than a continued search for peaceful coexistence and peaceful solution of problems. The peace dialogue could not be abandoned. However, India at this time was in the election mode that resulted in some dramatic changes. This will be discussed in the next chapter.

CHAPTER FIVE

FOREIGN POLICY UNDER MANMOHAN SINGH

The elections to Indian parliament resulted in a dramatic defeat of the NDA under Vajpayee and the victory of the United Progressive Alliance (UPA) under the leadership of Sonia Gandhi. Mrs Gandhi declined the office of Prime Minister and instead selected the eminent economist (who was also Finance Minister under Narasimha Rao), Dr Manmohan Singh to head the government. Sonia Gandhi was elected chairperson of the UPA. The Left supported the government from outside without participating in it. To a certain extent the election results constituted the electorate's rebuff to the use of Hindutva as a political plank and its endorsement of the secular polity in India.

So far as foreign policy was concerned, there was marked continuity under Manmohan Singh—more especially in relations with important neighbours like China and Pakistan and a big power like USA. Manmohan Singh carried forward the earlier policy of seeking better ties with them or raising them to a new level. The Government was also confronted with critical problems in Nepal and Sri Lanka. For continuity's sake we consider developments with Pakistan first.

Prime Minister Manmohan Singh not only stated his government's continued commitment to the peace dialogue but efforts were made to intensify the peace process.

Although the new External Affairs Minister, Natwar Singh met his Pakistani counterpart, a certain stagnation had been noted in the peace talks. The Prime Minister had an in-depth "constructive and frank" discussion with General Musharraf in New York on 24 September (2004) on the sidelines of their participation in the UN General Assembly. Reading out a joint statement at a joint press conference, the two leaders rededicated themselves to the pursuit of a peaceful solution to all the problems, including Kashmir, "in a sincere spirit and peaceful manner". They directed that all confidence-building measures (CBMs) between the two countries should be implemented in an attempt to normalise relations. They also renewed their commitment to the gas pipeline from Iran through Afghanistan and Pakistan to India. "Such a project would contribute to the welfare and prosperity of the people of both countries..", the two leaders affirmed.

The most significant aspect of the Manmohan-Musharraf talks related to what was ruled out, rather than what was ruled in. The Indian Prime Minister told the Pakistani President that he would not agree to any redrawing of the map and any further vivisection, more particularity on grounds of religion. He was open to any other proposals for a solution of the Kashmir issue. From all accounts General Musharraf had agreed with the Prime Minister's formulation. The General had himself been advocating thinking out-of-the-box, to use the current fashionable phrase. He had stated at various forums that any solution of the Kashmir issue should be acceptable to India, to Pakistan and to the people of Kashmir. The logic of this formulation, Manmohan Singh pointed out, itself ruled out a solution unacceptable to India. Repeatedly Manmohan Singh, in subsequent speeches and statements, emphasised the need to work towards a situation in which borders would become irrelevant. Musharraf had also occasionally referred to the same. If this were to happen the sting would be taken out of the acrimony over Kashmir.

Soon afterwards Musharraf, nonchalantly and almost as if he was thinking aloud, floated a proposal for the division of Kashmir into seven zones and their gradual demilitarisation. India's reaction was inevitably negative. For one, the basis on which Kashmir was to be divided into seven zones was ambiguous. Secondly no division on religious basis could be accepted. Moreover, demilitarisation at the border was not feasible until the border was completely peaceful and cross-border infiltration and terrorism had ceased.

The peace dialogue received new adrenaline and for a while the prospects appear to be more hopeful. Many confidence building measures were taken as well as measures to enhance normalcy at the Kashmir border. Manmohan Singh announced a troop-cut in Kashmir (12 November 2004) and within days 3000 soldiers left the state. Admittedly, there was some risk in the troop reductions, but the Prime Minister believed that it was a risk worth-taking. In his first visit to Kashmir Manmohan Singh announced a Rs. 24,000-crore aid package. He stated his willingness to hold talks unconditionally with all those who abjured violence. The offer was obviously directed towards the Hurriyat. But he reiterated that he had repeatedly made it clear that he would not accept any suggestion that smacked of a further division of the state. This categorical assertion was perhaps provoked by the immediate support given to Musharraf's proposal for division into seven zones and demilitarisation by Washington and hence the need to scotch it equally and immediately. The US Deputy Secretary of State Richard Armitage had found merit in Musharraf's proposal and described it as "forward thinking".

The composite dialogue sputtered along. Besides Kashmir, the two sides continued to discuss nuclear CBMs, differences over the boundary in the Sir Creek area—the only maritime dispute between the two countries, the Wullar Barrage and the Tulbul navigation project, the demilitarisation of Siachen and the Baglihar dam issue. We might clarify for the reader that the Wullar dispute related to a dam proposed to be built by India on the Wullar Lake to control the discharge of water into Jhelum river. The Tulbul navigation project was expected to ensure smoother transport of goods through the waterways. India believed that these measures would be beneficial to both the countries, but Pakistan was opposed to them as it was apprehensive that it was located at the downstream, and would affect its supply of water. Pakistan asserted that these measures violated the Indus Water Treaty. The Siachen glacier, on the Karakoram range, the scene of sporadic armed clashes between India and Pakistani forces since 1984, 76 km long and 2 to 8 km wide, with temperatures routinely dropping to –40 degrees and blizzards speeding up to 300 km per hour, is one of the most inhospitable places in the world. The Indian camps are located from 12,000 feet to 22,000 feet above sea level. Only 3 per cent of the Indian casualties have been due to hostile firing; 97 per cent due to the rigours of altitude, weather and terrain. Pakistani positions are at a lower altitude ranging from 9000 to 15,000 feet (the highest at 17,200 feet). Even so their major casualties could be put down to the ravages of climate and altitude. Normally it would be somewhat ridiculous for the two countries to be fighting over there, but all demilitarisation proposals have foundered on the rock of mistrust.

Both Indian and Pakistani officials held extensive discussions on all these issues but could not find common ground. Much less on Kashmir on which the gulf between the two remained quite wide. General Musharraf, whose penchant for casually floating unspecified proposals was well-known, in one of his more serious essays proposed self-governance in Kashmir. It was an interesting idea but the devil was in the details: the substance and the scope of this self-governance concept. Many in India claimed that there was already self-governing in India's Kashmir, but not on the other side. Nevertheless it was an idea that could be explored, but the understanding of the two sites was still poles apart. According to one Pakistani analyst, the self-governance or autonomy proposal rested on two pillars: phased withdrawal of the militaries from their respective Kashmiri parts and self-governance on both sides in its fullest meaning and spirit. The proposal, it was claimed, did not contemplate any change in the state's legal status, population or territory, but mutual troop withdrawals was the core requirement.

The concept of self-governance could be explored seriously but the "core" requirement of troop withdrawals required the complete purging of terrorism and the jehadis committing terrorist acts, often quite heinous, in Kashmir and elsewhere in India. India could not contemplate demilitarisation except in a peaceful atmosphere. Our Pakistani friends are unwilling or unable to accept the logic of their proposals. Nevertheless amongst the most significant confidence building measures was the launching of a bus service from Srinagar to Muzaffarabad, enabling Kashmiris of one side to visit their relatives on the other side of the divide. Both Manmohan Singh and Sonia Gandhi were present in Srinagar to flag off the first service. The Hurriyat leaders too were permitted to use the bus service and, unlike in the other cases, to proceed from POK to Islamabad to meet General Musharraf.

Manmohan Singh was in fact addressing the problem at two levels. He was engaging Pakistan and for the resolution of the Kashmir issue, but he was also trying to address the internal problems in Kashmir. The Hurriyat leaders were invited by the Prime Minister but they preferred to meet the General in Pakistan first before meeting Manmohan Singh. The Hurriyat had a certain support base in the valley, but not much outside Srinagar and a few other towns. They had not allowed their support to be tested in the last by all accounts as fair an election as possible amidst a flurry of terrorist acts and attempts at intimidation with a view to foiling the election process. The Hurriyat had to be a part of the eventual solution, but their own standpoint remained ambiguous and subject to changing equations within the Hurriyat and within the state.

The bus service provided immense relief to people from both sides and was enthusiastically welcomed from both sides of the divide. In addition there was the Samjhauta Express running from Wagha to Attari and much later Thar Express between Rajasthan and Sind. More heartwarming was the transformation in public opinion in both countries. There was a much larger what is referred to as the "peace constituency" now. Hardly anybody in India was a votary of war. In Pakistan also the people generally and fervently hoped for peace and good neighbourly relations. Most of them were not in favour of abandoning the quest for a Kashmir solution (which to Pakistan really meant the acquisition of the valley), but the overwhelming and demonstrative affection with which visitors from India were received was symptomatic of the mood change in Pakistan. Public opinion was running much ahead of the ruling elite. It is this desire for change in the relationship and for peace which could finally prove to be the catalyst for a fundamental re-evaluation of Indo-Pak ties. Let us make no mistake: the trust deficit between India and Pakistan has not been bridged. In general people on both sides remained highly distrustful of each other, each believing that it could not trust the other. But what had changed was that by and large opinion was growing against war in both the countries, as conflict leading to a war did not appear to be a viable option except to a small minority.

The summit-level talks gave hope and promise of a breakthrough. President Musharraf came to New Delhi for his second visit on 17 April (2005) to pursue the dialogue. Manmohan Singh declared with a flourish that the peace process had become "irreversible". The new confidence building measures listed in the joint communiqué included expanded contacts across the LOC, the possible start of Lahore-Amritsar bus service and the re-establishment of consulates in Karachi and Mumbai. The two sides agreed that terrorism would not be allowed to derail the peace process and they also pledged to resolve the Sir Creek and Siachen issues. On Kashmir, they agreed to continue the discussions "in a sincere, purposeful and forward-looking manner for a final settlement". President Musharraf told a breakfast meeting with the Editors Guild of India that the Kashmir issue could erupt again in the future if it was not resolved. "If you don't resolve it, don't blame me for what happens after 10 or 15 years", he warned. This was a rather odd statement for the problem was not what would happen in 10 or 15 years, but what was happening now—violence and mayhem by the jehadis not just in Kashmir, but in various parts of India.

Pakistan's leaders were increasingly complaining about the slow going on Kashmir talks. The issue bristled with complexity and emotion and admitted no easy solution. Nor was there much progress on other issues. Pakistan was also not willing to take the ASEAN route towards overcoming political problems. Initially relations among important ASEAN member countries, Malaysia, Singapore and Indonesia particularly, were troubled by many political and territorial issues. They concentrated on economic growth within ASEAN in order to overcome their political problems. Today the ASEAN countries are clearly economically integrated and equally fairly in control of their mutual political and territorial problems. Pakistan, however, is unmoved and is convinced that Kashmir was a different kettle of fish that had to be taken care of before economic relationship could develop meaningfully. It has consistently refused to grant the most-favoured nation status to India (which really means normal, non-discriminatory trading relationship), as required under the South Asia free-trade agreement (SAFTA) covering the SAARC (South Asian Association of Regional Cooperation) countries. "How can you do business with an enemy", Musharraf told a meeting of investors in Davos.

SAARC

The seven-nation South Asian Association for Regional Cooperation (SAARC) was established some two decades ago, December 1985 to be exact, but soon got embroiled in internal inter-members disputes. India, Pakistan, Sri Lanka, Bangladesh, Nepal, Bhutan and Maldives had formed themselves into a regional cooperation organisation, probably hoping to emulate the success of ASEAN and the European Union. More recently Afghanistan has been included as a member and it is now an eight-member organisation. From the start the organisation was plagued by internal political problems, mainly because the member-countries did not really follow either the ASEAN or the European Union model. Sometimes they tried to utilise the forum for sounding their bilateral enmities that occasionally deadlocked relations. In essence it has been the running feud between Pakistan and India that has thrown the spanners into the works. In one instance, however, the decline in security and the resurgence of the Islamist extremist elements in Bangladesh held up the SAARC summit.

It is not as if nothing had happened within SAARC and that no progress was made. A SAARC secretariat was established in Kathmandu with the post of its secretary general rotated among member countries. A number of technical committees were set up on a broad range of issues like drug trafficking, health care, poverty alleviation, cooperation in science and technology, women's welfare, and so on. They have quietly gone about their work within the limitations of capital resources and political spats. In April 1993 the seventh SAARC summit adopted the South Asian Preferential Treaty Arrangement (SAPTA) envisaging liberalised trade among the member-countries. The SAARC Council of Ministers have worked on identifying areas and commodities for such preferential agreements. All member countries listed commodities, items and goods for which preference would be available.

The 12th SAARC summit in Islamabad in January 2004 categorically condemned terrorism in all its forms and manifestations and a challenge to all humanity. It also recommitted itself to the decisions of the SAARC Regional Convention on Suppression of Terrorism. An additional protocol to deal effectively with the financing of terrorism was also concluded. The 13th SAARC summit in Dacca in April 2006 renewed the commitment to fight terrorism and accepted the Indian position that there could be no double standards in combating terrorism. The Heads of Governments also lauded the various measures that had been taken in the social field and declared the decade 2006-2015 as the Decade of Poverty Alleviation. The cooperation among member countries on social and some economic issues maintain steady, even if slow, progress.

Yet all said and done, SAARC has not fulfilled its promise. It has been the least of the productive regional alliances and the political deficit combined with insistence on prior solution of some of the political problems between India and Pakistan has hamstrung its functioning.

Continuing Stalemate

Manmohan Singh and Musharraf made yet another effort to push the peace process when they conferred in New York where they had gone to participate in the 60th UN General Assembly in September 2005. The joint statement issued by the two leaders confirmed the commitment of the two sides to ensure a peaceful settlement of all outstanding issues. Manmohan Singh said at the end of the talks: "We are very satisfied". Opinions differ on the results of the talks, but as *The News* of Pakistan put it, "the optimism (expressed by Manmohan Singh and Musharraf) was a little exaggerated, but pessimism over the fact that the discussions didn't make visible progress would be misplaced too". More so, to quote *Dawn*, "...It is often forgotten that for the first time in decades India and Pakistan are jointly attempting to address and resolve conflicts and differences of long-standing."

The peace dialogue was seriously disrupted by an increasing number of terrorist acts in India. Some of them may be recounted in view of the impact on India-Pakistan relations. Among the more serious ones was the terrorist blasts in Delhi markets on 21 October (2005) killing 67 and injuring some 224 people, including women and children. Followed on 8 March a terrorist strike on Varanasi at a temple and the nearby railway station which took 16 lives. Despite these terrorist acts, Prime Minister Manmohan Singh flagged off a landmark bus service from Amritsar to Nankana Sahib in Pakistan on 24 March enabling Sikhs to regain access to their holy shrines in Pakistan. Manmohan Singh took the opportunity to offer a Peace Treaty to Pakistan. He suggested that both sides in Kashmir could work out cooperative, consultative mechanism for mutual benefit with the active encouragement of the governments of India and Pakistan.

There were thus serious suggestions floating back and forth but they were battered against the wall of violence and indiscriminate killing by jehadis. The terrorists had no stake in peaceful coexistence. After the Delhi and Varanasi blasts came the attack on 28 December at the Indian Institute of Technology campus in Bangalore. Although only one scientist was killed and four persons were injured, it was the first indication of an attempt on the elite, scientific or commercial. This pattern was also obvious when on 11 July 2006 bombs ripped through packed first-class bogeys of suburban trains of Western Bombay railways in which a number of business executives were travelling, killing 200 persons and wounding more than 700. This was the second major attack on the city since the 1993 blasts.

Never, perhaps, since the attack on Parliament was the country so shaken by a terrorist assault, and there was a strong undercurrent of anger in India. As Barkha Dutt wrote in *Hindustan Times* (22 July 2006) the mood in the country was "brittle and impatient". The people wanted their leaders to speak loudly and unitedly and even angrily and would not accept the silence of the lambs.

Many wondered whether the peace process could be usefully pursued amidst such unabated terrorism. Pakistan condemned the violence and disclaimed responsibility. The needle of suspicion pointed towards Lashkar-e-Toiba which, although declared a terrorist organisation even by USA, freely operated within Pakistan under assumed names. The role of the ISI in financing and training jehadi organisations in Pakistan like Jaish-e-Muhammad, Lashkar-e-Toiba and al Badr has been a matter of considerable contention. Pakistan asks for proof. India replies proof has often been provided but Pakistan just blandly ignores and denies. However, so far as the functioning of jehadi camps in Pakistan was concerned, the Pakistani press itself has provided sufficient proof. To take just one instance, *The Herald* of Pakistan published a series of articles in July 2005 on the revival of jehadi camps in Pakistan. Its correspondent who was taken on a guided tour, spotted at least 13 major camps in just one region—Mansehra, to which "trained militants as well as new aspirants are flocking to enlist for jehad or holy war". Western correspondents have been ever so often reporting the presence and activities of jehadi organisations in Pakistan. Equally noticeable is the fact that most perpetrators of terrorist attacks from Ayodhya to London (7 July terrorist attack and subsequently the intended terror attack on British planes flying to USA) have been found to have links in Pakistan.

It was after these attacks that Manmohan Singh expressed acute concern over the safety of Pakistan's nuclear arsenal. A serious problem could arise if the nuclear weapons fell into the hands of jehadi elements, he told the CNN. India was also worried because the terror infrastructure remained "largely intact" in Pakistan despite Musharraf's commitment not to allow the use of Pakistani territory to plot terrorist attacks against India, he said. "Trust but verify", he told the CNN quoting Reagan on a query whether he trusted Musharraf. Musharraf's own quandary was that in many ways he was dependant on the support of the religious parties headed by the mullahs. But for their acquiescence he might not have been able to retain his uniform along with his office as President. Jurist Farooq Hasan of Pakistan put it perhaps too bluntly: "It is difficult to say whether the army is the military arm of the mullahs or the mullahs the political wing of the army". If there was an element of exaggeration in this statement, there was also a solid core of reality behind it.

Regarding Pakistan's involvement, the Human Rights Watch report released in September (2006), while sharply critical as before of Indian army's human rights abuses and summary executions in Kashmir, acknowledged that there was "considerable evidence that over many years Pakistan has provided Kashmiri militants with training, weapons, funding and sanctuary". Although under pressure from the US after 9/11 attacks, the report stated, Pakistan had banned some militant groups like Jaish-e-Muhammed and Lashkar-e-Toiba, "these groups continue to operate after changing their names".

Musharraf had his own domestic problems. The tribal area, Waziristan, North and South, on the borders between Pakistan and Afghanistan, a highly volatile tribal area, was virtually out of Islamabad's control. According to the noted Pakistani journalist, Ahmed Rashid, this region was considered by US commanders in Afghanistan "terrorism central" and was now a "fully operational Al Qaeda base area offering a wide range of services, facilities, and military and explosives training for extremists around the world planning attacks". The tribal regions along the border with Afghanistan, wrote Ahmed Rashid, an alliance of extremist groups that included Al Qaeda, Pakistani and Afghan Taliban, Central Asians, and Chechens won a significant victory against the Pakistani army which lost some 800 soldiers in the last three years, "has retreated, dismantled its checkpoints, released Al Qaeda prisoners and is now paying large compensation sums to the extremists". This was in lieu of the agreement signed by the Pakistani government with the tribal leaders of Waziristan on 5 September. Islamabad claimed that the agreement provided that the tribal leaders would not allow any infiltration across the border into Afghanistan and that, therefore, that tap had been shut. But there was no monitoring mechanism to check the movements across the borders. Musharraf had himself warned against the indigenous, that is Pakistani, Taliban as a bigger danger than Al Qaeda.

In addition, as a consequence of the military operations and the killing of the Baloch leader Nawab Akbar Khan Bughti, Sindh was also on the boil. Musharraf's own legitimacy was being increasingly questioned. Both the

Indian and the Pakistani leaders were under different domestic pressures. Manmohan Singh put it very frankly that unless Pakistan did more to control terrorist organisations functioning from its soil, he would find it difficult to persuade Indian public opinion to support the peace process.

The Havana Meet

Musharraf and Manmohan Singh met yet again in Havana, where both had gone to participate in the non-aligned summit, to infuse new life into the peace process. Manmohan Singh described his meeting with the Pakistani president as very good and asserted that Musharraf had made a commitment to fight terrorism. Their joint statement condemned the Bombay blasts and announced their decision to set up a joint anti-terrorist institutional mechanism, but gave no details. The two leaders decided to continue the "joint search for mutually acceptable options for peaceful negotiated settlement of all issues between India and Pakistan, including the issue of Jammu and Kashmir, in a sincere and purposeful manner". (This was a repeat of earlier joint statements). They asked the Foreign Secretaries to resume the composite dialogue and particular mention was made of Sir Creek and Siachen issues for settlement.

Although, an anti-terrorist mechanism has been established, it is too early to predict whether it would prove to be an effective instrument to check terrorist activities and nab their perpetrators. We may, however, pause and utilise this opportunity to consider certain basic issues.

Summing Up

The Indo-Pakistan relationship is a complex mix of national prejudices, inflated psyche, injured ego and plain rivalry. This was rooted in the history of partition and the manner in which the subcontinent was divided into two separate countries in which major roles were played by the imperialist policy of divide and rule of the British, the growing awakening of the Muslim middle class and the fear of the Muslim landlords of Hindu dominance, the spread of petty middle-class Hindu chauvinism symbolized by the Hindu Sabha and the RSS, and the diffidence of the Congress leadership in the face of these challenges to seriously struggle for the support of the Muslim masses.

The impulse—and much of the enthusiasm for partition—was provided by the Muslim elite of UP and Punjab (some from UP migrated to Pakistan subsequently). In fact very soon after partition West Punjab came to provide largely the ruling class of Pakistan and to consider it almost its natural right to rule Pakistan. West Punjab consequently came to dominate the other regions of Pakistan.

Religion provided the impulse for separation and formation of the State, but by itself could not resolve the problem of identity or of development and to keep the country emotionally integrated.

'The emotional divide between different linguistic regions of Pakistan has often been underestimated. It first led to the secession of East Bengal (now Bangladesh) and is apparent now in the ongoing conflict in Balochistan. West Punjab's monopoly of power and its domineering attitude exacerbated the regional and linguistic passions as the other constituents were made to feel second class citizens.

What was of greater import to the Indo-Pak situation was the conviction of the West Punjab ruling elite that it was superior to the "Hindu" ruling elite of India and must match its will and resolve with that of India. The urge for parity with India was deep and compulsive. The enmities and jealousies that the Indo-Pak relationship witnessed were an inevitable part of the psychology of separation and division.

India was the chief antagonist almost in the act of birth of the two states. There was nothing that India did that Pakistan could not and should not do better. The question of accepting to play a smaller country's role in relation to India did not arise. No sacrifice was too small; every effort was bent towards achieving equality with India. As it was, a smaller country's fears about a larger country on its borders would have influenced the relations between the two in any case, but the history and legacy of the two decades before independence added a peculiarly disruptive dimension of its own. Security considerations were overlaid with a strong sense of rivalry and competition.

The "testing of wills" came to be an unspoken, but no less real, struggle for some fundamental values and beliefs too. For Pakistan it was the theory of the two nations, for India at trial was the basic structure of her polity. In India the State was declared to have no religion of its own and all religions were to be honoured equally. In Pakistan the State was founded on religion and became its *raison d'etre*. India moved forward towards a parliamentary democracy, Pakistan towards initially bureaucratic and subsequently military dictatorship. Noisy and often chaotic Indian democracy stood in contrast with the occasional discipline and order of Pakistan. But above all the sense of rivalry, the fears, the anxieties dominated Indo-Pak relationship. These anxieties in Pakistan were often accentuated by the occasional pronouncements of Hindu chauvinists.

Pakistan' search for security and for parity with India has also led to divergent foreign policy perceptions and equally divergent goals in foreign policy. If India tried to block foreign intervention in the region, Pakistan invited it to get even with India. In the last three decades, with India in view, Pakistan made an alliance first with one big power, later sent overtures to a second one, made common cause with still another one and then with two of them together.

Thus India and Pakistan were set upon opposite directions, India towards non-alignment, Pakistan towards alignments, India towards minimizing foreign intervention, Pakistan towards maximizing it. Pakistan's urge for standing on the same mountain top as India and its continuing crisis of identity lent a particularly explosive dimension to the two neighbours' mutual dealings. It is in this setting that relations in the period under study have to be surveyed.

There have been two basic changes in this setting—the change in public opinion (in fact in both the countries) and the rise of terrorism against India. Kashmir is an important issue but firstly to find a solution acceptable to both the countries may not be asking for the moon, but is not a cakewalk either. Secondly, whether the dominant decision-making authority in Pakistan, the army, is the best instrument for reaching a settlement is also a moot point. The most encouraging factor, however, is the palpable desire in both the countries to live in peace. Public opinion has been running ahead of the governments. The international situation has also been transformed. An international coalition against terrorism is one new phenomenon. The search for economic growth is another that calls for peace and stability within and around the countries. The economic struggle has obliged countries to mitigate their political hostilities and to reach out to their rivals. India is a much bigger country with a crucial role to play in the international community and cannot allow itself to be cribbed, cabined and confined to a mere Pakistan-specific universe; Pakistan could momentarily indulge in such unproductive policies, but not India. There is no option but for India and Pakistan to keep engaged to find peaceful solutions to the outstanding issues, no matter how agonising and prolonged the search could turn out to be.

India-China: Continued Forward Movement Amidst Contradictions

India and China continued their journey towards a new and more amiable relationship. This relationship had ma positive and some contradictory aspects also. Before we consider the developing relationship and its various challenges, it is appropriate first to comprehend the bigger picture of China, its current basic motivations, and the State philosophy that would help put India-China relations in a better perspective.

In a way China is being ruled by two philosophies—one to which the Communist Party is wedded in theory at least, and the other espoused officially By the State. Of course it is a somewhat artificial division because the Communist Party does not separate itself from the State. Nevertheless the country's ruling elite is functioning on two parallel philosophies. Officially the Communist Party swears by Marxism-Leninism, and undeniably the Party is practising Leninism on the practical political plane in the domestic sphere. Simultaneously the State, including the Communist Party, has gone back to the country's classical roots, lauding the ancient world order that the Chinese historically believed in, predating even the most influential philosopher sage of China, Confucius. In fact, Confucius himself disclaimed any originality; he said he was only systematising the wisdom and beliefs filtering down from the ancients.

The traditional, classical world order was comprised of two immutable and transcendent concepts, *harmony* and *propriety* (*li* and *he*). Combined with the concepts of *yin* and *yang* (positive and negative) who were not in constant struggle but had to be present in a proper and appropriate proportion for the world to function harmoniously, they constituted the core of Sinology. The world, or rather the universe, had to be in harmony or should be brought into harmony and only if there was universal harmony, could the harmony of the society be maintained. One depended on the other.

Without going into a detailed discussion of China's ancient philosophy, which is neither the design of this book nor does the space available permit, the Chinese State has gone back to these ancient concepts to delineate its position in the contemporary world. A front-page article in *People's Daily's* overseas edition (23 March 2005) lauded the building of a socialist harmonious society. Harmony, it said, was an important characteristic of traditional Chinese culture, as well as "a precious cultural heritage of China". It was "rich in connotation and full of profound philosophy of great wisdom". Harmony meant the nurturing of diversity and practice of balance, "arriving at the same destination through different routes, reaching unanimity after taking many things into consideration", effectively advocating "tolerance, compatibility, honesty and moderation".

Harmony came to have three dimensions in modern-day China: harmony with nature, diplomatic harmony and harmony in society. Harmony with nature required a rational use of Nature's bounty, developing what civilisation had created, ensuring mutual growth and mutual prosperity with Nature and developing together with Nature in a harmonious way.

Harmony in international relations and diplomacy could "make all nations live together in peace". Harmony would thus be opening up "a broader world" for the future of humankind and "provide humanity with inexhaustible driving force for its development".

We have dwelt upon the conceptual framework China was offering because of its implications for the world as well as for India-China relations. Simply put, China was telling the world that it did not wish war or conflict. It strove for a peaceful environment around its borders and in the world. A harmonious society that China says it aspires to build obviously requires a harmonious international situation.

Of course the Chinese were going to defend their fundamental interests, no matter what. As the article on the new course noted that through the use of harmony, China had both safeguarded its own national independence and refrained from practising expansionism. "We would absolutely not allow other nations to commit aggression against our country". For China "our country" included Taiwan. Beijing would not permit secession of Taiwan at any cost, but would be willing to live with the status quo at least for the present.

The core message was that China would not like to get involved in conflictual situations—unless it was pushed to the wall. China wanted to continue with its preoccupation with economic development. As Chinese Premier Wen Jiabao said to foreign media in Beijing ahead of his visit to Finland, Britain and Germany: "We need peace, we need friends and we need time". This did not mean that China would not play its own kind of realpolitik, as we shall observe presently, but it did mean that China did not wish to be deflected from the pursuit of economic growth. That remained the principal priority.

India-China relations have also to be viewed in this context. China needed a harmonious relationship with India too, although this would not prevent it from pursuing a policy of containment within engagement. For its own reasons and its own interests India also desired a harmonious relationship with China while mindful of its own security needs. There was renewed harking back to their ancient civilisational links. In the words of Professor Yang Baoyun of Beijing University "we have much in common with India, we have both brilliant civilisations, a humiliating experience of occupation and a large population". Similarities were more important than the sources of conflict. Professor Amartya Sen, Nobel laureate, pointed out that India-China relations historically were pushed by trade, not Buddhism, although Buddhism also had considerable influence on China. Indian mathematicians and astronomers also influenced China.

We have already noted the transformation of the international situation. We need to consider another factor that has strongly impinged on this relationship—the economic struggle. Both India and China are determinedly pursuing economic growth. China started earlier, but India too is trying to move forward rapidly. Both have notched up huge successes, China more than India. Both have also accumulated huge social problems. The Indian picture is well-known but we take a momentary pause to examine the Chinese picture.

China: Domestic Factors

The phenomenal growth of the Chinese economy is now well-reported and well-recognised. The Chinese economy has been growing at the rate of 9.3 per cent for the last 25 years—three times the growth rate of the US economy. The World Bank has declared that China is now the fourth largest economy squeaking past Britain in 2006. In purchasing power parity the country's GDP was already the second highest in the world. In almost 5 years China will become as big a force as the 25 economies of the European Union put together. China produced $263,825 trillion in output, 0.004 per cent more than Britain. It has built a world-class infrastructure—highways and skyways and airports, hotels and shopping malls. It has become the world's biggest consumer of steel, coal, cement, copper and gold. It is the second most hungry consumer of oil. It provides the biggest market for mobile phones, with 400 million handsets and cellular phone accounts.

There are now more than 100 million middle-class Chinese and the number is growing. The total number of Internet users is the second highest in the world; China produces half the world's cameras and a quarter of its washing machines.

Since 2002, it's one of the major driving forces behind the big commodity boom in the world. The prices of copper, aluminium and many other commodities got a big boost as China rummaged the world for feeding its fast-growing economy. It is sitting over a mountain of cash—nearly $1 trillion worth of foreign reserves. China's Central Bank is holding nearly $ 400 billion of US Treasury bonds. China is now impacting on world economy. When on 27 April (2006) Beijing raised the 12-month lending rate by a tiny 0.27 points to 5.85 per cent, it led to a decline of more than 5 per cent in copper prices and 7 per cent in zinc prices in the world. Global stock markets also felt the impact.

The *People's Daily* reported as early as October 2004 that China had actually used $540 billion of foreign direct investments (FDI) since 1977 and was home to some 940,000 foreign-funded firms. China's economy was an export driven, not a consumer-based economy. China's foreign trade topped a trillion dollars. Fifty-five per cent of the export earnings came from foreign firms operating in China. The Daily noted that the country was unprecedentedly open to the rest of the world. Foreign firms were accorded preferential treatment over domestic private firms. They paid only 15 per cent tax whereas the native ones were charged 33 per cent. Only in September this year (2006) Beijing announced that the tax on native private industry would be reduced by half. The Daily also rued the fact that in more than 80 industries, some 60 were available to foreign capital but only 40 open to domestic companies.

China's economic growth has been driven primarily by foreign capital and large-scale state investments. Chinese economic system has been evolving into some kind of a hybrid system. According to the official Chinese figures released by the All-China Federation of Industry and Commerce, the proportion of private firms to the national economy was 65 per cent in 2005, and would be contributing three-quarters of the GDP by 2010. These figures, however, mask the reality that the State dominated the ownership of resources and capital which were allocated on a privileged basis to the State-owned enterprises (SOE). The four major banks were state-controlled and were saddled with non-performing loans of about $400 billion.

The Chinese miracle was, however, accompanied by a huge social implosion and some major economic problems: peasant and worker discontent on a worrying scale, huge disparities among individuals, regions and cities and villages, the ruthless exploitation of migrant labour, pervasive corruption and alarming environmental degradation. China had creditably lifted nearly 300 million people out of poverty, but some 200 million still remained mired.

The two classes that had brought Mao into power—the peasantry and the working class—are the most disaffected and disenchanted today. Peasant poverty has driven some 200 million to the cities. This migrant labour living in shanties or cubicles, 6-12 in a room, and enjoying no known legal rights as they do not qualify in legal terms as urban residents, have provided the chief workforce for the rapid economic expansion. In addition the peasant was being subjected to both land alienation and arbitrary taxation. A recently completed survey of six provinces conducted by the Chinese Agricultural University revealed that violation of farmers' rights was rampant at the local level. A joint China-US study showed that farmland seizures, mostly for commercial purposes, had increased five-fold in a decade. The Ministry of Land and Resources reported that between 1998-2005 there were a million cases of land seizures. Some 40 million farmers had lost their land.

They are now over 200 million rural migrant workers, 120 million in the cities and 80 million in the towns, seeking employment and shelter. Their average wage in January 2005: $50-$70 a month. As many as 15 million workers are unemployed in the towns and 10 times more in the countryside. The official count of the rural debt is about 800 yuan or some $110 per every rural resident who still number some 700 million. The *China Daily* (1 May 2006) published a central government survey to the effect that 68 per cent of employees in China's manufacturing sector and 80 per cent in the construction segment were rural migrant workers. According to a senior official of the Research Office of the Communist Party's Central School, the urban unemployment rate could be as high as 16 per cent. The economic growth was coming without major job expansion, he said.

The income gap between urban and rural residents, according to a senior functionary of the Central Committee of the Chinese Communist Party was as high as 3.3 to 1, and widening. The regional gap too was disturbing. In terms of relative development the east was rated 60.5, while the central region had fallen from 27.5 to 26.3 and the west had declined from 13.8 to 13.2.

The economic disparities had reached almost the red light level, with the Gini coefficient standing at above 0.45. The official Chinese news agency, Xinhua, quoted the National Development and Reform Commission in February 2006 that the poorest fifth of urban residents received only 2.75 per cent of the total income of urban areas, whereas the richest fifth commanded 20 times as much, clearly demonstrating that the rich-poor gap "is much more than a town-country divide", as Xinhua put it. Just about 320,000 people had snatched up $1.6 trillion, or nearly two-thirds of the GDP in 2005, according to an Asia-Pacific Wealth Report.

Both President Hu Jintao and Premier Wen Jiabao have shown very considerable sensitivity to the twin problems-rural exploitation and widening social and economic disparities. Beijing reported nearly 87,000 incidents of social unrest in 2005, principally peasant protests and some workers demonstrations. Prime Minister Wen said in a speech published on 20 January 2006 that land conflicts, unstable prices and backward conditions in China's farm sector were threatening the country's stability and food supply. Sustainable development and national stability depended on resolving such problems. The government has announced a number of measures to safeguard peasants' interests and boost farm production, including abolition of agricultural tax and a ban on illegal land seizures in order to set up commercial enterprises without adequate compensation.

Easier said than done. As in India the problem boiled down to implementation. The remedial measures had to be carried out through the same officials and cadres who were responsible in the first instance for such corrupt practices. Cadres had been evaluated on the basis of the economic gains they could show; the means were of peripheral consideration.

Two more serious social problems may be noted in passing. In a recent survey, 40 per cent of the urban residents mentioned corruption as the fundamental primary malaise of Chinese society. Corruption had become entrenched and intensified, a "high-level, high-stakes" corruption. Just one dimension of it could be seen from a report of the Ministry of Commerce in August last year (2005) revealing that 4000 corrupt officials had fled the country with approximately \$50 billion. China's National Audit Office has claimed in its annual report in September 2006 that no central government ministries or organisations were immune from financial misconduct and corruption. Hu Jintao launched a campaign against corruption, netting many high-level officials in its embrace, of which the latest victim is Chen Liangyu, a Politbureau member and secretary of the all-important Shanghai Communist Party. However, it must also be added that this case is somewhat suspiciously tied up with the ongoing factional struggle within the Communist Party and is perhaps directed against what is generally referred to as the "Shanghai gang" allied to the erstwhile secretary general of the party and president of the People's Republic, Jiang Zemin.

Yet another massive social problem facing the Chinese leadership that we may just touch upon is unprecedented degradation of the environment as a result of blind pursuit of economic development. The former Minister for environment, Pan Yue lamented that one third of the Chinese landmass was bathed in acid rain, half the water in the seven largest rivers was "completely useless", and five of the 10 most polluted rivers in the world were in China.

We have mentioned all these problems not to underestimate or denigrate China's phenomenal growth and progress, but to underline that these enormous social problems require the leadership's intense focus that make external war and conflict an unpleasant option. Indeed India too faces many of those problems like unemployment, corruption, agricultural stagnation, environmental hazards, and social disparities.

However, it is necessary to be clear about one major departure in polity between India and China. The two countries live under totally distinct political systems. India is ruled under a noisy, chaotic democratic system, relatively successful rule of law (warts and all notwithstanding), an independent activist judiciary, a boisterous free press, and, again relatively, free and fair elections, sometimes springing dramatic surprises. China is ruled under a Leninist political system that tolerates little dissent from the official Communist Party line, controls both the judiciary and the media, and empowers the Party to make virtually every single appointment in the country. There are no checks and balances, and the Party itself is supposed to rectify its own shortcomings. Hu Jintao, for all his reform measures, has taken to severe muzzling of dissidents and even what would in India be regarded as the most normal reporting has been harshly clamped down. Even foreign media has been asked to get prior clearance from the official news agency, Xinhua, for any news it disseminates in China.

Coming back to broad objectives of Chinese foreign policy, Hu Jintao and Wen Jiabao spelt out the foreign policy objectives in a three-day central meeting on foreign affairs work in Beijing that concluded on 23 August (2006). Foreign affairs work, they stressed, should centre on the primary task of "peace, development and cooperation", adhere to an independent foreign policy, "unswervingly" pursue the path of peaceful development and be multidimensional. The conference asked the foreign affairs officials to create a sound internal environment and favourable external conditions for China's reform, opening-up and modernisation and contribute to "pushing forward the building of a harmonious world of abiding peace and common prosperity".

India-China: Fast Progress

In this overall context we can now consider the further development of India-China relations. As we have already recounted, both countries were contributing to the rapid improvement of ties in various spheres. They kept intact the practice that had been set of high-level visits to each other's country. In addition they tried to give new momentum to finding a solution to a central problem, the border dispute, and raise the level of discussion on security issues. When Chinese Vice-Foreign Minister, Wu Dawei met Shyam Saran then Foreign Secretary, in Beijing on 17 February (2005) Xinhua, the official Chinese news agency, described it as the first "strategic dialogue" between India and China and claimed that they had reached common ground on a wide range of issues: the need to look beyond bilateral disputes and upgrade ties in a global perspective, reform of the UN and other international institutions, the danger of weapons of mass destruction and sensitive technologies falling in the hands of terrorists and the importance of international cooperation in combating terrorism. They also prepared the ground for Chinese Premier Wen Jiabao's visit to India.

The highlight of the relationship during this period was Chinese Prime Minister Wen Jiabao's visit in April 2005 and President Hu Jintao's visit in November 2006. Wen's visit consolidated the ties between the two countries. Both the countries believed that their relations had entered a new stage and agreed to establish a China-India strategic and cooperative partnership for peace and prosperity, a joint statement by Wen and Manmohan Singh said. It stressed the extension of economic relations, trade, services, investments and other areas, decided to further promote cooperation in the military field as well as intensify their cooperation in various other fields, like education, science, technology, health care, tourism, etc. The two sides led by Chinese Vice-Foreign Minister Wu Dawei and the Prime Minister's Security Advisor, M. K Narayanan signed what the Chinese official media describe as a landmark agreement on guidelines for resolving the border dispute, the guidelines having been enjoined upon them by the two Prime Ministers. The two Prime Ministers agreed that differences on this issue would not be allowed to come in the way of overall development of bilateral issues. They also declared 2006 as the India-China year.

The *People's Daily* put out a story with a lead on its English website that Premier Wen had supported India's bid for permanent membership of the Security Council. It said that Wen had conveyed this to Manmohan Singh. We are not privy to what Wen conveyed to Singh, but the actual language purported to have been used was somewhat more general and a little ambiguous. "We fully understand and support the Indian aspiration to play an even bigger role in international affairs and in the UN", Wen was reported by the Chinese official media to have told Manmohan Singh. Also that China attached "great importance" to India's role in both international and regional affairs and that "India is a very populous developing country, and also a very important developing country".

For the present, in any case, this is not an immediate issue as the various powers in the UN have not been able to arrive at a consensus. The fact of the matter is Pakistan hated to see India as a permanent member, China did not want Japan, Nigeria looked askance at South Africa, Italy would rather not have Germany in, Argentina was not keen to see Brazil joining the ranks of the permanent members, and USA did not want anybody else except Japan to be there.

Coming back to India-China relations, both countries had given considerable emphasis to finding a solution to the border issue, but the issue bristled with complications and complexities. The designated negotiators had held intensive discussions as directed by the guidelines set up by Wen Jiabao and Manmohan Singh, but had yet not been able to come up with a solution. It is reasonable to assume that they had considerably narrowed down the differences and had aligned their positions on a host of issues, but the final accord was still elusive.

In these high-level exchanges another notable visit was

that by the then Defence Minister Pranab Mukherjee in May 2006. Mukherjee inked an agreement with Beijing to boost military ties. The Agreement signed on 29 May envisaged a faster development of Sino-Indian military cooperation that could be regarded as an important confidence building measure. It focused on annual high-level exchanges of defence personnel, an annual defence dialogue embracing security and strategic issues and joint military exercises. The *People's Daily* noted that China and India had already established a strategic partnership. Sino-Indian military relations had increased the momentum of development and mutual trust had thereby deepened which created a favourable atmosphere for maintaining peace and tranquility on the border, the paper said.

Of considerable importance also was the summit meeting between the leaders of China, Russia and India in St Petersburg where Hu Jintao and Manmohan Singh had gone to meet with the G-8 members. Although the foreign ministers of the three countries had occasionally met earlier, this Putin-Hu-Manmohan meeting was the first summit of the leaders. They discussed energy security, the fight against terrorism and innovative education in the 21st-century, and allied topics. Hu said after the meeting that they had "so many common interests which help us reach consensus easily" and added, "after today's meeting, I believe that we can further develop our ties with each other very well".

Some misreading of these meetings should be clarified immediately. There is a tendency to pit this relationship against the US or Western countries. It would be a highly artificial perception to view these triangular talks in the context of any anti-US alliance. All the three countries had each a separate relationship with the United States which neither was going to put on the anvil in their trilateral deliberations.

However, as Jiang Yuechun, director of the division of

world economy at the China Institute of International Studies—a Foreign Ministry think-tank—commented, the close ties between China, Russia and India meant more clout for developing countries when they co-operated with rich countries on the international stage. That about sums up: clout, yes, confrontation, no.

Economic Relations: A Bright Spot

India-China exchanges were multiplying in virtually every field, but one area was particularly bright. Trade between the two countries had been leaping forward. India and China had earlier reached an agreement in 2003 on exchanging trade preferences under the Bangkok Agreement with China offering tariff preferences on 217 items and India reciprocating with about 188 items. The trade volume had touched $18.7 billion by the end of 2005—just a little short of the target for 2008 that the Chinese and Indian Prime Ministers had set in April 2005. China was now the second largest trade partner of India. However only in relative terms. The trade volume is as yet miniscule when viewed in terms of the total trade of China. There are also some structural weaknesses: India is largely exporting primary items like iron ore and marine products while China's exports revolved around machinery, electrical goods and industrial products. The business houses of the two countries set a trade target of $100 billion by 2015. For India the bright spot is that a number of business houses have set up shop in China, including some big names in information software, auto parts and pharmaceutical industry. Companies in each country are assessing the market potential of the other. The Chinese have been stressing that the two countries should combine their strengths to reach a higher level of economic relationship, pointing out that China's strength lay in information hardware and India's in software. A number of Chinese companies, like Haier,

Hauwei, Legend, TCL, and Sinosteel had made their presence in India.

However, the Chinese are complaining of discrimination on the plea by Indian authorities of security considerations and their bids are disallowed in some cases,whereas bids by companies of other countries are entertained. They are also unhappy at Indian visa regulations for Chinese nationals that obliges them to go back every three months and then reapply for a visa. Indian government sources believe the complaints are exaggerated. The official spokesperson, Navtej Sarna welcomed the growing investments by Chinese companies in India, but cautioned that India's security concerns had to be satisfied. According to government sources, Indian investments in China were much less than those by Chinese companies in India which were estimated at $2 billion or near about. It was pointed out that a particular problem with some of the Chinese investments was their insistence on bringing in Chinese labour for the completion of the projects they wished to undertake. The complaints about discrimination against the Chinese companies were considerably exaggerated. According to the Foreign Investment Promotion Board, 33 out of 38 FDI applications by Chinese firms since 2004 had been cleared by the Government. Additionally, on the eve of president Hu Jintao's visit, visa regulations were considerably relaxed for Chinese businessmen.

A useful step to boost trade was taken when the two countries decided to reopen trade links at Nathu la Pass in Sikkim on 6 July (2006) after a freeze of some 44 years. The Pass 4545 metres above sea level, or some 460 km from Lhasa and 550 km from Kolkata had accounted for nearly 80 per cent of the India-China border trade in the 1900s. Reopening the trade route was a helpful move to expand economic ties between the two countries. The severed trade contacts could not be re-established in a trice. The benefits would be garnered over a long-term. Moreover India had to ensure against cheap Chinese goods, often heavily subsidised and of unequal quality, flooding the Indian market. Nevertheless the potential is there and would show results over time.

Energy Security and India-China Relations

Prime Minister Manmohan Singh mentioned energy security as one of the primary areas of the country's focus in domestic as well as foreign policy. That is equally true of China. Beijing has been scouring the world for ensuring oil supplies for its rapidly growing economy and for establishing a stake in their oil production in countries as far as Venezuela, Sudan, Angola and many others in sub Sahara Africa ("we are in Sudan, Niger, Chad, Algeria, Mauritania and now Nigeria", a vice president of China National Petroleum Corporation claimed), Saudi Arabia and Iran in West Asia and the Persian Gulf, and nearer home in Central Asia, principally Kazakhstan and Uzbekistan. We need not concern ourselves with figures for each of these countries, but merely record that Beijing was spending billions of dollars in aid to many of those countries to secure the supply of hydrocarbons.

India, a latecomer in the game, has also been engaged now in the search for oil and gas around the world, given the importance of oil in its economic growth. India has far smaller oil resources within the country than China. Apart from the growing energy ties with Russia, India's roaming eyes have focused on Saudi Arabia and Iran in the Middle East, Kazakhstan and Uzbekistan in Central Asia and to a degree on Turkmenistan, the treasurehouse for gas, Sudan and Nigeria in Africa and has made tentative moves in some of the South American countries.

An important issue before the two countries was whether they would engage in unbridled rivalry and try to outbid each other as happened in Kazakhstan, Angola and Ecuador, or enhance their cooperation in jointly securing supplies, as for instance they did in Columbia where they made a joint bid for around $800 million to buy out Ominex de Colombia. Or the provisional agreement they arrived at to buy a Canadian oil company's 37 per cent stake in Syrian oilfields for • 444 million ($ 580 million).

Both countries have indicated that competition would hurt and cooperation—in fact not only between India and China but at the world level as well—would be beneficial for securing energy supplies for both of them. More formal agreements were signed in January this year (2006) when the then petroleum Minister Mani Shankar Ayer visited Beijing. The Memorandum of Understanding identified key areas for cooperation that included upstream exploration and production, refining and marketing of petroleum products and petrochemicals, promotion of environmental friendly fuels, trading in oil and joint bidding in third countries. The Memorandum called for the establishment of a joint committee to monitor implementation and facilitate dialogue and information-sharing.

Of course there is no guarantee except common sense and commonly perceived wisdom that they would not be tempted to go their own way in obtaining fuels from abroad, but their current realisation that unilateralism would turn out to be a blind alley can be regarded as a positive sign in their developing understanding.

Some Negative Factors

The border remains an unresolved issue. Although it has never been more peaceful than at present, as long as a final settlement has not been inked, the potential for trouble cannot be regarded as having been finally scotched.

No less serious the problem for India has been the Chinese policies towards our neighbouring countries, chiefly Pakistan, Burma and Bangladesh. Beijing has not been averse to playing realpolitik in these areas. Pakistan has been a particular focus of Chinese policy in South Asia. Beijing viewed Pakistan as an essential counter foil to India and has remained deeply committed to Islamabad through thick and thin. A special relationship has evolved between China and Pakistan over the years. Beijing made good Pakistan's military hardware losses in the 1965 India-Pakistan war and again after the Pakistani debacle in 1971. It has provided large-scale economic assistance to Pakistan and helped Islamabad in its manufacturing capabilities.

Beijing gave critical assistance to Pakistan in pursuit of its nuclear capability. It has helped develop Gawadar, Pakistan's naval port on the Arabian sea. It has built the Chashma nuclear plant and is extending its assistance in constructing more nuclear plants in Pakistan. It has developed trade with Pakistan on a relatively fast track, the trade volume reaching $4.25 billion in 2005.

Pakistan clinched a $600 million defence deal with China this year. That included construction of 4 F. 22 P frigates for the Pakistani navy, upgradation of the Karachi dockyard and transfer of technology for indigenous production of Chinese surface fleet. The two have jointly developed the FC1 jet fighter, designated as J F 17 Thunder, which Pakistan has already placed an order for 150.

These stray examples have been given to highlight the point about the nature of ties between China and Pakistan. The Chinese have similarly cultivated political, defence and economic relations—though not of the same intense quality—with Burma which is strictly speaking not a part of South Asia but still is an important neighbour, Bangladesh, Nepal and Sri Lanka. It does not need too much recounting, for the extensive military and economic relations developed between China and Burma are well-known now. Indeed this relationship, and one other factor, had obliged

India to dilute its support for the democratic forces led by Suu Kyi in Burma. The other factor has been the North-East insurgents' use of the Burmese border to carry on their militant activities. Both these factors have brought a perceptible change in India's policy and the consequent warming up with the Generals in Burma whose help is being sought to curb militancy in that region.

We take one more instance. Bangladesh refuses to supply gas to India, but has a defence supplies agreement with China. China is the largest supplier of military hardware to Bangladesh and has sold 65 fighter planes and 39 helicopters to Bangladesh's airforce. China has similarly supplied arms and ammunition to Nepal but there has been a major change in its policy there and elsewhere in the region also.

Undeniably China's approach towards South Asia has undergone a noticeable and notable change since Beijing embarked upon its economic reforms programme. It continues to develop extensive contacts and sizable aid programmes with all of the countries of this region barring Bhutan and perhaps Maldives, but unlike in the 60s and 70s Beijing is no longer egging them on against India. In line with its new policy all over the world, it no longer seeks conflictual situations, even those directed against India in the region. The special relationship with Pakistan remains intact, but Beijing no longer incites Pakistan against India. In all the recent Indo-Pak crisis situations, Beijing's advice has been in favour of conciliation and peaceful dialogue. Beijing condemned the attack on Parliament and other terrorist acts against India and, perhaps for the first time, gave no public support to Pakistan on Kargil. It does not any longer call for plebiscite in Kashmir or implementation of the UN resolutions of the 50s on the Kashmir dispute. It now regards the Kashmir dispute as the legacy of history and urges both sides to resolve the issue peacefully through bilateral negotiations. This in itself is a substantial gain for India, even though China continues to provide large-scale aid to Pakistan in the military and economic fields as well as in the construction of nuclear plants.

China has shown far greater caution in the case of Nepal. It had been supplying arms and ammunition and some economic aid to Nepal, but in the recent crisis, perhaps taking a leaf from its missteps at the time of the creation of Bangladesh, it stayed its hand and did not rush to the support of the King. A projected visit by its Foreign Minister was cancelled and Beijing let events work out their course.

Hu Jintao's Visit

President Hu Jintao paid a state visit to India on 20-23 December 2006. The atmosphere for the visit was unfortunately and unnecessarily vitiated somewhat by an indiscreet remark by the Chinese ambassador about Arunachal Pradesh on the eve of the Chinese President's visit. The general impression appeared to be that of a low-key, business-like visit. In fact the visit passed a number of benchmarks and could be described as fairly productive.

Let us consider what the two sides said both publicly and to each other and see whether that was a substantial advance on what happened earlier. According to Foreign Minister Pranab Mukherjee, President Hu Jintao characterised the present phase in the relationship as marking a "new historic beginning" and conveyed that his visit would send out a strong signal to the international community that India and China were willing to work hand-in-hand for long-term friendship and common development. China had taken a "long term and strategic view" of the relationship with India, Hu told the Indians. Without the simultaneous rise of India and China the Asian century could not be a complete one, he added.

On the border issue, the Chinese President and Indian

Prime Minister agreed that an early resolution of the boundary question would not only advance the basic interests of the two countries, but also invest their strategic partnership with further strength and dynamism, and should therefore be pursued as a strategic objective. They directed the Special Representatives to intensify their work to expeditiously explore the framework of a boundary settlement on the basis of the Agreement on Political Parameters and Guiding Principles signed in April 2005. They stated their commitment that pending the final settlement of the boundary question, they would maintain peace and tranquillity in the border areas and expedite the work of clarification and confirmation of the line of actual control.

We need to remind ourselves that India was in possession of Arunachal Pradesh and China of Aksai chin. The room for concessions was very narrow from both sides. Therefore the hype about the Chinese ambassador's statement was not really necessary. The Indian media's obsession about a border settlement was somewhat misplaced. Neither side was so strong compared to the other that the border positions could be changed by force. More essential was the building of trust and let time do the rest.

On the issue of permanent membership of the Security Council, President Hu reiterated the earlier assurance given by Chinese Premier Wen Jiabao to Manmohan Singh in April that China would be happy to see India succeed in its endeavour to become a permanent member of the UN Security Council. What that meant was that China would support, and not oppose, but it was for India to persuade the other UN Security Council members for such expansion.

On the Indo-US nuclear deal Foreign Minister Pranab Mukherjee replying to a question told a television interviewer (but he did not include it in his Parliament statement) that President Hu had indicated China's acceptance of the deal. If so, this was a major advance on the earlier Chinese position.

Hu said at the joint press conference: China and India are true friends and cooperation partners. Manmohan Singh summed up the Indian position when he said that there was enough space for India and China to develop together in a mutually supportive manner, while remaining sensitive to each other's concerns and aspirations. The two sides also agreed on regular summit meetings and mechanism for regular exchange of views at the Foreign Offices level. Hu mentioned that this was his fifth meeting with Manmohan Singh in the last 18 months.

No less a decision of import was the fixing of a trade target of $40 billion by 2,010 and to expedite the search for an India-China regional trading arrangement. It is this writer's view that the route to a really high level of India-China ties lies through economic relations. The day India-China trade approximates $100 billion figure, that day India-China relations would have become irreversible.

Hu Jintao's trip to India was compared to his visit to Pakistan immediately afterwards by the media in both countries. Certainly, there was far more hype and colourful festivity when Hu went to Pakistan. Hu called the people of Pakistan brothers. Pakistan believes and China encourages the belief that Beijing was an "all-weather" friend of Pakistan. India took comfort from the fact that Hu did not announce any new nuclear reactors for Pakistan. Of course China could provide reactors at a later date, or even without announcing it. But let us be clear China is the patron state of Pakistan, not of India. The nature of the relationship is different, India and China, two more or less equally placed neighbours, more in the nature of France and Germany, striving, it seems successfully for the present at least, to reach a *modus vivendi* and become good and closely connected neighbours.

Overall Assessment

Critics point to what they call Beijing's pincer movement surrounding India—Pakistan, Bangladesh, Burma in particular. The protagonists call for, if not immediate, as early as possible settlement of the boundary issue by more or less agreeing to the Chinese terms. Some of them berate the government for its somnambulance while the Chinese extended rail connectivity from Lhasa towards Nathu La, thereby, they believed, missing the bonanza available from trade on that route through lack of railway infrastructure. Both Confucius and Aristotle extolled the virtue of the golden mean. China and India need to build mutual trust and confidence to a level that would in a way automatically let the outstanding problems fall in their places. If China and India become stakeholders in each other's economic growth, common prosperity could do more to ensure a lasting peace than the approximation of their political and security perceptions. It may have become a cliche, but nevertheless a realistic one, that good relations between India and China were central to the maintenance of peace in Asia and the world.

India and Russia: An Enduring Relationship

We have noted in the previous chapters how India had developed a special relationship with the Soviet Union, how the breakup of the Soviet Union affected India and how the pieces were picked up to re-establish India-Russia ties, thereby highlighting the relevance of Kautaliya's dictum that neighbour's neighbour was a friend. The renewal of intimate contacts and relations with Russia also demonstrated that geopolitical verities were not subsumed by ephemeral, even if highly significant, developments. Despite some early hiccups after the dissolution of the Soviet Union, India and Russia were quick to find a friendly touch again.

The Putin era saw the virtual re-establishment of a special relationship, although of a somewhat different kind. The factors were many but some of them may be identified. There were no emotional irritants between the two, no territorial dispute, no race for parity with each other, no fear of dominance by the other, no serious differences on international issues and, more significantly, a commonality of approach and convergence of interests in the region surrounding India, the joint advocacy of a multipolar world and negotiated settlement of issues that divided the world.

Boris Yeltsin, as we noted in the last chapter, stabilised the relationship after the collapse of the USSR, but Vladimir Putin gave it more flesh and blood and added new dimensions to it. Putin had grasped the relative importance of India-Russia ties and knew how to nurse them without inviting hostility from others. This was clear from Putin's first visit to India in October 2000 soon after he took over as President. Putin told Indian media persons on the eve of his visit that he was "India's best friend" in the international community as well as within Russia. He underlined this Indo-Russian propinquity in his address to members of Parliament. He described India as "a long-term partner and ally". He did not consider Moscow's relations with other countries to be an alternative to friendship with India. Fighting terrorism was a common objective and there were no double standards. There was "verified information", he said, that the same organisations—"even the same individuals"—were responsible for terrorist acts from the Philippines to Kosovo, Kashmir to Afghanistan, and the northern Caucasus.

Putin and Vajpayee signed the Delhi declaration that replaced the 1971 Indo-Soviet Treaty. The declaration stressed their adherence to "the common ideals of peace, democracy, the rule of law, human rights and fundamental freedoms, non-violence and secularism" and went on to recognise "there are special responsibility by virtue of being among the largest multi-ethnic, multi-lingual and multi-religious States in strengthening international peace and security" and "democratisation of international relations". They reaffirmed their strategic partnership and called for progressive reduction of nuclear weapons with the ultimate goal of eliminating them. Equally importantly, they undertook to inform each other of any foreign policy initiatives in the international arena and not to participate in any military, political or other alliances directed against the other side or to conclude any treaties, agreements or understanding that infringed upon the independence, sovereignty, territorial integrity or national security interests of the other side. They stressed, however, that their relationship was not directed against any other country.

The Putin visit coincided with the huge military deal worth some $3 billion for the supply and eventual production in India of state-of-art T90 patrol tanks and Sukhoi 30 MK1 jet fighters. The military deal paved the way for a close defence relationship between Russia and India. Russia once again became the largest supplier of military hardware and retains this position currently, despite the growing military ties between India and Israel, India and France and now even with the US throwing its hat into the ring bidding for India's purchase of high-tech armament and arms-related items.

The propinquity of approach towards Afghanistan remained notable throughout this and the ensuing period. The two set up a joint working group on Afghanistan and acted in tandem with each other over the situation developing in Afghanistan. Russia also took initiative in bringing about closer deliberations between China, Russia and India on pressing world issues and in getting India invited to the Shanghai Security Organisation (SCO) as an observer along with Pakistan, Iran and Mongolia.

The Russian president's visit set the pattern for the development of a special relationship between India and Russia. Vajpayee went to Moscow in November 2001 and Putin returned the visit—even though for a day—in December 2002 and the summit-level talks became virtually an annual feature.

Vajpayee's visit came after the horrific attacks on the World Trade Centre in New York that transformed the world situation and witnessed the building of an international coalition against terrorism. India and Russia were in any case partners against terrorism and 9/11 only intensified their interaction. Putin came down quite hard on terrorism and quizzed George Bush on Pakistan's role during their meeting in St Petersburg on 22 November 2001. While he supported General Musharraf, he asked Bush, "what can happen with armies armed with weapons that exist in Pakistan, including weapons of mass destruction? We should not forget about this". Privately, Mr Putin was reported to have referred to the Pakistani military leadership as "a junta with nukes". (*New York Times*, 23 November 2002)

During Vajpayee's visit to Moscow an important agreement was signed on Russia's construction of a multi-billion dollar nuclear plant in Tamil Nadu. The agreement on the Koodankulam nuclear power plant's construction brought the Russians back into India's nuclear power programme. Russia undertook the supply, design and 90 per cent of the equipment for the plant as well as to provide 54 per cent of the cost as credit to be repaid in 14 equal installments one year after the commissioning of the plant. With this agreement Russia had also breached the international nuclear blockade against India.

Putin came back for a second visit in December 2002. The Russian Foreign Minister at the time, Igor Ivanov, emphasised on the eve of Putin's visit that Russia "shared the view that Pakistan must honour its obligations to dismantle the terrorists' infrastructure on the territory under its control". Putin came under very changed conditions from his first visit. Under his stewardship Russia had recovered from the economic meltdown of 1998 and had stabilised itself. It was now on the crest of an economic revival, a "resurgent Russia" in the words of a Japanese analyst. President Putin had revealed a deft touch at home and abroad, besting adversaries and winning new friends. He had gained immensely in self-confidence and had made himself and Russia an indispensable factor in world affairs. He had established a personal relationship with Bush without sacrificing Russian interests. The enhanced Russian role was evident from Putin's hosting of the G-8 meeting in St Petersburg where he invited both Indian and Chinese leaders to meet the G-8. He has made skilful use of Russia's possession of energy resources to increase Russia's clout. Today Russia is the top producer of oil outstripping even Saudi Arabia. The West has been increasingly critical of him, accusing him of recourse to authoritarian measures and misuse of the control of energy fuels. Many cases of suppression have been cited. But Russia's clout has not been dented.

Putin's second visit to India focused more on terrorism but, besides a MOU on fighting terrorism, a slew of agreements was also signed ranging from telecommunications to cooperation in science and technology. The Russian President emphasised that "our two countries share common views on the key issues in global politics". President Abdul Kalam equally warmly responded that with Russia, "we have a shared vision" of a multipolar world built on consensus and accommodation of different views and interests. Both countries stood for determined action for total elimination of international terrorism and religious extremism.

It was not as if no irritants came up to cause some

concern but they proved to be of a transient nature and generally did not leave any emotional hiatus. The Russian attempt to play with mediation between India and Pakistan was one such temporary irritant and the arrest and punishment of two Russian pilots involved in arms smuggling another one.

The first one related to the aftermath of the attack on the Indian parliament, 13/12 as it came to be known. Both the Indian Prime Minister Vajpayee and Pakistani President Musharraf participated in a conference on cooperative measures under the auspicious of the Shanghai Security Organisation that included Russia, China and the Central Asian states, at Almatti in Kazakhstan in June 2000. Putin tried hard to persuade the Indian Prime Minister to take a trip to Moscow where under Russian aegis negotiations could be held between Vajpayee and Musharraf to break the logjam between the two countries, but Vajpayee refused and India worried about the shades of Tashkent. Putin, however, had put aside Vajpayee's rebuff by the time he came for his second visit to India in the first week of December 2002.

The other incident that raised the hackles of the Russian elite concerned the detention and punishment of two Russian fliers caught in the act of smuggling arms to extremists in Purulia in West Bengal in 1998. The Russian media and parliamentarians were so worked up that reports even suggested that Putin might have to postpone his first visit to India. In the end, however, India acceded to the Russian pressure and released the two pilots. That cleared the way for Putin's visit in October 2000.

These constituted temporary hiccups and the basic vitality of India-Russia relations remained intact. Indeed, Russia's determination to remain faithful to its obligations under the Delhi declaration signed during his October visit was evident from the way Putin handled Musharraf's visit to Moscow in February 2003. He telephoned Mr Vajpayee before the arrival of General Musharraf to inform him about the nature of the visit and again after the departure of the Pakistani President he let Mr Vajpayee in on the substance of the talks. Many people thought he was trying to please India. The fact of the matter was that he was abiding by the obligation that the two sides had undertaken during Mr Putin's visit to India in October 2000 that enjoined on them to inform each other of any planned foreign policy initiatives in the international arena and not to participate in any military, political or other alliances or associations or armed conflict directed against the other side or to conclude any treaties, agreements or understandings that infringe upon the independence, sovereignty, territorial integrity or national security interests of the other side. Mr Putin was carrying out the letter and spirit of the decisions taken by the two countries earlier.

India-Russia relations can be divided into three segments: defence, energy and geopolitical. The defence dimension constitutes the core of India-Russia ties. The pattern was set by Putin's first visit. The defence ties continued to flourish in the subsequent years. India signed yet another deal in October 2003 for $1 billion with Russia and Israel—a first trilateral deal of its kind. The deal provided for Israeli-made Falcon radar to be mounted on converted high-powered Russian IL-76 transport aircraft. The Falcon was not merely a surveillance system to detect aerial threats, including missiles, from distances ranging from 800 km to 2000 km, but a command and control post in the sky, a switch-over from a paradigm of threat-based defence to a capabilities-based one.

After eight years of intense haggling India acquired the 44,750 ton aircraft carrier, Admiral Gorshkov, for $1.5 billion (or Rs 6900 crores) paid as repair and extensive refitting charges, a deal described by both sides as a "historic landmark" in bilateral strategic ties. This was a prelude to the leasing for 10 years in the first instance of a sophisticated Russian Akula 11 class nuclear-powered attack submarine—a multi-million dollar rental bargain that was to "buttress Indian navy's blue water profile".

We do not have to go into all the details as the general pattern has been outlined. We may only refer to two other characteristics of these defence ties. One was that in most cases the agreement provided for the manufacturing license within the country of the high-tech arms being purchased by India. The second related to joint research and production of some high-class weapons. To take one illustration, Russia and India had jointly produced the Brahmos supersonic missiles presently being inducted by the Indian navy.

There were necessarily glitches and irritants when such an extensive relationship is involved. From the Indian side the irritants concerned pricing and supply of spare parts. The Russians were driving hard bargains and the Indians believed the prices had been inflated. Moreover the Russians were often dragging their feet in regard to the supply of spare parts. That in fact related to Moscow's complaints about India dragging its feet on signing with it an intellectual property rights protection agreement. As the Russians were supplying India the very latest armaments some of which had hardly been inducted into the Russian army, they were worried about them being copied and the secrets being stolen by other countries. These were not minor glitches and had been holding up decisions on some important deals.

This was the subject matter of a marathon summit between Putin and Manmohan Singh in New Delhi on 3 December 2004. While they could not finalise an agreement on these issues, Manmohan Singh said the IPR rights would be respected for all future supplies of equipment and in the words of Putin one technical issue was left to be sorted out.

They energised the relationship through agreements on the energy sector and announcement of Russia's support to India's permanent membership of the Security Council (both these aspects we shall discuss presently).

The defence relationship was pursued by Defence Minister Pranab Mukherjee* visiting Moscow in November 2005 in preparation for the Putin-Manmohan Singh summit a few weeks later. Mukherjee, chairing India-Russia joint defence group, affirmed that defence ties with Moscow were robust and Russia would remain India's largest and most secure source of defence hardware. The ongoing deals with Russia ran into almost $9 billion. A 10-year defence cooperation agreement between India and Russia until 2010 included more than 200 projects worth $20 billion. New avenues were explored. Russia agreed to share the technology for an advance technology naval vessel (ATV) and an air defence vessel. The ATV was an indigenous project for the development of nuclear submarines. India also signed some other agreements, as for instance on the peaceful use of outer space, but space does not permit us to go into more details. In his meeting with Mukherjee, President Putin described the current level of Indo-Russian ties as "unprecedented".

Some of the glitches were sorted out and a new level of relationship reached at the summit talks held in early December between President Putin and Prime Minister Manmohan Singh. The two countries agreed on reciprocal protection of intellectual property rights clearing the way for further cooperation in the design, development and production of defence equipment. Manmohan Singh announced at a joint press conference that India and Russia had identified the medium range transport aircraft and the fifth generation of fighter aircraft as two such projects. After

* Now Foreign Minister.

Brahmos, this will be the second such project to be jointly produced by the two countries.

While on the subject of defence acquisitions, we may observe in conclusion that India had been diversifying its sources for the purchases of its defence needs. Israel, in particular, has become the second largest defence partner of India. France too has supplied substantial quantities and India has sometimes turned to Swedish and other firms. Now the US is also bidding in the Indian arms market. It is natural that India, even when keeping the core supplies from Russia secure, would wish to enlarge its options; it is equally natural that Russia would feel concerned lest it should slip from its marketplace in India. However, Russia seems to have accepted the reality that India would be purchasing its armament from other sources also and is more confident now that its niche is secure for many years to come.

Energy Dimensions

Russia was emerging as a major source of energy in an energy-hungry world. It was adroitly using its vast resources of oil and gas for an incremental role in the world. India's ties with Russia came to extend meaningfully to this vital area of India's needs and Russia became an increasingly important energy partner, in addition to being a defence supplier. Russia's deputy Prime Minister at the time, Alexander Zukov told the then Indian Petroleum Minister, Mani Shankar Aiyer in February 2005, "we regard India as our strategic partner, including in the sphere of energy cooperation. Russia is interested in getting Indian investments in energy projects". Aiyer responded by asserting that India could invest up to $25 billion in Russia's oil industry. Already in 2001 India had concluded an agreement with Russia by which ONGC Videsh invested $1.7 billion for a 20 per cent share in one of the biggest hydrocarbon treasure houses in Russia's Far East, Sakhalin.

The gigantic Sakhalin 1 fields in Russia's Far East, India's single largest investment abroad, began oil and gas production by 1 October 2005. Sakhalin 1 where India has a 20 per cent stake would produce 23,000 barrels of oil and about 58 million standard cubic feet of gas a day rising to 50,000 barrels and 200 million standard cubic feet of gas a day by the end of 2006. ONGC Videsh made an additional investment of $1.7 billion in Sakhalin 1 and was banking on the import of 700,000 barrels by the end of 2006. Prime Minister Manmohan Singh said after the meeting with Russian Prime Minister Mikhail Fredkov that, in view of Russia's experience, he was hopeful of finding ways and means of involving Russia in the construction of the proposed Iran-Pakistan-India oil pipeline.

While on the subject of India's search for oil and gas requirements abroad, we might note in passing that ONGC Videsh had by now presence in Sudan, Vietnam, Angola and Brazil, apart from Sakhalin. It also proposed to commence pumping in Brazil, Cuba, Venezuela, Qatar and Burma in the next few years.

Besides traditional and non-renewable energy sources, Russia was also a partner of India in the nuclear power field. The Tarapur atomic power station was running with the help of low-enriched uranium supplied by Russia—it might have otherwise closed down. Russia, as we have already mentioned, had provided two 1000 MW reactors for the Koodankulam nuclear power plant in Tamil Nadu. Russia had given this assistance despite the stringent regulations obligated by the Nuclear Suppliers Group regime.

However, there was no doubt that Russia was constrained by these regulations. Further cooperation could come only through an agreement by which the NSG made an exception for India which, again, depended on a nuclear deal with the United States. There was equally no doubt that Russia supported the proposed deal with the United States and wished to expand the nuclear power relationship with India. Putin had pledged Russia's support for India to get international restrictions on civilian nuclear technology transfers lifted and expressed confidence at a press conference after the summit-level talks in Moscow in December 2005 that the moment for broadening the scope of the nuclear relationship would soon be at hand.

Geopolitical Dimensions

Undeniably Russia was building up a geopolitical relationship with India, just as Moscow was also building up a geopolitical relationship with China. It was essentially through Russian efforts that Russian, Indian and Chinese Foreign Ministers began holding joint periodic discussions on world issues and it was through Russian efforts that India-China-Russia held a summit of their own on the sidelines of the G8 meeting in St Petersburg in 2006.

We have used the words geopolitical partnership deliberately, for these relationships did not constitute, and were not intended to constitute, a military alliance, or in fact any kind of alliance, against the United States or any other country. Each of the three countries had their separate relationship with the United States. It would be fanciful for anyone to believe that any country or any combination of countries could substitute for relationship with the United States. But the deliberations among the leaders of the three fastest growing economies on world issues and their common problems could help promote peace and development and provide them with more leverage on the world scene.

India-Russia strategic partnership was beneficial to both countries in meeting the challenges of economic development, terrorism, emerging energy crisis, nuclear challenges, and the unilateralism involved in the current structure of world politics. This did not mean that they had no differences. Sometimes they had different requirements. To give one instance, even though Russia supported permanent membership for India in the Security Council, they differed on the means to achieve it. India had joined hands with Japan, Brazil and South Africa to form what came to be known as G4 to press their demand for inclusion in the Security Council as permanent members. Jointly they moved a motion at the UN for achieving this objective. All the three major powers, USA, Russia and China opposed the motion for different reasons and it had to be dropped. But Russia still strongly supported India's bid for the Security Council.

There are substantial differences in the political and economic structures of India and Russia, but there is a rare complementarity of interests in international relations. This complementarity keeps intact their very close and very friendly relations, no matter which government ruled in either country. The missing link, however, was the economic relationship which stood at a meagre figure of Rs. 1841 crores worth of exports to and a little over Rs. 959 crores of imports from Russia between April-November 2005-2006.

India and the United States: That Nuclear Deal

Bush's reelection was soon followed by the victory and induction of a new government in India. The NDA (National Democratic Alliance) government headed by Vajpayee was voted out and a United Progressive Alliance (UPA) government took over. Mrs. Sonia Gandhi, the leader of the largest formation in it, Indian National Congress, declined the post of Prime Minister and, instead, selected the eminent economist Dr. Manmohan Singh as Prime Minister. Sonia Gandhi was elected chairperson of the UPA. The Left parties in Parliament decided to support the new government without participating in it.

In terms of foreign policy there was little change of substance. The UPA government continued with almost the same policy as the NDA, and in some cases, like relations with USA and to some extent with Pakistan carried the process of building a new relationship much further than the NDA was able to do. The continuity in foreign policy was both marked and significant.

India and US continued and expanded their cooperative activities between the militaries of their two countries. They kept the negotiations ongoing during the second phase of the Next Step in Strategic Partnership (NSSP).

And not only in defence cooperation, the new Government was eager to expand relations in every area. We shall presently examine some of the prime reasons for this effusiveness, but here we may take note of the rationale offered by Prime Minister Manmohan Singh himself in perhaps the frankest analysis by an Indian political leader of the justification for a new Indo-U.S. relationship.

Talking to the media persons on board his special plane during his first visit to Europe as Prime Minister in November Manmohan Singh said, "we have to look at the realities of the world. International relations are, in the final analysis, power relations. And we are living in a world of unequal power. We cannot wish away the realities of the situation. We have to use the available international system to promote our interests". It was, therefore, necessary to engage the U.S. The U.S. played a preeminent role in the world economy and in the world political system and "we cannot wish that away. Our effort will be to have a constructive dialogue which enlarges the scope for autonomous decision-making in our country". The U.S., he said, was a super power and its interests did not always coincide with Indian interests but he believed that there was "enormous scope" for constructive engagement to "the mutual advantage of both countries".

The most important and visible development in the shaping of a new relationship was Secretary of State Condoleeza Rice's visit to India in mid March (2005). It was then that the ground and the basis for an entirely new ball game in India-U.S. ties was laid and Washington's policy and strategy in this regard was spelt out. Rice told Manmohan Singh that it was "the policy of the United States to help India become a major world power in the 21st century". Rice had come to India at the request of President Bush. Revealing this U.S. ambassador David Mulford wrote in an article for a U.S. embassy press release soon after: "The U.S. and India are poised for a partnership that will be crucial in shaping the international order in the 21st century. In her meetings with Prime Minister Manmohan Singh, Foreign Minister Natwar Singh, Congress President Sonia Gandhi and Opposition Leader, L.K. Advani, Secretary Rice addressed the practical steps that need to be taken to make this happen. In each meeting there was a clear agreement that the U.S. and India must not only broaden their strategic partnership, but move into new and substantively more complex issues".

The new Defence Minister Pranab Mukherjee's visit to Washington was a prelude to the signing of a far-reaching agreement with the U.S. Mukherjee signed with U.S. Defence Secretary Donald Rumsfeld in Washington a defence cooperation agreement. The "New Framework for the U.S.-India Defence Relationship" signed on 29 June envisioned a 10-year programme of accelerating cooperation in the defence field including the sale of F-16 and F-18 fighter aircrafts, if India so desired. This was reported to be in pursuance of the Bush administration's pledge to help India become a major world power in the 21st century.

The agreement was broad in its scope, even including collaboration in multinational operations, "when it is in their common interests". This became the most controversial clause in the agreement. The critics, particularly the Left, were aghast at the absence of any mention of UN involvement or UN sanction for such multinational operations which they believed was a departure from the traditional Indian approach. The government defence: any such operations would be undertaken only if it were considered in India's interests. That still left the question why was UN's consent not included in the text of the agreement. Pranab Mukherjee additionally argued that the agreement was only a framework agreement, it was not a treaty.

This was only the beginning of a new debate over the direction of India's foreign policy. The debate became sharper with further developments in Indo– U.S. relations, the agreement signed between George Bush and Manmohan Singh and the subsequent vote on the Iran issue at the IAEA. All these issues became enmeshed in the debate on India's foreign policy. We shall first take note of all the developments before we analyse the pros and cons.

Pranab Mukherjee's visit was followed by Prime Minister Manmohan Singh's trip to Washington to a red carpet welcome and an even more significant agreement. President George Bush and Prime Minister Manmohan Singh signed a joint statement on 18 July in which they pledged to transform Indo-U.S. relationship and establish a global partnership. President Bush "conveyed his appreciation to the Prime Minister over India's strong commitment to preventing WMD proliferation and stated that as a responsible state with advanced nuclear technology, India should acquire the same benefits and advantages as other such states". The President told the Prime Minister that he would work to achieve full civil nuclear energy cooperation with India as it realizes its goals of promoting nuclear power and achieving energy security. The President would also seek agreement from Congress to adjust U.S. laws and policies, and the United States would work with friends and allies to adjust international regimes to enable full civil nuclear energy cooperation and trade with India, including but not limited to expeditious consideration of fuel supplies for safeguarded nuclear reactors at Tarapur. In the meantime, the United States would encourage its partners to also consider this request expeditiously.

On his part the Indian Prime Minister undertook that "India would reciprocally agree that it would be ready to assume the same responsibilities and practices and acquire the same benefits and advantages as other leading countries with advanced nuclear technology, such as the United States. These responsibilities and practices consist of identifying and separating civilian and military nuclear facilities and programs in a phased manner and filing a declaration regarding its civilian facilities with the International Atomic Energy Agency (IAEA); taking a decision to place voluntarily its civilian nuclear facilities under IAEA safeguards; signing and adhering to an Additional Protocol with respect to civilian nuclear facilities; continuing India's unilateral moratorium on nuclear testing; working with the United States for the conclusion of a multilateral Fissible Material Cut Off Treaty; refraining from transfer of enrichment and reprocessing technologies to states that do not have them and supporting international efforts to limit their spread; and ensuring that the necessary steps have been taken to secure nuclear materials and technology through comprehensive export control legislation and through harmonization and adherence to Missile Technology Control Regime (MTCR) and Nuclear Suppliers Group (NSG) guidelines".

The two leaders "agreed to establish a working group to undertake on a phased basis in the months ahead the necessary actions mentioned above to fulfill these commitments. The President and the Prime Minister also agreed that they would review this progress when the President visits India in 2006".

The U.S. also agreed to seek the "expeditious consideration of fuel supplies for safeguarded nuclear reactors at Tarapur", an atomic power station near Mumbai that had been under threat amid dwindling stocks of enriched uranium from Russia. In addition, the joint statement referred to steps to be taken for accelerating economic cooperation and boosting trade, investment and technology collaboration, energy security, prevention of nuclear proliferation and various other fields.

The agreement widened the differences and the domestic debate on foreign policy. The divide became sharper when it became enmeshed with India's vote in IAEA general body in favour of a resolution warning Iran that its case could be referred to the Security Council for possible sanctions if it did not fully cooperate with the IAEA on its investigation about any secret efforts at enrichment of uranium to a degree that would make it possible for Iran to develop an atomic device. It must be added in parenthesis that Iran, unlike India, was a signatory to the NPT. The resolution and India's vote came in the wake of official Iranian reports that Tehran had removed all the seals placed by international inspectors at Isfahan Uranium Conversion Facility. Iran's deputy head of atomic energy agency, Mohammad Said had said on 10 August that the conversion facility was fully operational.

Before the vote the newly elected president of Iran telephoned Prime Minister Manmohan Singh who reportedly advised him to be flexible in the matter in order to stave off a crisis. India defended its vote on the ground that it had agreed to do so only after the EU-3 had agreed to defer any decision on the Security Council referral until the next meeting of the IAEA board in

November thus gaining time for Iran and the International community to strive for a peaceful solution to the issue. By that time in any case the EU-3 had managed to defer the issue temporarily without referring the matter to the Security Council for sanctions.

However, the Iran vote opened the floodgates of a heated division of opinion among the elite in India. From former Foreign Minister Yashwant Sinha of the rightist BJP to the Left in India sharp opposition was mounted against India's vote. Even the main English newspapers were divided in their opinion and analysis.

The critics accused the government of surrendering to the United States. The vote, they alleged, was given under U.S. pressure to protect the Indo-U.S. agreement. The India vote was almost denounced as a shameful betrayal of the non-aligned movement. Iran was a friendly country, hugely important to India as supplier of energy for a fuel resource-short India. Questions were also raised about India's sincerity in implementing the earlier agreement with Iran for the construction of an oil pipeline that would run through Afghanistan and Pakistan.

Some analysts asserted that what Iran was doing was permitted under the NPT agreement. The NPT which Tehran signed in 1974, allowed a signatory country to build facilities involving all aspects of the nuclear enrichment (for peaceful uses) subject to international safeguards. The caveat of course was "under international safeguards". The spreading suspicion was that Iran was trying to erode or evade the scope of the international safeguards by limiting the role of the international inspectors. It does need some stressing that two of the EU-3 countries that were negotiating with Iran—France and Germany—(the third being UK) could in no sense be described as subservient to the United States. Moreover the chairman of the IAEA board was an independent person least wanted by the United States.

But there was also a well-grounded suspicion that the U.S. was deliberately exaggerating the Iranian proximity to the possession of a nuclear device. A major U.S. intelligence review was reported by *Washington Post* on 2 August (2005) to have projected that Iran was at least a decade away from manufacturing the key ingredient for a nuclear weapon. Similarly around the same time the UN nuclear agency tests had concluded that traces of highly, enriched uranium on centrifuge parts discovered in Iran were from imported equipment (obviously from Pakistan) rather than from any enrichment activities by Iran.

An official Iranian announcement on 7 January informed the world that Iran was ending its two-and-a-half year suspension of nuclear fuel research. Tehran asked the international inspectors to remove the seals on the research centers. Tehran maintained that it would only pursue a peaceful programme and that the research could be carried on under the supervision of the IAEA's cameras. Some of the scare around Tehran's announcements was due to a number of well reported hawkish, in fact indefensible, statements by the new President Mahmoud Ahmadinejad denying the historical fact of the holocaust against Jews and asserting that Israel should be "wiped off the map."

Before we analyse some deeper issues involved in this situation a few more troubling caveats need to the added.

The critics of the Indian vote on Iran were not sufficiently addressing the core issue of the clandestine transfer of nuclear technology from the nuclear proliferation machine of A.Q. Khan to Iran, among others. Iran's progress towards nuclear development had the stamp of Pakistan on it. The documents given by Iran itself to the IAEA provided the clearest proof that Khan delivered the design of a nuclear bomb to Tehran. Even the Americans, while loudly complaining of Tehran's nuclear ambitions and demanding its disciplining by the Security Council, go on a silence fast when it comes to the question of investigating the Islamabad-Tehran nuclear link.

Undeniably India had to strive for mutual fruitful relations with Iran. There were historical linkages between the two countries and there were present needs that demanded close relations—all this was so evident that it need not be dwelt upon : India's energy requirements and Tehran's search for modern technology, avenues for the sale of oil and, no less, reducing its isolation. No matter, what the American pressure, India had to be pursuing the oil pipeline proposal from Iran through Afghanistan and Pakistan, and it is inconceivable that Americans would kill the Indo-U.S. agreement because of it.

India could not shut its eyes to recent developments. India voted only once against Iran. Tehran voted many times against India on the Kashmir issue in the Organization of Islamic Countries. It was unhistorical to forget that Iran had until very recently been the most vocal critic of India and supporter of Pakistan on the Kashmir issue. It had not happened too often in contemporary diplomatic history, but Iran managed just to do that. Almost on its eve, the then Foreign Minister I.K. Gujral's visit to Tehran was cancelled in 1996 by the Iranian authorities because, as the Iranians officially put it, India was "oppressing" Muslims in Kashmir. Tehran did not even try to come up with a lame excuse which is the normal diplomatic practice. And this at a time when India and Iran were coordinating their policies on Afghanistan.

Necessarily one did not just live in history, and in the present international situation India and Iran needed to develop closer relations, but we must keep our perspective.

Undoubtedly Russia and China had been trying to restrain the U.S. from hasty action and Russia proposed a compromise that would enable Iran to enrich uranium for peaceful purposes within Russian territory but despite continuing negotiations Iran was unwilling to accept the proposal that the entire process be carried on in Russia alone. How long and to what extent Russia and China would continue to protect Iran diplomatically was an open question. The problem was not the acceptance or otherwise of this proposal. The problem was the confusing and changing signals that came from the Iranians. One day they indicated they might accept the Russian proposal, the next day they would not. One day they were prepared to discuss the issue of suspension of enrichment uranium; the next day that was out of the question. One day a proposal comes from a high-level Iranian that France, or may be including one or two other countries, could organize the enrichment of uranium within Iran so that it remained under supervision; the next day there was no mention of it. It is these ambiguous responses that has obliged China and Russia to agree to some sanctions against Tehran.

Now, consider the U.S. position or positions, here too there were larger troubling questions.

The United States never tried to understand or accommodate Iran after the Shah was overthrown. It has only offered unmitigated hostility to Tehran. As we have noted earlier, and as is well-known, USA gave covert and overt support to Saddam Hussein in his war against Iran. As a task force of the Council for Foreign Relations admitted (much before the nuclear issue became compelling), USA had been trapped in a "self-perpetuating cycle whereby mutual distrust begets uncompromising assertiveness and unyielding negotiating positions". People, particularly in the West, forget that the Persian civilization is a very ancient civilization and that the people of Iran are as proud inheritors of their civilization as any other people with such ancient civilization. One of India's senior diplomats with great understanding of the region, Hamid Ansari pointed out "the sheer impracticality of ignoring Iran in a wider scheme of things covering west and central Asia". It should be obvious to any observer with the most ordinary common sense that any attempt to pursue a violent solution or apply the Iraq approach to Iran world be fraught with the most incalculably dangerous consequences. The more Washington threatened the more determined Tehran would be to acquire nuclear bombs. The nuclear bomb was perceived as conferring security against American invasion, as the world watched the case of North Korea.

The most troubling question, to this writer's perception, is that the nuclear powers were violating both in letter and spirit the NPT. They had formed a cartel, laying rules and conditions for others, but none for their own conduct. The NPT was negotiated on the express understanding that while non-nuclear powers would refrain from attempting to produce nuclear weapons, the nuclear powers would undertake a process of gradual reduction of their arsenals with the ultimate aim of eliminating them. That understanding was now a faint and distant dream. They were refining and re-refining their nuclear weapons so as to make then more accurate and more devastating. USA had carried out more than a thousand nuclear tests and had more than 7000 operational thermonuclear weapons of its own while it preached nuclear abstinence to everyone else. Both Britain and France had been suspected of stealthily modernizing their ageing nuclear arsenals (Britain now proposes to do it openly) and Paris had threatened nuclear retaliation against any terror attacks on France. China had been steadily and ambitiously expanding its nuclear armoury both in reach and lethality. Russia had announced the development of new missiles that would be impervious to the nuclear shield being put in place by the Americans. In fact the five nuclear powers had made a mockery of the international nuclear regime.

Having considered all aspects of the Iran nuclear issue,

we can come back to a consideration of the Indo-U.S. agreement of 18 July (2005). The agreement could be looked at within the context of the needs and requirements of both the countries. So far as India was concerned, the economy was growing at a fast pace, creating a bigger hiatus between the needs, the domestic fuel resources and the financial resources for ensuring speedy supplies. As the world demand for energy, including that of fast-growing China, was leaping, oil prices were hitting the ceiling. India's hopes lay in rapid development of nuclear power but its quest for pursuing that road was seriously constrained by the limits and conditions imposed by the nuclear suppliers through their regulatory regime. India was finding it hard to keep running even the existing nuclear power plants and Russia too was being restrained by the rules laid down by the nuclear suppliers regime that it had as a member of the cartel agreed to abide by. This was equally true of other nuclear fuel suppliers like France and Canada, besides USA.

Unless India surrendered its nuclear weapons capability, the going was getting more difficult. The agreement appeared to provide a way out, without India having to surrender its nuclear arsenal and capability. It could help New Delhi break out of the shackles with which it had been bound after its explosion of nuclear devices. The agreement conferred on India an implicit nuclear weapons power status and as visiting Senator and former Democratic Party presidential candidate, John Kerry said in New Delhi in response to a media question that it would be "disingenuous" to suggest that it was not so if the agreement went through.

The *New York Times* even derided the Bush administration with the rhetorical question: "Why (Not) Sell Nukes to India ?" President Bush had "legitimized" India's nuclear arsenal by offering to sell it technology "that had long been forbidden to any one who played outside the world's nuclear states", it wrote. This in itself suggests the rationale of the Manmohan Singh government in signing the agreement apart from various others factors some of which we have already alluded to.

So even while India had had serious differences with the U.S. on various issues, including Iraq, the government claimed that it had acted in the larger and long-term interests of India.

But what about the American side? Why did the Bush administration strive to reach this agreement. What was the rationale on the U.S. administration's side in pursuing this kind of agreement which, many felt, was compromising the non-proliferation regime so dearly held and advocated by the US establishment. That India had had a singularly good record in preventing the spread of knowledge about nuclear technology and had passed laws to further tighten possible leakages (in fact India was a better non-proliferator than most other countries, including China and USA, not to speak of the nuclear shopping mall set up by A. Q. Khan) helped but was not the driving factor.

Many U.S. and Indian analysts (among others) took the view that the agreement came in the context of U.S. desire to contain China, and India was being helped to become stronger in the hope to use the relationship to put pressure on Beijing. This was only a half-truth.

Undoubtedly Washington had in mind a new balance in Asia in which China did not run away with dominance and which would also secure its own continued central role in Asia. According to two well-informed U.S. correspondents, much of the plan was conceived by Robert Blackwell, former ambassador to India and an erstwhile deputy national security adviser under Condoleeza Rice, along with his close confidant Ashley B. Tellis, a specialist on U.S.–India relations at Carnegie (and much earlier at the Rand Corporation).

Tellis, the correspondents reported, had earlier in the year laid out a broad vision for India-U.S. relations in a paper titled "India as a New Global Power". It advocated geostrategic cooperation between the two countries rooted strongly in U.S. defence and military sales to India and U.S. support for New Delhi's growing nuclear arsenal.

"If the United States is serious about advancing its geopolitical objectives in Asia, it would almost by definition help New Delhi develop strategic capabilities such that India's nuclear weaponry and associated delivery systems could deter against the growing and utterly more capable nuclear forces Beijing is likely to possess by 2025," Tellis wrote.

Certainly the U.S. strove for a balance in Asia that would help maintain its primacy in the region, but not just by isolating China. Moreover, the mainstay for the security aspect in the region for the U.S. was not India, but Japan. Washington and Tokyo had tightened their alliance by many notches. A new relationship with India would be of considerable significance but it was not and was not going to be a military alliance.

India too desired a stable balance but not an anti-China front. The kind of balance India had in mind was one that would put constraints not only on China but on USA too. India was expanding its relations with China and Russia while striving for a new relationship with the United States. It was a new ballgame in international relations. The Chinese call it a "win-win" situation in which mutually beneficial relations, particularly economic, were pursued with almost everyone, a policy of engagement, and not confrontation.

In any case, even the George Bush regime, for all its hawkishness, had no intention of disengaging from closer contact with China. Not only was China militarily stronger than ever before, but what counted more was the emergence of China as one of the most powerful economies in the world. The U.S.-Chinese economic relationship was too important for either country to disregard.

USA strove for a balance in Asia but not just an anti-Chinese front. Deputy Secretary of State, Robert Zoellic Washington's pointman, then in China, told the National Committee on U.S.-China Relations that USA wished to boost China's international role and make it "a responsible stakeholder" in the international system to ensure its growing power produced cooperation, not confrontation. It is not without significance that USA has already had two high-level strategic talks with China and that their pointman was at the level of Minister of State (Zoellic, Deputy Secretary of State), whereas the pointman in India had the rank of a secretary in our MEA (Burns, Under Secretary of State). Even more significant was the message sent by the United States to congratulate Shinzo Abe on his induction as the new Prime Minister of Japan. Washington, while sending its warm felicitations to Abe, hoped that he would improve Japan's relations with neighbouring countries, particularly China. This message made it evident that the US wished to continue a policy of engagement with China.

The real factor behind Washington's decision to vastly upgrade its relations with India was not just India's strategic position but because India was now being seen—all over the world—as a rising power particularly in economic terms. The U.S. and world opinion was agog with two fast rising economies, those of China and India, which would in a few years reach the top, behind only the United States. India's growing economic and military strength provided a new perspective for Washington, as it did for Beijing (indeed Beijing realized this earlier than Washington did). This perspective and the anticipation of participation on a major scale in this growing economy was a principal driving factor, the other being the rise of India as a political and military power that could contribute to a better balance in Asia. It also helped, at least with U.S. public opinion, that India was a parliamentary democracy with a free press and an independent judiciary.

So what the Bush administration was doing was what it regarded as in its long-term interests—a kind of long-term investment, and what the UPA government was doing was what it perceived to be in India's long term interests.

The fact of the matter, or rather, the heart of the matter was that there was deep distrust in India of the Bush administration as a consequence of the worldview expounded by Bush and his powerful aides and their unilateralist policies, particularly the flawed invasion of Iraq. This distrust was not confined to the Left but was shared by large sections of the intelligentsia. Moreover, the scientific community, more particularly those associated with the development of the nuclear programme, were strongly opposed to the U.S. effort to "change the goal posts" in the implementation of the Indo-U.S. nuclear accord in violation of its letter and spirit.

Prime Minister Manmohan Singh in a forceful speech in the Rajya Sabha on 17 August (2006) made it abundantly clear that for him there were only two goalposts and that none other would be accepted. One was the Bush-Manmohan Singh agreement (joint statement of 18 July) and the other the announcement on the separation plan of the Indian civil nuclear programme from the military one on 2 March, known as the Separation Plan. The civilian nuclear reactors were specified and those would be put under IAEA inspection after the US had completed its processes of giving legal shape to the agreement, but the military part of the nuclear programme would be kept independent under the country's own control.

Manmohan Singh made it clear that he would not accept any additional conditionalities but would stick to the obligations he had undertaken in the joint statement and the Separation Plan.

The Prime Minister also refuted the critics' claim about the dilution of India's independent foreign policy. As an instance of his faithfulness to the basic parameters of India's foreign policy, he said he had made it clear in the full glare of the American media and had also told President Bush that India did not favour the policy of regime change in Iraq and that India believed it was wrong to have gone to war in Iraq. Whatever the Government had done, it had done in the larger interests of the country, he said.

At the same time he stoutly defended the nuclear deal, which was actually a civilian energy deal, as in the interests of Indian energy needs. Subsequently talking with some of the senior nuclear scientists, who had expressed apprehensions about the attempt by US legislators to change the goalposts, but had expressed satisfaction with his Rajya Sabha statement, Manmohan Singh requested them to help end nuclear apartheid being practised against India.

The fact of the matter was that the nuclear scientists had been unable to deliver all that they had hoped to. At present the nuclear reactors essentially used uranium for keeping them in operation. India was woefully short of uranium and was almost exclusively dependent upon imports, although it has built a substantial stock for the present. There was, therefore, need for breaking through, if possible, the constraints of the nuclear suppliers strict regime for the supply of uranium.

The other route could possibly be thorium-based nuclear reactors. India is richly endowed with thorium resources but the sting is that the scientists have yet to discover the technology to set up cost-effective thorium-based nuclear reactors, and going by the past record, there was no knowing *when* and *if* they would be able to come up with the technology for thorium-based nuclear reactors. In the meantime uranium was needed to keep the reactors going.

After prolonged deliberation and interaction with the Bush administration, the US Congress has passed what has come to be known as the Hyde Act pertaining to a civilian nuclear energy agreement between USA and India. The final legislation was hailed by the administration but divided opinion in India. Without going into too many details, many critics, including some senior scientists, have strongly advocated its rejection by India, while some others have expressed strong reservations about some of the conditions that form part of the Act. Many people wanted the Prime Minister to stand firm on his 17th August statement in Parliament.

These fears particularly related to three aspects. India had declared a voluntary moratorium on further testing of the nuclear bomb, but if in the future India came to the conclusion that in the interests of its basic security, it must undertake a nuclear test, the US would be obliged by its laws to stop all assistance in the supply of technology and fuel to India's civilian nuclear programme, and would ask for the return to all the materials supplied. The Hyde Act apart, the US laws have been in place for many years obligating the administration in such circumstances. What then happens to the commitment of assured fuel supplies as envisaged in the original joint statement? Would the US administration also be obliged to lobby with all the other members of the NSG to cease all cooperation with India in India's civilian nuclear energy program?

The second apprehension related to the use of spent fuel. The Act did not permit its reuse by India nor did the question of what was to be done with the nuclear waste accumulated through nuclear power reactors clarified by the Act.

The third reservation was a broader question. The

critics' apprehension was that the congressional legislation attempted to get India's foreign policy aligned to that of the US. The Americans would use the agreement to put fetters on India's autonomy in foreign affairs and India's foreign policy would have to subserve American objectives and requirements.

These are serious concerns that cannot just be waved off. Of course, as Pranab Mukherjee asserted in Parliament on 12 December (2006) the civilian nuclear energy agreement, now known as Agreement 123, was being negotiated between India and the US, and India would be a party only to what was agreed upon between the two sides. India could not concern itself with what the US did internally. He also quoted Condoleeza Rice who had assured that USA would meet all the commitments it had made. The Prime Minister repeated the assurance in Parliament that the strategic segment of the nuclear programme and the research and development connected with it would be off limits for other countries and no intrusive inspection would be allowed. It was the civilian part which would be under IAEA safeguards.

The critics pointed out that any agreement between USA and India would have to conform to US laws made by the US Congress. They had a point, but they were ignoring some crucial aspects. Firstly, as President Bush clarified, the Hyde Act had portions that were prescriptive, some were advisory, and some others were recommendatory, and that in the final analysis foreign policy was the prerogative of the President. There would have to be hard and hard-nosed negotiations for Agreement 123*, but if India could get some of its most serious concerns addressed in the final agreement, that accord would have to be taken back to the

---

* So called because it was being negotiated under Section 123 of the U.S. Atomic Energy Act.

Congress as provided by the Hyde Act. If the agreement was approved, it would have the stamp of Congress on it. If it was rejected there, the deal would be off and the onus would be on the United States. If the US insisted on unacceptable conditions, the deal would be in jeopardy.

There are two other aspects that many of the critics had not taken into consideration. If this deal came through, India would have broken out of the India-Pakistan syndrome in world affairs. India would have cut loose off the Indo-Pak straitjacket that many countries, chiefly the US, had been trying to fit us into for the last half century. The notion of an artificial parity had finally been given the short shrift that it deserved. Moreover, the nuclear deal would enable India to secure defacto proximity (even though not complete equality) to the other nuclear powers.

As regards the fears that India's foreign policy would become subservient to US policies and objectives, there was no way in which another country could dictate India's policies unless India itself keeps permitting them to do so. Every country, chiefly the big powers, wished to influence other countries' policies; it would be entirely for us to decide how much to be influenced. It was a measure of lack of confidence in ourselves to believe that our country could be sat upon. As an instance, the US would like us to cooperate with it in controlling proliferation of weapons of mass destruction, particularly concerning Iran. A fair enough objective, but it would be up to us to decide where and to what extent we need to cooperate. There should be no fetters on our other relationships with Iran.

Economic Dimension

In considering the Indo-U.S. relations, not excluding the nuclear agreement, the economic dimension cannot be ignored. The United States was India's largest trading partner. Between 2004-2005 India exported goods worth

Rs. 48,303 crores and imported nearly 40,200 crores from the US. USA had over 11 per cent of India's foreign trade. Baring Mauritius which fell in a different category, U.S. was also the largest investor in India, cumulative FDI by the end of 2005 being some $ 5.038 billion. American corporations operating in India multiplied from 14 in 1991 to over a thousand in 2004. USA occupies a central position in India's economic relationships, although India is only marginal to U.S. foreign economic relations. What counts for the U.S., however, is the potential of the emerging Indian market.

Outsourcing, controversial it may be in the U.S., has become one of the largest income-earning occupations for Indians. A number of "tradeable jobs" in US are going offshore—a large number to India. As *Business Week* of USA has noted, under pressure to increase profits, American companies from General Electric (GE) to IBM were changing their business processes so that they could take advantage of cheaper foreign labour wherever it was possible. A surprising amount of activities for higher-end functions were being carved out, many of them being transferred to India. General Electrics had the largest R&D center in India, employing some 22000 people, including 1800 computer engineers in Bangalore. Many US banks and automobile companies had their accounting and much of their back office activity done in India.

Perhaps the best summing up of the potential of India's economic growth and its implication for US and the developed world was provided by Finance Minister P. Chidambaram in his 2005 Trumbull lecture at Yale University:

"Between 1997 and 2003, World GDP grew at an annual average growth rate of 3.5 per cent. The US economy was a major engine of growth for the world economy by contributing 40 percent of world growth. China contributed

6.7 percent. India's contribution was marginal in this period. However, India is now coming to a point where its contribution to world output growth will be significant. With a GDP of nearly $800 billion, each 10 per cent rise in India's GDP will contribute $80 billion to world output.

"India now has a roughly 25-year track record of an average annual growth of 5.8 per cent. This has brought millions of people out of the depths of poverty to a better situation. The nominal GDP is now about US $800 billion. With a little more than a billion people, this translates to a per capita income of approximately US $750 a year. Measured in terms of purchasing power parity, the five biggest economies of the world are the US, China, Japan, India and Germany. There is, of course, a long way to go before every Indian is pulled out of poverty and deprivation.

"How far has India come? Just a few weeks ago, the Fraser Institute in Canada, released the Economic Freedom of the World 2005 report, which has data as of 2003. This report measures economic freedom in 127 countries and ranks them. The measurement for India was done by the Centre for Civil Society, a think tank in New Delhi.

"The US is at third rank. India is at 66th rank. India is closer to a country like Italy, at 54th rank, or Israel at rank 50, than to China or Brazil which are at the 86th and 88th ranks respectively. This may give you an intuitive flavour about the kind of economy that we now have—freer than China or Brazil, but less so when compared with Israel or Italy, though closer to the latter pair. This measurement of economic freedom also shows that India has improved steadily, from a score of 4.9 in 1990 to a score of 6.4 in 2002 and 2003. If we take this measure seriously, then it suggests that China or Brazil today (with a score of 5.9 or 6.0) is roughly where India was in 1997."

Demands of International Power Relations

Overall one can conclude by drawing attention to a basic feature in the contemporary international situation. The US is a superpower, the lone superpower, and India like China has to deal with it, even though China has had bigger problems with Washington than India. India needed to expand relations with the US while safeguarding its fundamental interests. International relations is all about give and take as long as giving is not incommensurate with taking. The concessions that you make should be consistent with your national interests and preservation of autonomy in decision-making. That is where India would have to be careful in exploring new relationships with USA, China, Pakistan or other countries and powers in the world.

Nepal: New Challenges for India

We have already discussed in an earlier chapter the various aspects of India-Nepal relationship. But new and more difficult, and perhaps more dangerous, challenges came in the last three years for India.

King Birendra and a number of his family members were assassinated by his own son, Prince Dipendra, who then killed himself in June 2001. Birendra's uncle Prince Gyanendra ascended the throne and soon after began the problems. Not only was Prince Gyanendra's son a maverick and playboy, but apparently he himself nursed the ambition of becoming an absolute ruler, not content with his role as a constitutional monarch. On the other hand, driven by Nepal's poverty, lack of development, the alienation of the poor, the authoritarian measures gradually taken by the King and to some extent ineffectualness of the democratic parties, a Maoist armed movement under the rubric of Communist Party of Nepal (Maoist) arose within the country. Undeniably the movement had considerable grass roots support, but it also often took recourse to strong-arm tactics, dragooning young boys and girls into their armed movement, extorting money and requisitioning food, holding "people's courts" and sometimes wantonly killing those not with them. The King relied on his army whose brutal measures further fed the insurgency against the Crown. There was, unfortunately, considerable bloodletting in Nepal. Then on 1 February 2005 the King dispensed with all constitutional niceties, staged a royal coup, dismissed the Sher Bahadur Deuba-led coalition government and took direct control of Nepal to, as he ironically put it, "protect the system of democracy and multi-party rule". We need not concern ourselves with all the day-to-day developments in Nepal, but we may note that with this action and the subsequent brutality of his rule the King hastened the denouement and brought together diverse political and social parties and groups against the unconstitutional but ruthless monarchy.

Both the political parties and the Maoist leadership realised that individually and severally they would not be able to overcome the might of the monarchical state and that they must concert their strengths and struggle unitedly against the dictatorship of the Royal Palace. The mainstream political parties had already come together to form the United Front for the restoration of multi-party democracy, what came to be referred to as the seven-party alliance (SPA). In November 2005 the mainstream parties and the Maoists reached an agreement on an alliance against the monarchy by which the Maoists committed themselves to parliamentary democracy, and the mainstream parties to a possible constitutional change. Not only did this raise the stakes for the King, it converted the struggle for the restoration of parliamentary democracy into a people's movement, drawing in large numbers of young and middle aged men and women into the movement. It was now the Nepalese *janta* against the Palace.

There were, of course, many imponderables and loose ends in the understanding between the Maoists and the mainstream political parties. The Maoists wanted to do away with the monarchy altogether, while some of the mainstream political parties were not yet sold on their Republican agenda. The more difficult and complex question of how the Maoist arms were to be tackled or how they were to be disarmed was still to be resolved. The King, on the other hand, took recourse to more violent and ruthless measures to suppress the struggle.

India's Dilemma

The rapidly escalating situation in Nepal put India on the back foot. On the one hand, there was extreme sensitivity in Nepal about an interfering big brother and, on the other hand, inactivity or passivity on the part of India could result in a chaotic situation in Nepal and earn ill will of the Nepalese parties and people because it also raised the more piquant question of whether India should continue with its military (and economic) assistance which would necessarily be used by the Palace, and how far the ties with the monarch should be maintained. Ideally India preferred a Nepal with parliamentary democracy under the throne that would function as the symbol of Nepal's unity and state entity. The King's attempt to smother democracy and impose his own dictatorship dismayed India and posed painful choices before it. India's dilemma was further confounded by the Maoist insurgency in Nepal as India was itself facing a Maoist insurgency within the country. There were widespread suspicions of a link between the two. The Nepalese Palace attempted to play upon these fears and make it out as if the choice before India was: us or the Maoists. For a while India flip-flopped towards a viable policy.

First India made it known that military aid to Nepal

had been suspended from 1st February (2005) and then in May delivery of arms was resumed on the ground that the King had assured New Delhi that democracy would soon be restored. The Palace was obviously conveying to New Delhi that arms suspension would only help the Maoists. New Delhi had yet to overcome the antipathy towards the Maoists. The Nepalese Maoists were leading an armed insurgency, and so were the Indian Maoists. It was not an easy transition for the government to make a distinction between the Nepalese Maoists and the Indian variety.

In a way this was a problem mutual to New Delhi and the Nepalese Maoists. Instinctively suspicious of India and often cashing on latent suspicions in Nepal for populist purposes, the Maoists also moved cautiously from hostility to ambivalence to a reluctant acceptance of a necessary Indian role in taming the monarchy.

For a while there was even a split in their leadership over various ideological issues, the attitude towards other political parties, the approach towards India and the role and the extent of armed struggle, one faction led by Pushpakamal Dahl and the other by Baburam Bhattarai. But they managed to patch up their differences and the movement changed track. Their leadership decided to accept multi-party democracy and in fact advised their Indian counterparts to do likewise. They also put aside for a while their antipathy towards India and held secret parleys with CPI (M) leader Prakash Karat, not without the knowledge and concurrence of the Government.

Dr Manmohan Singh changed the disastrous course of hunting with the hounds and running with the hare almost at the eleventh hour. The wake-up in South Block led to the dispatch of a special envoy, Dr Karan Singh, to Kathmandu where he had one-to-one dialogue with the King on 19th April (2006). According to Dr Karan Singh's own account, he conveyed a strong message to the King on behalf of Prime Minister Manmohan Singh advising him to restore democracy and emphasised the element of urgency.

The Palace was coming under inordinate pressure. The Americans and Europeans were strongly urging the King to retrace his steps. The Chinese also, after some hobnobbing with the King, perhaps learning from the experience of the emergence of Bangladesh which they had initially strongly opposed to show their solidarity with Pakistan, stepped aside from the scene in view of the popular surge against the Palace. Indian pressure was becoming increasingly difficult to resist, but above everything else the internal struggle was too widespread for the King's comfort.

The international pressure was somewhat divided. The US policy was in a way unworkable. Washington stood for the restoration of democracy but was utterly opposed to any role for the Maoists. This had, however, become untenable in the Nepalese situation. India's policy, recognising the Nepalese realities, moved away from that of the Americans and faced with the choice of the Palace versus the people, opted for support to the people. The divergences between the American and Indian policies became apparent.

The King finally buckled under internal and external pressures, restored parliament and, on the last day of April (2006) inducted the unanimous choice of the political parties, the veteran Nepali Congress leader, Girja Prasad Koirala, as the new interim Prime Minister. We say "interim", because the understanding among the political parties was that the new government would hold elections for a constituent assembly which would decide the future constitutional structure of the country. The new government moved quickly to prune the powers of the King. The army was taken out of the King's control and made subordinate to Parliament. The King's power to dissolve parliament was taken away. India welcomed the developments, reopened its purse strings and announced a new economic package for Nepal.

With the Government playing somewhat of a second fiddle, the CPI-M leader Sitaram Yechuri made a vital contribution in bringing the various Nepalese political parties, including the Maoists, together on a common platform, thus defusing simmering tensions and bringing about a measure of normalcy in the strife-torn Himalayan country. His role was highly appreciated by all the political parties in Nepal.

The Maoists agreed to a 25-point code of conduct, thus ending—at least for the time being—the insurgency that began in 1996 and took a toll of more than 1200 people. They promised to end extortions from the people and also announced the suspension of the holding of people's courts. They also agreed to "deposit" their arms under UN supervision. The bringing in of the UN was not an easy pill for them to swallow.

So far so good. But many challenges remained and could confront India again with unpleasant choices. Negotiations were on between the Nepalese Prime Minister and the Maoist leadership and even though various parties have reached a settlement for the present on many crucial issues, many thorny issues had yet to be resolved. The Maoists had to be brought into the political mainstream but not as an armed movement. Elections to the constituent assembly had to be held, but the Maoist army had to be disarmed before the elections took place. The Nepalese army had to be depoliticised while the Maoists army had to be disarmed. How would the UN ensure that this had been genuinely and effectively achieved—was a crucial question. There was need for arms management, but this was easier said than done. The future of monarchy was still undecided.

India's policy in Nepal could suddenly and rapidly face

new pitfalls. The dilemma for India in a nutshell could be how far to go and how far not to go. Any aggressive intervention would be highly unproductive, a passive policy could also be hurtful in terms of India's security as well as Nepalese peoples' expectations. Highly sensitive and easily aroused, the people, pulsating with nationalism, bristle at any suggestion of Indian overlordship and yet hope for Indian interventions in certain situations and of a certain kind. India would have to be clear about its goalposts and carefully negotiate the landmines in Nepal.

ASEAN, Japan and European Community

We have earlier considered Jawaharlal Nehru's vision in foreign policy and its continuing relevance, continuity and change, Indira Gandhi's practice of it, and we have examined the various challenges at various times to our foreign policy from Rajiv Gandhi to Manmohan Singh. This does not exhaust the gamut of our foreign policy relations. There are many more important relationships which we have only touched upon, and some not even that. They are by no means less significant. So far we have dealt with major challenges. We now consider a few of the other relationships in broad outline to round off our analysis of India's foreign relations.

Relations with ASEAN (Association of South-East Asian Countries, comprising of Singapore, Thailand, Malaysia, Indonesia, the Philippines, Vietnam, Cambodia, Laos, Brunei and Burma) are among the important relations of India. For India, Southeast Asia is like what Russians describe the Caspian and Central Asian states as "near abroad". Historically, politically and economically the Southeast Asian countries, now formed into ASEAN, have had intimate, fruitful and generally cordial relationship with India. We have seen how Indira Gandhi nursed the relationship. Narasimha Rao also made efforts to restore closer contacts. There was no real acrimony, but many political problems hampered closer ties. In the early period most of the Southeast Asian countries (Vietnam, Laos, Cambodia and Burma joined ASEAN much later) had drifted towards USA and the Western camp, wary of both the Soviet Union and (ironically) China, while India driven by its own geopolitical compulsions had a warmer relationship with the Soviet Union. The Vietnam war and developments in Cambodia had widened differences. Serious efforts were made after the demise of the Soviet Union—India becoming a sectoral partner of ASEAN and then a full "dialogue partner" in 1995 and increasing participation in Asian Regional Forum (ARF) from 1996—, but political roadblocks have not been completely cleared and some temporary economic obstacles also came in the way. India's nuclear tests in 1998 and the financial crises that hit most of Southeast Asia in 1997-98 slowed the reigniting of closer ties.

It was economics that set the tone for the development of a new period in their relationship. It helped that there was no serious political divide between them. ASEAN is focused on economic development and with India emerging as an important country both strategically and in economic terms, the momentum in the expansion of relationships has been building up and is now acquiring a meaningful dimension. Some focal points in relationships have emerged in the development of these relationships: Singapore, Thailand, Malaysia and Indonesia. Ties with Burma constitute a separate category as Burma is an important neighbour, affecting India's security, and we shall touch upon India-Burma relations in a separate section.

A sub-regional economic cooperation group was formed, consisting of Bangladesh, India, Myanmar (Burma), Sri Lanka and Thailand, subsequently joined by Bhutan and Nepal. Although founded in 1997, its first leadership summit was held in Bangkok in July 2004. Going by the acronym of BIMSTEC (Bay of Bengal Initiative for Multi-Sectoral Trade and Economic Cooperation), its purpose was to concentrate on six key sectors from tourism to technology. Earlier in the year, the member countries had signed a free trade agreement at Phuket in Thailand. India, Sri Lanka and Thailand committed themselves to trade liberalisation by 2012 while the rest would follow within five years .

Prime Minister Manmohan Singh, in his first overseas speech since taking office in May, said that the group was a key part of India's "look East" trading policy. But he believed the group would have to tackle other key issues as well, such as terrorism, religious extremism, gun running and drug smuggling. The areas of conflict were coming closer to us, he said. The group representing some 1.3 billion people was so far big on symbolism and small on actual results. It's inter-group trade was only $7.3 billion, constituting only four per cent of their total overall trade.

Singapore has become the focal point in relations with ASEAN and is also the largest trading partner of India in the region. The former Singapore Prime Minister, Goh Chok Tong, was the first ASEAN leader to recognise the potential of India and the first to urge India not only to fully open up its markets but also to invite it to make Singapore its linchpin in promoting relations with ASEAN. The new Prime Minister Lee Hsien Loong continued Goh's policy towards India and signed a Comprehensive Economic Cooperation Agreement with India in June 2005. India's trade with Singapore stood at $10 billion and as Lee noted in June 2005 was growing by 50 per cent every year. As he remarked, if the two countries could sustain this momentum, the economic relations would become very meaningful. There were nearly 1500 Indian companies based in Singapore. Manmohan Singh described Singapore as India's "Gateway to Southeast and East Asia". Singapore also supported India's bid for a permanent seat in the Security Council.

India's trade with ASEAN was expanding rapidly from $2.38 billion in 1990, and nearly $16 billion in 2004 to over $23 billion in 2005, with exports at $8.6 billion and imports at $14.6 billion—the trade being heavily in favour of ASEAN. ASEAN's share in the total trade of India touched nearly 10 per cent in 2006. ASEAN supplied some 7.6 per cent of the FDI flowing into India in 2005, while the outward flow of direct investments into ASEAN was touching nearly 12 per cent by 2006. India had currently a billion dollars invested in Malaysia and had sent over 200,000 Indian visitors in tourist trade to that country.

India had already in 2003 acceded to the Treaty of Amity and Cooperation in Southeast Asia. There were also various working groups functioning for development of relations. A landmark beginning in India-ASEAN relationship was the third India-ASEAN summit in December 2004 at Vientiane in Laos taking a giant step forward in strategic terms. India and the 10-nation ASEAN signed an "ASEAN-India Partnership for Peace, Progress and Shared Prosperity" wherein they pledged to boost trade, investment, tourism, cultural exchanges, sports and people-to-people contacts. They also vowed to jointly fight international terrorism and to work together for the reform of the United Nations to make it "more reflective of the contemporary realities" and in addressing common challenges of economic, food, human and energy security. The document called for taking full advantage of the geographical integrity of Southeast Asia and India in implementing a Free Trade Pact by 2011 for the ASEAN and India and progressively bringing in member-states by 2018. The Partnership Pact included the entire range of political and security cooperation, including food and energy, finance and science and technology. Prime Minister Manmohan

Singh quoted Jawaharlal Nehru's speech of 1947 at the Asian Relations Conference in New Delhi exhorting Asian leaders to work jointly to chart out a new future for Asia.

ASEAN accounted for 8.56 per cent of India's global trade. This, however, should be compared with a 130 billion dollars volume of China's trade with ASEAN. As Singapore Prime Minister Lee remarked, India could not replace China just as China could not replace the US. The importance of East Asia was apparent from the exclusive forum that was set up to comprise ASEAN and China, Japan and Korea, referred to as ASEAN +3. In December 2005 an East Asia Summit was called into being that included ASEAN + 3 plus Australia, New Zealand and India. Although very general issues were discussed and a great many problems had yet to be resolved, yet a beginning has been made.

That also shows how far India has yet to go in developing relations with ASEAN. India was invited to the first East Asian Summit but, despite Japan's efforts, not yet to the exclusive club of ASEAN + 3. India's free trade pact with ASEAN had also not been given enough substance as yet. It was still limping because ASEAN believed India's offer of items for free trade was unacceptably small, while India was insisting it must protect its farmers from the fallout of such agreements. Anyway the various hurdles have yet to be crossed.

However, there is a certain importance to the India-ASEAN relationship that transcends the current figures of trade. ASEAN by itself has become a significant economic entity. Add to that ASEAN + 3 (China, Japan and Korea) and now the ASEAN's bid to form a single market by 2015—an economic powerhouse was in the offing, even though there were numerous political and economic hurdles yet to be overcome. If India maintains its rapid economic growth, a fairly meaningful economic relationship would be established. But transcending that is the political and strategic partnership.

India was now working at three levels with the greater East Asia, that is including ASEAN plus 3, Australia, New Zealand, Hong Kong and Macau. One was the strengthening of economic relations and it is notable that India had already a trade volume of over $67 billion with this region, constituting some 28 per cent of India's total foreign trade. India is also negotiating free trade agreements with a number of countries of this region. The other level was the security level. India had strengthened security dialogues with many countries of this greater East Asian region, more particularly with Singapore, Thailand, Indonesia, Japan and Australia. All these countries have shown some keenness in a broader cooperation with India within the East Asian region. The third level was the cultural level, like repairing and saving heritages in Cambodia and Laos and cultural exchanges with many countries like Indonesia, Thailand and Malaysia.

The US has many reservations and is considerably wary of the emerging East Asian community chiefly because it excludes the US. ASEAN countries have shed their earlier inhibitions about China, but they do not want a Chinese dominance. They remain pretty friendly with USA, but realise that regional cooperation is central to their development. It is in this context that India can play a helpful role. Besides economic cooperation, India and ASEAN were partners in combating terrorism and promoting peace and stability. India does not engender any real fear of dominance. ASEAN wishes for a balanced relationship in Southeast Asia, focused on economic development and political tranquility. Development of a substantial India-ASEAN relationship could help promote that kind of amity and cooperation mutually beneficial to all countries and be of some use in establishing a healthier balance of forces in this region.

Burma: Painful Choices

Although Burma (now officially known as Myanmar) is a member of ASEAN (admitted into it in 1997), for India it is in a different league altogether. Next door neighbour, not "near-abroad", and India's security is bound with developments in Rangoon (Yangon is the official name). Both geography and history binds them together. Burma was a part of the British Indian empire. During the struggle for freedom, the Indian National Congress decided to accept Burma's independence and to support the Burmese freedom movement. We may also note that there was a large Indian community in Burma in 1947. But, partly as a result of the Burmese policy, many of them left for India and their influence declined over the years.

Along with India, Burma emerged as an independent democratic country, even as the dawn of independence was blighted by the assassination of some of its topmost leaders, like Aung San and a number of his colleagues. Finally democracy was extinguished by General Ne Win in 1962 and Burma slid into a hermit, isolationist state. The students revolted but were massacred in thousands in August 1988. Ne Win was himself displaced by another group of generals who ruled by martial law under the framework of a military government calling itself SLORC. The generals decided to hold national parliamentary elections on 27 May 1990 that resulted in a landslide victory of the National League for Democracy led by Aung San Suu Kyi, daughter of Aung San, who had studied in India and married an English academician, but had returned to Rangoon to head the movement for the restoration of democracy. The military junta now assuming the rubric of State Peace and Development Council refused to accept the results of the elections, kept Suu Kyi under house arrest and continued their repressive rule over Burma. After Nelson Mandela, Suu Kyi may soon become the longest serving political prisoner. She has been in custody for the last 11 years and was awarded the Nobel Peace Prize in 1991.

There was palpable sympathy and support for the democracy movement and for Suu Kyi at both the government and the popular levels. India extended political shelter to hundreds of Burmese activists. Suu Kyi was honoured with the Jawaharlal Nehru Prize for Peace and Understanding. Relations with the military junta became quite frosty. However two things happened to bring about a noticeable change in India's approach towards the military government. One was the China factor. India watched with considerable apprehension rapid and increasing Chinese penetration in Burma. Beijing became the biggest arms supplier to the Burmese army. It developed roads linking its border areas with Burma and expanded trade with it. Investments flowed in. More worrying was the perceived Chinese activity in Burma's Coco Islands overlooking the Indian Ocean. New Delhi believed that the Chinese were developing naval facilities there which could bring Chinese naval presence right into the Indian Ocean and pose problems for its security.

The second factor was the insurgency in the North-East. The Naga and Mizo rebels, particularly the two factions of the National Socialist Council of Nagaland (NSCN) and to some extent the ULFA rebels of Assam were using Burmese territory as sanctuary to carry on their armed struggle against India. The government came to believe that it could not effectively contain insurgency without the active cooperation of the Burmese authorities. So began the visible change in India's policy. The foreign ministers of the two countries met. The Foreign Secretary, the army chief and the Home Secretary trooped to Rangoon to repair and advance the ties. Military supplies wound their way to Rangoon. Border roads were repaired or constructed to promote trade and greater coordination with the Burmese army. The Burmese Home Minister came assuring the Indian Home Minister that Burma would not allow its territory to be used by the extremists for any anti-Indian activities. New Delhi rolled out the red carpet for the vice-chairman of the State Peace and Development Council, General Maung Aye, the second most powerful member of the ruling military junta. Burma's Foreign Minister came on a week-long visit and renewed the assurance even adding, "I want to tell the Indian public that any island in my country, or Myanmar's soil, will not be used as a military base by any power against India". To top all this came the visit of the number one strongman of Burma, General Tan Shwe in October 2004 cementing the burgeoning new relationship. The exchange of high-level visits, marking the new relationship, was capped by President Kalam's visit to Burma in March 2006.

To some extent India's policy was paying off if we consider it in the context of India's security concerns. Not only was India becoming a larger factor with the Burmese government, there was far greater cooperation available from the Burmese army in containing the insurgents' use of the Burmese territory for their operations against India. India also received assurances that no foreign (read Chinese) sea or land bases would be allowed to be set up in Burma and that Rangoon would pursue a balanced policy.

The economic links came to be revived. General Than Shwe invited Indian businessmen to invest in Burma, pointing out that Indian share of foreign direct investments in Burma barely exceeded 1 per cent of the total FDI in Burma. By the end of 2005 India-Burma trade volume rose up to $500 million and a target of $1 billion was set up for 2006-2007. India came to be the second largest supplier of goods to Burma. India constructed the hundred-mile Kalay-Kalaywa-Kyrigon-Tam road connecting Burma with Manipur, facilitating trade from the border to central Burma. In addition, India constructed 170-feet long bridge connecting Mizoram with the Chin state of Burma. Burma was also an important constituent of BIMSTEC as well as of the projected trans-Asian highway and railway projects. India also had an eye on Arakan offshore gas exploration in northwestern Burma.

To conclude, in the short-term India's new approach has yielded fair results in terms of balancing Burmese foreign policy and in enhancing perceived security interests. But whether in the long run this policy would continue to be of help is an open question. The military government is under intense international pressure to loosen its grip, release Aung San Suu Kyi and observe democratic norms. The generals are fiercely resisting the pressures and in the process Burma remains an impoverished country. Sooner or later they would have to submit to the domestic movement and foreign pressure. Hopefully India's geographical advantages, domestic democratic polity and economic potential would help in mitigating the disappointments of any emerging democratic regime and maintaining fruitful links with it that are so necessary for India's own security and progress.

India-Japan: Unfulfilled Potential

No ideological divide hampered India's relations with Japan, but geographical compulsions and perceptional differences have not so for allowed the realisation of the full possibilities in their ties. Historically China, Japan and Korea formed a unique geographical entity, generally referred to as East Asia (it is only now and that too for economic reasons that the East Asia concept is being extended to include Southeast Asia). China was the mother civilisation and Confucianism a common philosophical tradition. But both Japan and Korea developed distinct civilisations even while bonded together in many ways.

Japan emerged as an Imperial power in the late 19th

and early 20th century. It occupied Korea and a large part of China in its attempt to create an "East Asia Coprosperity Sphere". Japan's occupation ended with its defeat in the Second World War that led to the division of Korea and the emergence of new China. It left a legacy that is still haunting their relationships. It brought the Americans in and they have stayed there. Japan began its own long march towards democracy and development, rising in time to be the second largest economy in the world.

India was among the first countries to acknowledge postwar Japan as an independent country, signed a separate peace treaty with it and renounced all reparations claims that many other countries in Asia put up to Tokyo. With no aggravating disputes between them and being distant neighbours, democracies both of them, the two countries should have been on a binge of a close relationship. But that was not to be for a variety of reasons.

Japan became allied with the US in both strategic and economic terms, the alliance sanctified by the security treaty signed by Tokyo with Washington. India was an active non-aligned country which while defending its interests sometimes found itself on the wrong side of USA, the relations often troubled by the US alliance with Pakistan. Japan was hugely wary of the Soviet Union whereas India came to nurture its relationship with Moscow as a counterweight to the US-Pakistan alliance. Tokyo also had a schizophrenic approach towards China. It harboured doubts about Communist China but because of its prewar colonial rule in China suffered from a guilt complex that often produced an ambivalent kind of fascination. Geographical proximity added to the fascination and to the focusing on China. The other area Japan gave very considerable attention to was Southeast Asia. Relations with India just limped along. India's wars with China and Pakistan and its policy on mixed economy and a large state sector contributed to further diminishing Japan's interest in India. The grouse against the state's role in economic affairs in India was somewhat ironic, for Japan's private industry was firmly "guided" by the state bureaucracy with the Ministry of Trade and Industry (MITI) supplying some of the post-war prime ministers of Japan.

Nevertheless efforts were made from both sides to build up relations. Indira Gandhi had gone to Japan in 1969 to give a boost to ties with Tokyo and the foreign offices remained in touch. Prime Minister Nakasone ended the drought of visits by Japanese high-level dignitaries visiting India in 1984 followed by Rajiv Gandhi's visit to Japan the next year. In fact three times he went to Japan in his five-year rule. The Japanese Prime Minister, Toshiki Kaifu, undertook his first visit abroad as Prime Minister to Asian countries, among them to India in April 1990. Kaifu remained associated with the India-Japan Committee.

Japan's economic relations with India also expanded in the eighties and nineties. India was amongst the highest recipients of Japanese Overseas Development Assistance (ODI). Japan remained the top donor to India on a government level. Many Japanese industrial houses started their businesses in India, either by themselves or in joint ventures, like Sony, Toyota, Toshiba, Suzuki, Honda, Mitsubishi, and some others. Economic reforms introduced by Manmohan Singh as Finance Minister in the early nineties attracted considerable interest from Japanese corporate world. However the reality was that Japanese investments in India in the late nineties was a mere 0.1 per cent of their total overseas investments. The lion's share went to USA-about 44 per cent. Some 16 per cent went to Asia, principally Southeast Asia and China and Korea. The share of China has been increasing year by year.

A major setback in relations came with India's nuclear tests in 1998. Japan's reaction was sharp and swift. It cut off official assistance to India and was in the forefront of the international pressure on India to roll back its nuclear programme, join the Nuclear Non-Proliferation Treaty as a non-nuclear state, or later to sign up on the Comprehensive Test Ban Treaty (CTBT). This came to be the most difficult period in India-Japan relations. For a while Japan held its entire relationship hostage to India's nuclear programme. India wanted Tokyo to understand the challenges to its security that had prompted it to undertake nuclear tests. Most observers, including former Indian diplomats, were of the view that India should show understanding, even when not submissive, of Japan's sentiments in this regard. Japan had the harrowing experience of atomic strikes on Hiroshima and Nagasaki which ended World War II and in which hundreds of thousands of Japanese men, women and children perished or suffered from long-term ailments as a consequence of the radiation released by the atomic blasts. But such is the irony of history and international relations that today, in view of the security threat posed by North Korea's nuclear test, the Japanese Foreign Minister is openly asking for a public debate on whether Japan should also go nuclear.

Gradually Japan began to rethink. It became obvious that Tokyo could not keep its relations with India in the cold storage for too long a period. It started feeling its way towards restoring normalcy in its ties with India. Prime Minister Yoshiro Mori took the initiative. Visiting in August 2000, Mori skirted the nuclear issue and focused on information technology. He also revived the Eminent Persons Group to advise the two countries on expansion of relations and announced resumption of aid in some select projects, like Delhi Metro and Samadhri power project in Andhra. This could be regarded as the turning point in relations after the low of post nuclear blasts. Mori came back a second time in October 2001, this time as the personal envoy of Prime Minister Koizumi, in a second important move in the direction of normalcy. The sanctions were lifted, although the continuing tense situation with Pakistan brought a blunt message through Mori: reduce tension with Pakistan.

The international situation was changing rapidly and with it Japan's requirements and understanding of it, the same was true of India. Vajpayee visited Tokyo in December 2001 and issued a joint statement that clearly put the nuclear tests behind and express their resolve to work together for stability and prosperity, regular exchange of views on all security-related matters and strive together for the total elimination of terrorism and fight against all those who provided support and sustenance to terrorists.

The problems were really from the Japanese side, not from the Indian side. Indians harboured the most friendly feelings towards Japan. A Centre for Media Studies poll in 2002 rated Japan at the top with 33 per cent among the developed countries that Indians liked the most, with USA next at 29 per cent. It is inconceivable that India would have a similar rating in Japan among developing countries.

The economic link was also picking up. To put it in summary form and telescoping the years, Japan's total loans to India amounted to $4.2 billion by 2004 end; grant aid was to the order of $399 million, and technical aid totaled $179 million. In 2005 India exported goods worth $2.5 billion to Japan and imported from Japan goods worth $4.1 billion—a rather strong adverse balance of trade. Japan's FDI in India was valued at over $2 billion by December 2005. Of course all this pales into insignificance when compared with the $200 billion a year Sino-Japanese trade. But the positive aspect was the increasing awareness and desire for hiking economic relations in Japan as well as in India.

Not only economic cooperation, but even more so in

political and strategic relations. That Tokyo had decided upon a new path in relations with India was noticeable when the then Foreign Minister Ms. Kawaguchi visited India twice in the space of a little more than a year between January 2003 and August 2004 without waiting for the reciprocal visit by an Indian foreign minister, as is the normal practice, the second time soon after the new government headed by Manmohan Singh assumed office. During this period new assistance was announced for some seven projects in the power sector, urban transport, environmental protection and preservation of cultural heritage. India was a strategic partner, she said.

India and Japan opened a new chapter by conducting a joint exercise of naval warships in September 2004. India had the largest navy of all countries between the two commercial straits of Harmuz and Malacca through which half the world's maritime trade passed, crucial for countries dependent on free passage through them for their oil and export-import requirements. Cooperation with the Indian navy was an important factor. Even the US was seeking Indian help in fighting piracy and terrorist activities in these waters.

This was one factor in Japan's change of tack in relations with India. There were other weighty factors that we discuss presently. But while on high-level visits, we may cap it by noting Prime Minister Junichiro Koizumi's visit on 30 April 2005. Koizumi said on the eve of his visit that Japan and India were bound by shared values and principles, such as democracy as well as the convergence of strategic interests. They needed each other "as a strong, prosperous and dynamic partner". It was his intention to reinforce this relationship with a new strategic relationship in a new Asian era and "to take our partnership to a new height of regional and global significance". He also noted that trade figures were about 16 per cent higher in 2004 over

2003 and that the number of Japanese companies had increased from 222 in 2001 to 301 in 2005.

Koizumi and Manmohan Singh agreed upon an eight-fold initiative as part of Japan-India Partnership In the New Asian Era, that envisaged comprehensive economic engagement, enhanced security dialogue and cooperation in ushering in a new Asian era. Japan was also now co-opting India in the campaign against nuclear proliferation. Defence cooperation was also further enhanced when the then Defence Minister (now Foreign Minister) Pranab Mukherjee signed a joint statement in Tokyo with his Japanese counterpart that spelt out cooperation ranging from regular dialogues between the defence ministers and defence secretaries, comprehensive security and military-to-military talks and goodwill exercises.

The most notable aspect of the new relationship was their decision to support each other's candidacy for a permanent place at the high table of the Security Council and their moving together a resolution in the UN for ensuring this. The resolution had to be withdrawn because of opposition for varying reasons from the three big powers. India and Japan joined hands with South Africa, Germany and Brazil to work towards the expansion of the Security Council to include all of them as permanent members.

We have discussed two factors—maritime safety and restructuring of the UN—in this process of the coming nearer of the two. There were more profound reasons for this transformation of relations. The Japanese establishment had made a deeper appraisal of the fundamental changes taking place in Asia and the world. China was fast emerging as an economic powerhouse. India was behind but was also a rising economic power. South Korea and some of the ASEAN countries were registering fair levels of economic growth. USA and Europe were huge economic entities, but the economic momentum had shifted to Asia. Japan had extensive economic relations with China and ASEAN, already becoming the largest trading partner of China, even though the relationship was beset by political troubles. It made economic sense to stake a larger presence in India, already the fourth largest economy in the world in terms of purchasing power parity. Both China and Japan were pitching for increased relationship with ASEAN and both wanted a larger role in any East Asian Community. The inclusion of India could help in bringing about more balanced economic relationships in Asia. That was how Tokyo viewed the situation.

For Tokyo this kind of balancing was even more relevant in the political and security fields. Japan was undergoing a generational change. For China—as for the number of other countries in Asia—history was still a present perception and Japanese aggression in World War II not yet a distant, forgotten episode. Chinese nationalism was very much alive and the Chinese Communist Party leadership made intelligent use of it to buttress its legitimacy while keeping the manifestations of nationalism strictly under its control. To the Japanese younger generation now gradually in power positions wartime history was a forgotten epoch and it was no longer obsessed by a guilt complex that haunted the older generation, no longer a felt need to constantly worry about offending China. Japanese nationalism was now a factor. Ways had to be found to bring about harmony in the nationalisms of Japan, China and Korea. Tokyo understood the need to smoothen the ruffled feathers in Beijing and Seoul, but no longer was it willing to be obsequious. Tokyo realised that a larger balance had to be established in Asia.

Japan was facing agonising situations. If North Korea enlarged its nuclear posture, the domestic debate on its nuclear options would become sharper and more divisive. Despite its extensive economic relationship with China,

Tokyo was wary of a rising China, just as China was anxious about the increasing demonstrations of Japanese nationalism.

Japan was firmly ensconced in a security relationship with the United States. The threat from the nuclear ambitions of North Korea further cemented this relationship. But Tokyo knew it was not enough in the new Asian situation. India gained some importance in Tokyo's perceptions in meeting the challenges of the new dispensation in East and South-East Asia. For the first time shared democratic values worked as a bridge between the two countries. Japan became the most vocal advocate of India's inclusion in the ASEAN + 3 as well as in the Asia-Pacific Economic Community (APEC). Tokyo was trying to bring about a better balance not through an exclusionist policy but through an expanding inclusionist strategy.

India and Japan had a long way to go before it could be claimed that they had established a deepened, irreversible economic and political relationship. But in the transformed Asian and world milieu the prospects for an expanding Indo-Japanese relationship are bright.

India-Europe and the European Union: A Changing Relationship

The re-emergence of Europe has been a significant development in the last quarter of the last century. Bonded together as the European Union with the treaty of Maastricht on 31 December 1992, now comprising 25 sovereign countries, it is one of the economic pillars of the world. It constitutes the world's seventh-largest territory and represented its largest economy in GDP terms (over $13 trillion with a per capita income of $28,000) and the third largest in population. These figures tell their own story about the importance of Europe. So far 12 of the European Union countries, including France and Germany, have formed themselves into a common market with common customs union and a single currency. The European Union (EU) now has a Council of the European Union, the European Commission, the European Parliament, the European Court of Justice, the European Council and the European Central Bank.

With more limited success, the EU has been engaged in evolving common stances on foreign policy and security issues. Some see a division both politically and economically between the so-called old Europe, as for instance France, Germany, Belgium and Italy, and the "new Europe", comprising mostly the East European countries who recently joined the EU. France and Germany continue to provide the backbone to the European Union.

India has had a substantial relationship with many countries of Europe, like United Kingdom, France and Germany, and its various formations, beginning with the European Economic Community, the predecessor of the European Union. A wide-ranging agreement was signed on 20 December 1993, known as the 1994 Cooperation Agreement that went well beyond trade and economic cooperation. Along with it was signed a joint political statement which fixed annual ministerial meetings and provided the basis for a political dialogue between the EU and India. Various subcommissions were set up, and are functioning presently, ranging from trade to development cooperation.

A significant step forward was taken in June 2004 when the EU adopted a Communication that proposed to build an ambitious strategic partnership with India. This was followed by the EU-India Joint Action Plan adopted by the EU-India summit in September 2005 envisaging an expansion of cooperation in trade, investment, transport, environment, science and technology, including space technology, and various other areas. Apart from trade and investment, we note two or three other significant areas of cooperation. One is the agreement on science and technology that allows scientists to participate in each other's research programme. The other is collaboration in space technology, particularly in EU's Galileo programme, the European satellite navigation project, and the international thermonuclear experimental reactor, otherwise referred to as ITER, set up by a consortium led by the EU comprising, besides EU, China, Japan, Russia, South Korea, USA and now India. Both were ambitious and long-term scientific projects that would change the face of the global transport and energy sectors once implemented, in the words of the President of the European Commission, Jose Brosso.

Combined, the EU is the largest trading partner of India, although trade varied from country to country within the EU. In 2004 the EU's imports from India were valued at • 16.2 billion and exports at • 17 billion (one euro is about $1.2). The total trade of the value of • 33 billion was roughly balanced. The EU accounted for 22% of India's exports and 18 per cent of its imports. But taking EU's total trade, India's exports were just about 1.8 per cent of EU's imports and India's imports only 1.6 per cent of EU's exports. India was as yet a marginal trade partner of the EU, although EU played a much larger part in India's total trade.

The EU collectively was also a source of FDI—some • 2 billion in 2002. Between 1991 and 2004 FDI inflow from EU member states totaled about • 5.27 billion. It was a pittance so far as the EU was concerned, constituting only 1 per cent of its total FDI. But with the rise of the IT and Biotech sectors in India, there was also an outward flow of FDI from India valued at $5.1 billion in 2003. With the forays abroad made by Indian industrialists, this volume was rising rapidly. It is estimated that India is already the second largest investor in the City of London.

Politically, especially on world issues, India shares many common perceptions with the European countries. Whether on Iraq or on restructuring of the United Nations or broadly on international issues, there is a fair amount of convergence of the Indian and EU stances. However there are some important differences on a few economic issues. Talks on a new trade and investment agreement under aegis of the World Trade Organisation (WTO), known as Doha round of talks have been stalled on two major areas of disagreement between the EU and developing countries. One is the EU's insistence on retaining agricultural subsidies while insisting on the developing countries removing or reducing their trade restrictions (or the subsidies) in agriculture, industry, banking and other areas. The other point of discord relates to the EU seeking inclusion of social issues, like labour standards, and environmental safeguards and non-proliferation in any agreement on trade and investment which the developing countries regard as extraneous issues and a red herring to reduce their access to the markets of the developed countries. India was among the countries leading the fight against these discriminatory demands.

However, the importance of Indo-EU relations lay in its potential as well as in a fast growth of relations in the last five-six years. The EU was revisiting India as the country was seen as an emerging market and an emerging power. Consequently India was being co-opted as a strategic partner. The EU began to adopt a tougher approach towards terrorism in Kashmir and in India often emanating from across the border and India was assured that the EU had conveyed to Pakistan the need to check the use of its soil for terrorist activities against India, including Kashmir. Many countries in Europe were struggling with the fallout of multi-culturalism and India's example was a laudatory one. The change that was taking place in the approach towards India in many countries could perhaps be summed up in Tony Blair 's speech to the World Affairs Council in Los Angeles in August 2006: "Think ahead... think China... think Russia... think India" because "all these great emerging powers want a benign relationship with the West".

It was the emerging India inviting attention. But in the new era it was also in India's interests, economic as well as political and strategic, to expand its ties with the EU. The most fruitful step from both sides was the India-EU summit in Helsinki in October 2006 where Manmohan Singh and the EU leaders were able to find common language on many issues, including terrorism and strategic partnership. There were still outstanding issues on labour standards, mentioned earlier, but the path ahead was being smoothened to reach a new level of relationship.

India had stronger relations with some of the EU countries, like UK, France, Germany and Italy than with others. With the United Kingdom India had a long colonial relationship. But independent India retained close political and economic relations with Britain and its membership of the Commonwealth. India and UK share a relationship which India did not have with any other western country. Despite differences over the Iraq war with Tony Blair, India and the United Kingdom have a consensus on many international issues. India and Britain have a huge common problem of being targets of the terrorists whose mentors reside in the same country and they shared an approach which is different even from that of the United States. A think tank close to the British Defence Ministry had concluded that Pakistan had become the hub of international terrorism (of course that did not mean with the approval of the Pakistani government) and although the British government distanced itself from the report on the eve of Musharraf's visit to London, particularly in view of Musharraf's sharing of intelligence that made it possible for Britain to thwart a planned attack on flights to USA, the report was indicative of the thinking in the British security establishment.

The UK had a large Indian community, nearly 1 1/2 million strong; some 500,000 visitors were received by the two countries annually; and 25,000 students were studying in each other's educational institutions. This gave a different dimension to this relationship. The political relationship was accompanied by a fair economic link. The United Kingdom was India's largest trading partner in Europe and India occupied the 15th position in UK's export market. In 2004 India's export volume totaled £ 2.340 million while the imports from Britain totaled £ 2.243 million. The UK was the second largest investor in India and India the eighth largest in the UK.

Britain had pledged that it would continue to work for India's permanent membership of the Security Council. We may also note that Britain has been a strong supporter of the Indo-US nuclear deal. Defence relationship has also perked up after India signed an agreement in March 2004 for the purchase of 66 Hawk Advanced Jet Trainers (AJT) for the Indian Air Force with a price tag of nearly 800 million pounds. The agreement was signed by the NDA government which lost the general election a couple of months later. There have been some questions about the agreement as a new government took over, but unquestionably defence ties were picking up.

With France also India had developed a strong political and military relationship and somewhat more limited economic ties. Their worldview converged on many issues as both stood for a plural world order and the resolution of world issues through peaceful dialogue and negotiations. France had recognised that along with China, India was an emerging power and backed a permanent place for it in the

Security Council. More significantly, France was among the largest suppliers of nuclear fuel and technology and had a robust defence relationship with India. It may be mentioned that France had a larger nuclear power complement in its domestic electricity supply than most other countries and was, therefore, in a better position than the US in assisting India in its nuclear energy quest. Consequently, France was a strong supporter of the Indo-US nuclear deal and of a waiver from the nuclear suppliers regime so that India's energy needs could be met partly from sources other than oil. President Jacques Chirac pledged nuclear technology assistance to India for its civilian nuclear energy program under the safeguards of the IAEA during his important visit in February 2006, but as he made it clear, France would have to wait for the clearance of the nuclear deal in Washington.

What basically had happened for the change in relationships was evident from the French President's remarks to the media in New Delhi that India was one of the world's main engines of growth, with a growth rate of 7-8 per cent, a market of several hundred million consumers and a purchasing power multiplied by five in 25 years. The French President declared his resolve along with India's Prime Minister to double Indo French trade in the next five years. Indo-French trade in 2004-2005 stood at $1858 million—a growth rate of some 70 per cent over the previous year.

India's acquisition of Mirage 2000 and the recent decision to purchase French scorpene class submarines worth about $3 billion and 43 AirBus aircraft for the Indian Airlines worth another $2.5 billion further cemented the strategic, military and economic cooperation between India and France.

Another relationship of note was that with Germany. Considerations of space do not permit any detailed discussion. The same two factors we have noticed with the EU, UK and France—India's economic development and the fast changing international situation—constituted the impulse behind the developing relationship with Germany. In the financial year 2004-2005 Indian exports to Germany were valued at Rs. 11,880 crores and imports at Rs. 17,380 crores. If we take the base year of 1991 Indian exports had increased 120 per cent and imports by 135 per cent. To remind ourselves of the limitations, we should recall that India's share in German foreign trade was less than 1 per cent. However, the positive aspect was that it was growing rapidly. Germany was the fourth largest investor in India. More notably, the collaboration agreements and joint ventures numbered more than 2000 and that these collaboration companies were market leaders in at least 24 product groups, either occupying the first or the second spot.

A notable aspect was the new political relationship that was developing between the two countries. Both candidates for permanent membership of the Security Council, they locked hands, along with Japan, Brazil and South Africa, to work for the restructuring of the UN Security Council. Both India and Germany were now very much more alive to the opportunities and challenges of the new international era enfolding in the 21st-century and were exhibiting a new willingness to enhance their cooperation so as to maximise their advantages. Symptomatic of the new relationship was the first ever defence agreement signed between the two countries in September 2006 and an institutional framework was put in place to transform the buyer-seller relationship to a strategic one. Although no details were made available, officials of the two countries said that it would involve training of officers, purchase of equipment, platform for high cooperation, including the navy, and items of high technology.

Return of Africa

We have noted in our earlier chapters how Jawaharlal Nehru, Indira Gandhi and Rajiv Gandhi took up the cause against racialism in Africa and the independence of the African countries. India had established close political relations with African leaders and the freedom movements. Most of Africa was able to shake off colonial rule but for a long time many of the African countries could not take off in economic development. Civil wars, large-scale tribal killings, brutal and acquisitive dictatorships, dependence on single-source economic base, and terrorist machinations to some extent and many other factors hampered and stunted economic development. There were exceptions like South Africa, Mauritius and some others that were evolving a civil society and gaining economic momentum. But the general picture gave the impression of hopeless poverty combined with a greedy ruling elite.

Africa began falling off the radar internationally. Many analysts, particularly in the West, described it as a "lost continent". India's relations with African countries also did not rise to the level that was earlier expected. India became more preoccupied with neighbouring countries, Pakistan for one, Sri Lanka and Nepal too, and with China and USA, and later with some of the South-East Asian and Gulf countries.

The return of Africa in world focus is an important development of the 21st-century. Many countries of Africa are on the path of commendable economic growth. As a World Bank report says, Africa is turning the corner from poverty and debt to prosperity and wealth. There are now 16 countries that have achieved annual growth rates in excess of 4.5 per cent for more than a decade. Even more than that, the resource-rich continent is inviting attention from all over the world because of its tapped and untapped black gold—as oil is often described as—and vast mineral resources that have become the necessary ingredients of economic growth. As a result most countries have woken up to the importance of Africa. Commodity producing countries like Nigeria, Ethiopia, Sudan and the Congo and agricultural powerhouses like Kenya and Tanzania and rapidly globalising countries like South Africa, Mauritius, Tanzania and Benin, many African countries were richly endowed with commodities like natural gas, oil, copper, iron, coal and timber, etc.

Many developed and developing countries were now giving considerable attention to Africa—USA, China, Japan, Europe and now India too. Above all oil in Africa was the new magnet attracting many countries to seek economic opportunities in Africa. The USA was importing 15 per cent of its oil requirements from Africa, China nearly 30 per cent, mostly from Sudan, Angola, the Congo and Nigeria, with its heavy investments in these countries. The US would be investing nearly $50 billion in the Gulf of Guinea's energy sector. China's energy firms were the largest state-owned investors in Africa. Just two examples, the $2 billion low-interest loan to Angola and the commitment for $1 billion investment in the Nigerian energy fields. But the most dramatic and significant step it took was to hold an Africa summit in Beijing November 3-5, 2006 attended by nearly 48 African countries. China offered $5 billion aid and economic cooperation to the African participants.

India too is now making significant investments, though not on the same scale, and is establishing new and building up on the old links. Indian efforts ranged from diplomatic and political to economic. Minister of State for external affairs Anand Sharma asserted that Africa and South America were not off India's radar. India had institutionalised partnership with major subregional groups of Africa and he mentioned meetings with South Africa Development Community, Economic Community of West

African States and Common Market for Eastern and Southern Africa. India had pledged nearly $1 billion in socio-economic assistance to African countries, Sharma said in a media interview.

However, India's efforts were actually renewed in the last few years. India's exports to Africa in 2003-2004 totalled a little over $3802 million and imports about $ 3185 million. (China had a $50 billion trade with Africa). While the exports surged by over 25 per cent from the previous year, imports in fact fell by nearly 7 per cent. But India's political and economic activity in Africa gained quite some momentum during the last five years. New Delhi launched the "Focus: Africa" programme under the Exim policy 2002-2007. The target countries in the first phase were Mauritius, Kenya and Ethiopia. According to press reports, the Oil and Natural Gas Corporation (ONGC) had committed $2 billion in an oil field in Nigeria which was believed to have reserves of over 300 million barrels of oil and 2.5 trillion cubic feet of gas. Production by the ONGC could reach the peak of 225,000 barrels a day by 2008. India also negotiated energy deals with Libya, Sudan and the Ivory Coast.

Undoubtedly India expended the largest diplomatic and political effort to develop a strategic relationship with South Africa that was sanctified during Prime Minister Manmohan Singh's visit in October 2006. Visiting South Africa on the occasion of the 100th anniversary of the launching of satyagraha by Mahatma Gandhi in South Africa, Manmohan Singh and President Mbeki issued a joint statement reflecting their commitment to Gandhian vision of peaceful resolution of disputes, the elimination of nuclear weapons in a comprehensive, universal, non-discriminatory and verifiable manner, and sending a strong message of non violence contained in Gandhi's satyagraha that had inspired leaders and renowned personalities like Martin Luther King, Albert Luthali, Oliver Tambo, Nelson Mandela and

Desmond Tutu. Their joint statement pledged the two countries to raise to a new level their partnership and co-operation in the fields of trade and investment, defence, science and technology and cultural and educational exchanges.

More significantly, they reiterated their support to each other for the restructuring of the Security Council and permanent membership for both of them. In this regard and to promote closer cooperation in the three continents of Asia, Africa and South America, they had already established what came to be known as IBSA (India, Brazil and South Africa) whose first summit was held in Brasilia. The India-South Africa joint statement welcomed the emergence of IBSA as an effective instrument for promoting "ever-closer coordination on global issues between these influential and diverse democracies of Africa, Asia and South America". India and South Africa also agreed to "intensify consultations and cooperation in multilateral forums such as NAM, Commonwealth, G-77, G-20 and New Asian-African Strategic Partnership (NAASP) with a view to jointly addressing global challenges".

No less important was President Mbeki's nod for the Indo-US nuclear deal and his stated willingness to support India's case for a specific relaxation from the Nuclear Fuel Suppliers Group for the supply of nuclear resources and technology for India's civilian nuclear energy program under IAEA safeguards.

India in a way is revisiting Africa. The efforts have only recently gained momentum. It will be some time before India can establish a new kind of and a more durable presence in the vast, diverse and resource-rich continent of Africa.

Gulf, Oil and All That

Prime Minister Manmohan Singh said famously,

"diplomacy has changed and today it is about economics, trade and petroleum". There may be a slight exaggeration in this statement, but there is also a solid kernel of truth in it. Today many relationships have come up, or been reinforced or reinvented, as a consequence of the essential requirements of resources and energy. We have already considered this in relation to Africa as well as some other countries and regions. This holds equally true of our relationship with the Persian Gulf and West Asian region to which we have alluded earlier. Let us consider a few more facts.

India has had strong historical contacts, economic, social, cultural and religious, with a number of countries in that region, like Iraq and Iran for instance. Their cultural and economic interaction with India through the ages is well-known. Now there is a new immediacy and urgency to this relationship in the light of the new international situation as well as India's own economic requirements—India's rising demand for energy and those countries' need for investments and technical skills.

There are some 4 million Indians in the region whose nearly $ 5.5 billion worth of remittances home lubricated India's foreign exchange reserves. The trade bill with India could be in the region of $20 billion a year in 2005. India is closing the political gap with most of those countries and further expanding the economic relationship. India's oil import bill was calculated at $45 billion out of the total import value of $140 billion in 2005-2006. Some 73 per cent was imported from abroad, two thirds came from the Gulf region and growing, particularly from member countries of the Gulf Co-Operation Council comprising Saudi Arabia, UAE, Kuwait, Qatar, Oman and Bahrain established in February 1981.

India burns 1.4 million barrels a day and its oil consumption is expected to touch 5 million barrels per day by 2020. It is projected that by then India could become the fourth largest consumer of energy after USA, China and Japan. Saudi Arabia, with the highest reserves in the world, supplied over 26 per cent of India's crude oil requirements. India was Saudi Arabia's fourth largest trading partner ($8.8 billion was the value of trade in 2004). India has sought to strengthen its relationship with Riyadh. The high point was the visit of King Abdullah in January 2006. Prime Minister Manmohan Singh himself broke protocol to receive the King at the airport while the King broke protocol in himself signing the joint statement with the Indian Prime Minister. India desired to enhance its energy relationship with Saudi Arabia through diversification of the Indo-Saudi relations, while the King wished to expand his options outside of an almost total political dependence on the United States. (Abdulla travelled first to China and after India to Pakistan). After signing the joint statement with India, the King hugged and kissed a shy and "embarrassed "Prime Minister.

The King told the Vice President: "I know many countries will be jealous but India is special to me".

The joint statement of the two sides pledged them to "closely and actively cooperate to fight the menace of terrorism and other international crimes". India was assured that Saudi Arabia would be a "trusted and reliable source of oil supplies" and that its needs would be looked after. The Prime Minister invited Saudi Arabian corporates to invest in India, in the areas of power, telecom, airports, railways among others.

India also expanded its relations substantially with other Gulf countries—UAE, Kuwait, Qatar and Oman. India takes about 11 million tons of the black gold a year from Kuwait. With Qatar, India negotiated agreements to purchase 7.5 million tons of liquefied natural gas (LNG) in 2005 and 1 million tons of oil annually. India has been upping both the political and economic antenna with these countries. The UAE, supplying about 6.5 million tons of oil a year, is also among the top three trading partners of India, the trade volume in 2003-2004 being over $ 7000 million, more than with any other Gulf country. However the UAE essentially serves as a facilitating ground for commercial engagements with other countries in the region. Interestingly, with all the difficulties in Iraq, we are still importing nearly 7.5 million tons of oil every year from that strife-torn country.

India is also looking towards Russia and Iran for its energy needs. Russia we have already discussed earlier in this chapter. Despite certain problems as India came somewhat in the crossfire between USA and Iran, New Delhi has been developing its relations with Tehran on various levels. Let us not forget that Iran is the second largest producer of oil in the world and that we have had strong historical links and interaction with the Persian civilisation. That India sought the Iranian source for its petroleum needs was evident from the $22 billion agreement for the purchase of 5 million tons of LNG annually from Iran starting 2009 going up to 7.5 million tonnes by 2011 for the development of two Iranian oil fields and one gasfield. Presently, Iran is supplying some 9.6 million tons of oil yearly to India. The ONGC will help develop the Iranian oil fields in exchange for 900,000 barrels a day of crude oil. This is besides the talks that are going on with Iran and Pakistan for the construction of a 2775 km-long gas pipeline from Iran through Afghanistan and Pakistan to India. This is still in the negotiating stage.

While we are on the subject of energy needs, we may also take into account of the fact that India is looking at various other sources to satisfy its energy hunger. In the east it has mended fences with Burma and is negotiating with it to build a pipeline to bring its natural gas to India. To the west India has secured energy presence, as noted earlier, with a number of African countries. It is now attempting to forge durable relationships with many South American countries. Venezuela is the world's fifth largest oil exporter. Both China and India are keen on expanding relations with Venezuela. President Hugo Chávez visited India in April 2005 and signed six energy and cooperation agreements with New Delhi. The ONGC and Gail are set for a 49 per cent stake in the Venezuelan oil field of San Christobal and PDVSA, while Venezuelan state-run oil company is investing in India's Mangalore refinery.

Conclusion

Foreign policy in the contemporary world has become more and more complex. It has strategic elements, political connotations and a huge economic content. First, the strategic elements. Of course the time-old consideration to secure peaceful borders and deter any aggression from abroad remains the chief objective of a country. To this has been added a new element: terrorism, cross-border terrorism, international terrorism. This has brought many countries together as it has divided many others. Also, the neighbour's woes do not necessarily mean your welfare. Globalisation has made us inextricably interdependent. Globalisation provides opportunities but also has its "discontents". Its downside is glaring disparities and the creation of two or three societies within one country. Real security must provide for an uplifting from the bottom upwards, and not remain content with the growth levels of the upper 20 per cent.

National cohesion is an essential component of security in its broadest and most enduring sense. The Chinese call it harmony. But harmony cannot be imposed with a fist. It breds best in an atmosphere of trust, tolerance and freedom of choice and at least a relative equality of opportunity. Unless every part and every community in the country feels secure and confident about the state's benign impartiality and has faith in the legal and political institutions of the country, the country's security could more easily be subverted from within or without.

While these various dimensions of security remain important, no less relevant in today's circumstances is economic security. The struggle for economic development is now rated as high as the other requirements of security. A country's place in the community of nations is determined as much by its economic strength and the immediate prospects as by its military clout. In fact its political clout is increasingly the function of its economic clout. Only a few years ago India was being dismissed as a chaotic democracy, something to be patronised, but little else. Even the nuclear blasts, significant as they were over the long run, elicited some hostility at the time. How the world's way of looking at India has been transformed within less than a decade ! India's military strength is now appreciated only in the context of its economic growth. The world over the talk is about the rise of China and India. 'Chindia' is the word now in universal currency, essentially because of their rapid economic growth and "emerging markets".

China is far ahead of India in economic growth, but around 8 per cent rate of growth in India has set the elites of the world writing about China and India in the same breath. China has been the favourite destination of foreign direct investments (some $60 billion in 2005 against nearly $5 billion for India), but India is now said to be the second most attractive destination. India was also "inching back as a favourable trading destination of the world". India's advances in the knowledge industries have put it in the top league, despite the woeful inadequacy of its infrastructure.

We have talked about the transformed international situation. Among the various trends already mentioned, yet another stands out prominently. To put it in slightly exaggerated terms the exodus of money from West to East—and some power along with it. Money and power generally go together! The 19th century saw the rise of Great Britain and Europe; the 20th of the United States of America; and the 21st bids fair to be that of Asia. Take the case of wages. They were rising sharply in India and China but stagnating in the US and Europe. According to the *Financial Times* of London, real hourly incomes in the US are lower today then they were five years ago.

According to the projections of the US rating agency Goldman Sachs, by 2025 India's GDP would go past that of the United Kingdom, even if still very much behind USA's GDP. But by 2050, India's projected GDP of $ 28,000 billion would not be too far away from $35,000 billion of the US. Of course if we take the per capita income, even by 2050 India's per capita income of $18,000 would be much lower than that of the current UK's $24,000 and USA's $35,000. Still if these projections turn out to be correct, the population of over a billion people with $18,000 per capita income would strongly impact on the world.

Yet as the noted historian Paul Kennedy raised the question: "is the distribution equitable? Or does it consist of many multibillionaires, a good number of well-off middle-class folks and a billion people still at meagre standards of living?.... Energy dependence is a big constraint on rapid growth. The sinews of power also include the social fabric, a flourishing democratic system and factors which make a country comfortable with its own growth". Foreign policy will continue to be constrained if 200 million people remain below the poverty line.

We have already discussed at some length the energy issue. Undeniably the quest for energy—for a long time of the nonrenewable nature—would provide a strong input in the development of foreign relations. Increasingly India would look for establishing stronger links with countries that helped satisfy its growing energy needs. India would have to spread its wings far and wide—from the Persian Gulf region to Africa and to South America. The world would become smaller for us in this quest while relations would have to be deepened with the existing suppliers.

Foreign policy is not a zero sum game. It's positive quality lay in its ability to evolve multidimensional relationships. Since Jawaharlal Nehru's time we have striven to maintain friendly relations with as many countries as possible. The renewed wave of globalisation makes expansion of relations, the enlargement of friendships and the diminution of enmities a priority. Those who remained mired in wars and conflicts are being left behind by decades together. Today all countries are trying to reach out to others. China and USA may be hugely wary of each other's objectives, but this does not deter them from remaining strongly engaged. Relations with one country cannot be to the exclusion or detriment of relations with another. The objective necessarily is the diversification of relationships, the opening of new opportunities and the availability of increased options, even countervailing chips, balancing factors, or even large forums which could make ever a little contribution to restrain the trend towards unilateralism and hegemony.

It was these considerations that apparently prompted Manmohan Singh to skip the UN session and attend the summit meeting of the member countries of the non-aligned movement (NAM) in Havana in September 2006. There was some illiterate criticism about the Prime Minister attending an "irrelevant" organisation's meeting in preference to an address at the UN. NAM, flabby as it has become, might have lost some steam and could do with some blood transfusion, but for India, the founder member, to disdain an organisation of some 118 members could only be described as the height of folly. NAM needed to pursue some new directions, economic and political. The economic direction was clear: the non-aligned countries, almost all of them developing, had to and were indeed trying to make common efforts to ensure a more equitable economic order, an effort in which countries like India, China, South Africa, Brazil and some others were taking the lead jointly to secure the interests of the developing countries. As far as political direction was concerned, as Manmohan Singh said at the NAM summit, the movement should serve as the voice of "moderation, harmony and reason" and as a "bridge of understanding", among cultures so urgently needed to curb the waters stirred up by the votaries of the "clash of civilisations" on both sides of the struggle. The NAM summit's resolution came out strongly against terrorism and urged countries to refrain from extending political, diplomatic, moral or material support to terrorism and to combat this menace by various means, including by prosecuting and extraditing its perpetrators. The 91-page final document expressed deep concern that the terrorist groups, including the former Taliban, were regrouping in the southern and eastern parts of Afghanistan. It also expressed concern at the lack of progress in the restructuring of the United Nations and equitable representation in the Security Council.

The more forums the country can operate through, deliberating and finding consensus on world issues, the more effective it can be in advancing its point of view in world councils. It was the same logic that induced India, South Africa and Brazil to bond together and form the IBSA. They came together from three continents to promote what they considered as their common interests and the common interests of all like-minded countries. IBSA was formed in 2003 with various commissions set up to focus on alleviation of poverty and hunger, sustainable development, and expansion of trade among the three countries as well as on security issues. The first summit, attended by President Lulu da Silva of Brazil, President Thabo Mbeki of South Africa and Prime Minister Manmohan Singh of India, was held in Brazil on 13 September 2006, just before the non-aligned summit in Havana. The joint statement affirmed that "the IBSA Dialogue Forum plays an increasingly important role in foreign policies of India, Brazil and South Africa" and "has become instrumental in promoting ever-closer coordination on global issues between the three large multicultural and multiracial democracies of Asia, South America and Africa". This puts in a nutshell the driving objectives and the relative importance of such forums.

Without going into too many details, yet another significant aspect was the summit level talks between Brazil and India. This was the first visit of an Indian Prime Minister after Indira Gandhi went there in 1968—a gap of some 38 years. A new bond had been created, with India making Brazil as one of its key relationships in South America whose importance ranged from political, strategic to energy areas.

We have said foreign policy is not a zero sum game. It is not a one upmanship game either.. Nor is it heads I win and tails you lose. Nor still is it a game of all give and no take. In fact foreign policy is serious business and not a game at all. It is a business of engagement, engagement with neighbours, engagement with world powers, engagement with as many countries of the world as possible, engagement for political reasons, engagement for economic reasons, engagement for security reasons, for peace and development, and now engagement for energy considerations.

You can neither be on your front foot nor on your back foot all the time. Compromises and accommodation are the essence of foreign policy. Accommodation is not tantamount to capitulation, but the reverse of capitulation is not inflexibility. One cannot take the view that in order to accommodate, one must just accept the others' point of view or demand, as some analysts seem to be suggesting. Accept whatever the US says, accept whatever China asks, accept whatever Pakistan wants. This is not how foreign policy can be run. Nor can it be run, as Indira Gandhi once said to me, on the basis of: here we stand and here we shall stand for all time to come. Rightly she rejected that kind of rigidity in foreign policy. National interests are not immutable; they change with changing circumstances. We recall what Jawaharlal Nehru said: no government can adopt a policy which is demonstrably to the disadvantage of the country. But, at the same time, he pointed out, we must strive to harmonise the national interests of various countries while advancing our own. That is the sum and substance of foreign policy.

PART IVA

Article 51A

Fundamental duties

It shall be the duty of every citizen of India -

(a) to abide by the Constitution and respect its ideals and institutions, the National Flag and the National Anthem;

(b) to cherish and follow the noble ideals which inspired our national struggle for freedom;

(c) to uphold and protect the sovereignty, unity and integrity of India;

(d) to defend the country and render national service when called upon to do so;

(e) to promote harmony and the spirit of common brotherhood amongst all the people of India transcending religious, linguistic and regional or sectional diversities; to renounce practices derogatory to the dignity of women;

(f) to value and preserve the rich heritage of our composite culture;

(g) to protect and improve the natural environment including forests, lakes, rivers and wild life, and to have compassion for living creatures;

(h) to develop the scientific temper, humanism and the spirit of inquiry and reform;

(i) to safeguard public property and to abjure violence;

(j) to strive towards excellence in all spheres of individual and collective activity so that the nation constantly rises to higher levels of endeavour and achievement;

(k) who is a parent or guardian to provide opportunities for education to his child or, as the case may be, ward between the age of six and fourteen years.